LIFTOFF!

PRACTICAL DESIGN LEAD
YOUR ORGANIZATION, AN

Chris Avore
Russ Unger

Rosenfeld®

NEW YORK   2020

"Finally, a book that provides detailed and practical advice covering the entire lifecycle of hiring, integrating, and nurturing a team of designers to excel."

—Bruno Figueiredo,
Director, Xperienz and curator of UX Lisbon

"This book is full of advice and guidance covering vital topics like inclusion and team mental health that I wish I'd had. Managers, read it to uncover your weak spots. Aspiring managers, read it to ensure that you lead well."

—Katja Forbes,
Design leader

"Whether you're a new design leader or have spent years herding mountain lions, this playbook smartly helps you elevate your game and reminds us all how to utilize the biggest tool in our leadership toolkit: heart."

—Kara DeFrias,
Director of Experience Design, Obama White House

"Design is hard, but managing is harder. Don't miss this concise and effective handbook for growing your skills so your team can thrive."

—Scott Berkun,
Author of *How Design Makes the World*

Liftoff!
Practical Design Leadership to Elevate Your Team, Your Organization, and You
By Chris Avore and Russ Unger

Rosenfeld Media, LLC

125 Maiden Lane, Suite 209

New York, New York 10038

USA

On the Web: www.rosenfeldmedia.com

Please send errors to: errata@rosenfeldmedia.com

Publisher: Louis Rosenfeld

Managing Editor: Marta Justak

Illustrations: Deb Aoki

Interior Layout Tech: Danielle Foster

Cover Design: The Heads of State

Indexer: Marilyn Augst

Proofreader: Sue Boshers

ISBN: 1-933820-80-2

ISBN 13: 978-1-933820-80-4

LCCN: 2019950033

Printed and bound in the United States of America

To everyone out there who had to figure out
a bunch of this stuff as they went along,
and everyone who had to work with them and us
along the way.

HOW TO USE THIS BOOK

Who Should Read This Book?

This book is for anyone who wants or needs to step into design leadership or design management. You may be someone who is eyeballing a promotion, or who just landed that sweet manager or director role that you've worked so hard to achieve. Or you may just be the most logical person remaining after the exit of your most recent supervisor. Regardless of the reasons why you find yourself leading and managing, if you're seeking guidance that comes from hard lessons learned, valuable insights, and inspiration from others across the industry, this book is for you.

And if you're not a designer, or in the design industry, we're pretty sure there's a lot in here that will be valuable to you as well.

What's in This Book?

We did our best to organize this book into a sensible, linear reading experience. However, we fully recognize that the first time you crack the spine on this material might be because you need to address a very serious, very *right now* need. As such, we've prepared the following brief guide to tell you what's going on throughout these pages.

Chapter 1, "Surprise! You're in Charge of People Now," introduces you to what may be an entirely new set of skills that you'll need to learn in order to be successful in a new role. There can be a lot of uncertainty, and in some cases, not a lot of support, as you move forward in support of others, and we're here to help.

It's not lost on us, two Caucasian men, that we're far from unique in the leadership and management book space. At the same time, we also know that everything in life and work benefits from true diversity and inclusion, and as such, Chapter 2, "Designing Diversity and Inclusion in Your Teams," was written with the direction, input, guidance, and counsel from a lot of stand-out, exemplary folks who have breadth and depth of experience.

Collectively, we have spent a lot of time playing different roles in the hiring process of organizations we have worked with and for.

If you're seeking some additional guidance and insight into how to design or enhance your own hiring processes, you'll find that the five chapters we've written on this topic share some great ideas that you can use or modify to springboard into something that fits your situation and environment. Definitely start with Chapter 3, "Designing Your Hiring Process," to get started and evaluate where your process is today.

Then take a look at Chapter 4, "Performance Profiles and Interview Guides," for a thoughtful way to create a description of what success looks like in the roles you are seeking to fill, as well as consistent ways to interview and evaluate candidates. Chapter 5, "Screening Designers," demonstrates a solid approach for moving candidates forward in your interview process, after you've cast the right net, of course.

We wrote Chapter 6, "Interviewing Potential Team Members," to take advantage of your interview guide and your team in order to identify the best candidates to add to your team. We didn't shy away from an industry hot topic—design exercises—either. Chapter 7, "Offers, Negotiations, and Onboarding," wraps everything up nicely and helps you get an offer that everyone agrees upon (or doesn't) and then sets up your new employee for success in your organization.

Chapter 8, "Unifying the Team Culture with Charters," identifies a way to build coalition and agreement across your team. At certain points in any team's trajectory, purpose and messaging can get a little muddled or fragmented, and the team charter can bring your team together. While we're bringing teams together, it's also important to bring the individuals on your team to you, so we wrote Chapter 9, "Designing the One-on-Ones," to guide your check-ins with the people you manage, the people managed by the people you manage, and your peers across the organization. That's a lot of meetings!

As Adam Connor, coauthor of *Discussing Design: Improving Communication and Collaboration Through Critique* said, "Critique isn't just a design skill, it's a life skill." Chapter 10, "Leading Continuous Critique," shows you how to provide structured, continuous critique throughout your team and across your organization. Critique is a natural lead-in to how you share your work more formally, so Chapter 11, "Presenting Work," will highlight all of the effort that goes into preparing for and leading meetings where designers show their work.

We included Chapter 12, "Saying No," because sometimes telling people no can be a lot more challenging than it should be, and we've seen and heard from others that guidance on this topic would be helpful.

While the topics in the book have been all about helping you help others as a leader and manager, Chapter 13, "Developing Designers," provides an explicit focus to help continually level-up the people you work with and assist them in growing into their next role.

In some cases, design will just be finding its footing in an organization. In others, Chapter 14, "Scaling Design," can provide guidance on how to take an established design practice and grow it to meet the needs of a much greater demand.

Successful leaders know that it's important to build coalition, collaboration, and trust across the entirety of their organization, so we've included Chapter 15, "Designing Influence," to navigate that path beyond your own design team and into the C-suite of your company.

Lastly, Chapter 16, "Escape Velocity," explores what's next for design leaders and the new skills and perspectives they'll need as they lift off to leave the old ways of designing far behind.

Throughout the book, you'll be introduced to a myriad of other expert design leaders across design and other industries. It was important to us to include insights and perspectives beyond our own. These different perspectives, delivered based upon the topics of the chapters, are meant to inform your own decision-making as you design the best path forward for you and your organization. We've been really lucky to find amazing people who deeply cared about sharing their time and craft. We truly admire them, have been influenced by them, and have been made better by knowing them.

What Comes with This Book?

This book's companion website (⚑https://rosenfeldmedia.com
/books/ux-leadership/) contains additional content. The book's
diagrams and other illustrations are available under a Creative
Commons license (when possible) for you to download and
include in your own presentations. You can find these on Flickr
at www.flickr.com/photos/rosenfeldmedia/sets/.

FREQUENTLY ASKED QUESTIONS

Is this a how-to book?

Of course not! And, well, maybe. We've included a lot of what we've learned based on our own personal experiences and our collaboration with each other—and others—which we view as a framework to help you on your way. You certainly might be able to take what we've written and apply it as-is, especially when it comes to the hiring process (see Chapters 3–7). There's step-by-step instructions to facilitate a design charter workshop (Chapter 8). And Chapter 15 includes specific ways to tweak generally-used user experience design activities to include executive leaders, which may elevate your influence in the company. But there are also a lot of tips, stories, and experiences in this book that aren't necessarily meant to be applied directly. Instead, use them to build your own foundation for how you make decisions relevant to your situation and environment.

Why did you include a chapter on designing diversity and inclusion into teams?

A diverse team where individuals can be their full selves in a psychologically safe, inclusive environment will be better prepared to design solutions to ambiguous, complex problems (see Chapter 2). We promote diverse teams working together in an inclusive environment throughout the entire book, not just in one chapter. By the end of the book, we hope audiences will feel more prepared and comfortable committing to intentionally building and supporting diverse, inclusive teams.

Are you using management and leadership interchangeably?

Usually, until we don't. Management and leadership are not synonyms, yet in many cases the two terms represent similar means to similar ends. In Chapter 1, we provide a breakdown of the differences between a design leader and a design manager. Throughout the book, we use *design manager* intentionally to refer to the person responsible for managing their teams of direct reports, and ultimately the people who report to them. Think org charts, hierarchy, and bosses.

We often will use *design leader* when we're referring to anyone in the organization who identifies as a designer and is trying to improve their team, their team's delivery, or their workplace, whether or not they have official management responsibility.

Does the world really need another management book?

We're familiar with the litany of books about management and leadership—some of which have helped shape the views we share here. Many recent management books have focused on managing technical teams or software development teams. However, there are far fewer books that can help new or experienced design managers with both short-term and longer term paths to improve their design practice. For instance, design leaders can likely see positive short-term results by trying the ideas in Chapter 10 on critique and Chapter 11, which focuses on presenting work. But we also cover complex topics that may take months to see organizational change, such as Chapter 14 on scaling design and Chapter 15 on influencing cross-functional partners and senior leaders.

Why did you write so many chapters on the hiring process?

A good, solid hiring process (Chapter 3) is truly at the foundation of how a team works. Hiring includes thoughtful descriptions of the types of work to be done and what success looks like in a role (Chapter 4), well-defined and consistent interviewing practices (Chapters 5 and 6), and a thorough onboarding process (Chapter 7). It's easy to focus on only one aspect of the hiring process; however, we see the pieces as interconnected and extremely important to be aware of. A strong hiring process shows candidates what it's like to work on your team at your organization, and everyone should strive to put their best foot forward.

What's up with a whole chapter on saying no?

Chapter 12 reinforces what many of us already know well: saying no is rarely easy in the workplace. We investigate power and social dynamics, risks of telling the boss no, and ways to help make saying no a little easier. We even share advice on planning (and cleaning up after) birthday parties!

CONTENTS

FOREWORD

A successful transition from individual designer to design manager requires a fundamental change in mindset. As an individual, you were expected to come up with great design solutions or actionable research insights. As a manager, you have far more complicated deliverables. The first one is a healthy, effective team that can meet the organization's evolving needs. The second is an environment where that team can thrive and grow.

The skills required to produce these results can be overwhelming for new managers and frustrating even for experienced ones. The good news is that if we take the time to understand our colleagues as we would our users and customers, then it's possible to design their experience accordingly. What should it be like to get hired at your company? How can team members understand their career progression (and how to move it along)? What should it be like for other teams to work with yours? These are all complex design problems, but they're still design problems.

The other good news is that Chris Avore and Russ Unger have distilled their collective decades of management experience into this book. It's a collection of great advice and practical tools for everything from recruiting and coaching to influencing—(and even learning how and when to say no). New managers will find it offers a starting point from which to build their own management practice. Experienced managers can use it to fine-tune whatever isn't working today.

Effective leadership is hard. It's a mindful, daily practice—some days you'll be good at it, and some days you won't. What works in one culture or with one team member doesn't always work with another. No book will answer all of your questions, but this one will equip you with some good tools to start answering them for yourself.

—Kim Goodwin, design and product executive;
author, *Designing for the Digital Age*

INTRODUCTION

Being a design manager or leader isn't getting any easier. Despite more organizations needing design leaders, there are limited resources available to learn how to lead teams in an environment where valuations, expectations, and public sentiment are now more closely watched than ever. Executives in the C-suite, in the board rooms, and the general public all have an opinion on design, and those opinions are more sophisticated than ever.

The challenges that design managers face come from all angles, including from designers on high-performing teams who know their skills are in demand. The struggles are real: integrating design at scale to better serve their organization and its products, coaching and training executives on how to understand the value and the ROI of design, staying ahead of the changing demands of customers, and warding off competitors who are using the same tactics for the same reasons from the same shallow pool of design talent.

Heading into 2016, we set out to write a book that could help address only a few of these angles. We thought we had accomplished enough in our own work lives without too many battle scars so that we were ready to share what had worked for us. Russ had already written a number of books on practicing effective design, but had yet to really dive into writing about, well, everything else that designers face in their careers.

Our own experiences have changed quite a bit since then. Chris went from managing one team in one company to helping teams all over the world improve their design maturity. Russ adapted the skills he was using in the federal government to help other companies design their own design organizations. These experiences, while delaying the book by about four years, ultimately helped us shift the course of the book to a new direction.

As a result, what started out as a book intended for first-time or early-career managers has evolved into a book to help all design leaders address a spectrum of challenges they may face throughout their careers.

We didn't want to limit the lessons in this book to our own lived experiences, though. To reflect a diverse range of experiences, we talked to a lot of people at various stages of their careers and experiences in managing teams. Unfortunately, we couldn't use everything that so many people generously shared, but they should know that their conversations, survey results, or emails all helped shape this book.

Our *Advice from the Field* sidebars are contributions from design managers and leaders who shared especially insightful and relevant experience. We made sure we weren't only asking our pals, or others we saw every few months at Yet Another Design Conference. There's a great chance you probably haven't heard of some of these folks because they've been busy building teams, leading design, and creating an impact in their organizations instead of talking or tweeting about it. We're especially excited to have their experiences captured here.

Liftoff! prepares current and future design leaders to meet these challenges directly so they can thrive while organizations continue to expand their expectations and reliance upon design practices. In this book, we'll explore the following topics:

- How to grow and nurture a team by redesigning the hiring process

- How to keep your teammates feeling like part of the broader organization in a design-literate workplace culture

- How to scale the practice of design throughout your various lines of business so that design can make a difference at all levels of the organization

- How DesignOps and Design Systems can be integral parts of your practice to create operational efficiencies at scale

- How to grow careers—not just skills—as designers learn to adapt and confront new challenges in their ever-changing workforce and ever-evolving organizations

- How to influence and educate your executive team in order to create an environment where design positively influences how the organization succeeds

With the right leadership and culture, design can continue to ascend to heights that people who entered the profession only 25 years ago couldn't imagine. But it's not guaranteed. Organizational priorities may shift, funding and resources may get reallocated, and your design champions may find their own paths changing. Designing resiliency into your own systems—your teams, your goals, and your practices—will prepare you for those almost inevitable shocks and disruptions.

Design is now succeeding in places where it used to be an after-thought, if it was present at all. Governments, banks, management consultancies all want design to help them view the world differently and address their most glaring business problems. When the companies that were previously synonymous with dead zones of design now practice high-performing, effective design, it's safe to say that design must be ready for the next phase of maturity.

Regardless if a company understands design's possibilities or is just beginning to get it, these organizations will need leaders to shepherd their teams on that journey toward elevating their design practice and the designers themselves.

Liftoff! prepares design leaders and managers, their teams, and their companies to adapt, evolve, and ultimately thrive in this new environment. You can do it, too—you just don't have to do it alone.

CHAPTER 1

Surprise! You're in Charge of People Now!

The founder of a high-growth technology company approached Megan, a designer who had joined the organization just a month earlier, and asked her to take a walk. Megan was apprehensive—convinced that she was getting fired, despite thinking she had done well in her new job.

Surprisingly, the founder praised her performance, offered her a promotion, and asked her to begin managing the design team. Megan also learned that her current manager would remain on the team and would now be reporting to her—instead of the other way around. In a split second, Megan went from being a team player to a team manager.

Megan's first experience at managing designers was similar to many other practicing designers who are asked to begin managing teams without prior experience—it was a disaster.

"Let's face it—I was totally in over my head," she said. "I was a few years out of college and knew how to deliver as an individual, but I was *not* yet a good collaborator. I had really only seen management styles that I didn't like. I had a brand new set of responsibilities, which I didn't fully understand, and I certainly didn't know how to deliver on them. If there was a mistake to be made, I made it. I didn't know how to build coalitions. I didn't know how to relinquish control to others. And I didn't know how to get out of my way and the team's way in order to help delivery happen as it should. The company's leadership saw me as a high performer, and as such, they were sure that I was the right person for the role."

Within a couple of months, Megan left the organization, frustrated that she didn't have more support and that she wasn't feeling successful. She knew she should never have accepted the position. She felt that she had let her design team down. Because of that disastrous experience, she retreated from leading and managing teams for several years. "It always felt to me that there was an unwritten language of management and leadership that no one told me about and that I was supposed to guess what the correct answer was."

* * *

Unfortunately, Megan's story is more the norm than the exception. She was identified as a leader by upper management—even though she had never been a manager and recognized herself that she wasn't ready to fulfill that position.

On the other hand, if you've been leading designers for years, you've probably experienced your share of changes as well. The teams of designers reporting to you may expect more career development or visibility into the rest of the company. Executive management may be turning to you to scale product development across the organization. Or perhaps your employer doesn't necessarily understand the value of design, and you need to evangelize how effective design and high-performing design teams contribute to the health of the company.

If you're frightened, it's probably justified—because design leadership is a new field compared to many other roles. It's a tenuous position without a lot of guidelines to get you started in the right direction, or to show you where to steer decision-making once you've had some success.

In fact, many organizations simply don't know how to position or lead people toward a successful career as a manager or how to nurture design leadership.

But fortunately, you aren't alone. We're here to help you navigate both leadership and management, whether you just started managing your first direct report, or you've been leading multiple teams across several lines of business throughout a long and successful career.

Calculating your approach to design leadership and design management should provide the tactics you can use to deliver better products in an organization that values effective design and its methods. You'll be better prepared to build diverse teams, hire amazing designers, and scale the design practice to meet the growing needs of the larger organization.

Defining Design Management and Design Leadership

Before we get much further, let's define how we'll be using the terms *design management* and *design leadership*. For the purposes of this book, *design management* refers to the act and responsibility of managing designers. To get reflective, design managers manage designers. They may have been designers earlier in their career, or have never designed anything at all, yet they are expected to support a healthy, functioning team that produces great work.

Leadership, conversely, is the practical skill of influencing others, without mandate or decree. *Design leadership*, as we'll be using it, refers to creating and nurturing an environment where curiosity, growth, inclusivity, innovation, discovery, and iteration can thrive, both within the design team itself and beyond. Design leaders don't need designers reporting to them, but they do need followers.

Throughout the book, we'll use *design management* when referring to tasks that are the responsibility or expectation of the manager, such as hiring designers and conducting one-on-one meetings with their team.

We'll use terms like *design leaders* or *design leadership* to refer, well, to basically everything else. If you're reading this book, chances are you're a design leader, even if you're not managing designers.

What Is a Design Leader?

Design leaders may be everywhere in organizations large and small. They challenge the status quo to improve how their company develops products. They build bridges that connect departments and other leaders who may have never spoken to each other. They implement and evangelize practices that their organization had previously only heard about, like conducting research with real customers.

Unfortunately, not every organization recognizes its design leaders, and not every organization enables design leaders to thrive and grow. Many organizations don't provide the air cover that design leaders need to experiment with different methods and approaches to design. In some cases, design leaders exist *despite* the company itself, not because of the organization's investment in the design leader.

As a design leader, ask yourself if any of these situations sound familiar:

- You've conducted guerilla usability testing or sent out your own survey when research wasn't officially approved.

- You led an effort to articulate your team's design principles and values.

- You wrote the job description for an open position on your team rather than using what HR provided.

- You tried using better software or other tools to get the job done.

- You invited other teams to participate in design workshops.

- You shared design-related articles, blog posts, and conference talks with coworkers and partners.

- You helped nondesigner stakeholders improve how they provided useful and actionable feedback.

- You advocated for your team to write blog posts and speak at conferences.

- You wrote the career bands defining the differences between a junior designer and a senior designer, or what's expected of a team lead.

All of the above actions are supposed to improve the individual, team, company, or the practice of design itself. Some of these examples are risky. Depending on who you are, your standing in the company, and your own inherent privilege (or lack thereof), these risks can be catastrophic to your job, because as a change agent, changing how design is done can be threatening to many organizations. Some of those companies may only want to work with people who fall in line and don't ask questions.

A design leader, then, is a person who can picture a better team, work environment, and world. They calculate what steps (and what risks) they *can* and *cannot* take to help themselves and their team get closer to that improved state from where they are today.

These actions that design leaders take can grow trust among the members on their team, their partner teams in product management, marketing, and engineering, and their senior executives. In turn, these design leaders become more influential. More folks inside the organization follow the design leader's vision and trust their decision making. We'll explore more about tactics and building influence within the organization in Chapter 15, "Designing Influence."

As a result, design leadership is often an exercise in balancing mindsets that are diametrically opposed: in one instance, the design leader must be *proactive*, spotting where change needs to be made. Then on the other end of the spectrum, the design leader must be aware of their surroundings to see when and how they must *react* to their changing environment and the expectations of others. And that's exactly why so many of us are looking for more answers, experiences, and help.

What Is a Design Manager?

Design management may seem more straightforward than design leadership since it's a role and responsibility. Many organizations now have *design manager* as a title.

Design managers focus most of their time on monitoring the team itself—the development of the designers, how they work, and what they're working on. The *management* aspect will almost always suggest hierarchical or supervisory relationships with a number of designers, researchers, and other product development professionals, including other managers. In many cases, *management* also connotes the overseeing of the delivery of work to reach an outcome, probably on a schedule and budget. Even delivery as a management function may be different to modern design teams with mature design operations functions. We'll examine design operations and managing delivery in Chapter 14, "Scaling Design."

The challenges facing design managers today are more complex and critical to the business than just approving timecards and who gets a new computer.

Consider just a few of these gnarly cases that design managers might be asked to navigate:

- Identifying, sponsoring, and coaching teammates who may be interested in management themselves

- Creating a work environment conducive to flexible, remote, and distributed work

- Building and nurturing a diverse pipeline of prospects who may interview to join the design team

- Defining the hiring process, including interviewing practices, establishing bias-free compensation bands, and onboarding into the organization

- Nurturing a psychologically safe environment

- Sustaining an inclusive team culture

- Articulating roles, responsibilities, growth, and outcomes for career paths across junior, senior, team lead, and other roles

- Intentionally defining DesignOps expectations and responsibilities to systematically establish routines, processes, and best practices

- Clearly defining quality design work

These situations can vary across design managers and their organizations. As more companies embrace design, it's not a stretch to assume that companies will need more design managers to address these challenges.

Design management also needs a similar proactive mindset similar to design leadership when deciding to create change, despite not being advised or directed to solve a problem. "Recognizing my own [position's] lack of structure led me to create more structure for my team. My team got 1:1s, regular feedback, reviews, and raises (which I negotiated directly with the CFO—valuable experience I wouldn't have had with a layer above me). We held team meetings and outings in a culture where this wasn't the norm," said Helen Keighron, Director of Product Design for HubSpot.

Many high-performing designers are tasked with leading projects or teams based on their ability to design, sometimes without even being asked if management aligns with their own goals. The prospect of designing less while increasing your responsibility of managing others can be daunting. "It took me a while to become comfortable with the idea of becoming a manager. I loved the hands-on creative process and was afraid of losing connection with the actual making. In my mind, I had framed management as the not creative path. My perspective on this slowly shifted during my time at *The New York Times* R&D Lab, where I eventually stepped into a leadership role as creative director," said Alexis Lloyd, Vice President of Product Design at Medium and co-founder at Ethical Futures Lab.

Management isn't for everyone. Many successful designers prefer to hone their craft, their practice, and their ability to deliver amazing work for interesting, challenging audiences, problems, or industries. Other reluctant managers assume that design management is the only path to the next step in their career. Instead, you should start by asking what you hope to learn as a design manager, rather than what you can get out of management.

Chelsey Glasson, a user research lead at Facebook, in her Boxes and Arrows article "So You Want to Be a UX Manager?"[1] wrote "Ultimately, this is a question that requires a lot of exploration and that comes down to factors such as your values, your personality and strengths, and how you derive energy." It will also require answering what you don't want and won't tolerate as well.

What Makes Design Management Unique?

Design management is different from other management positions in the corporate world today because the field, the participants, the expectations, and the outputs and outcomes it yields are all maturing as demand increases, despite many companies still not fully understanding effective product design. While ergonomics, human factors, and industrial design disciplines have been practiced and studied throughout the 20th century, many of us are learning today what's still relevant and what lessons need to evolve.

The differences are stark: in highly functioning product development organizations today, design is now involved early and after a product has been released. Teams interact with customers frequently instead of after a product has been released. The discipline collaborates with more teams than even a decade ago. Competitors embracing design can emerge at any time, from anywhere in the world. And the workforce itself is more diverse, distributed, and in more demand than ever before.

This evolution adds to the challenges facing design leaders.

"The nascency of design as a function means that the VP or Head has to do more diplomacy (cross-functionally), educating, and stakeholder management than other functions, whose maturity allows them to be more easily integrated and understood," said Peter Merholz, design leader and coauthor of *Org Design for Design Orgs: Building and Managing In-House Design Teams*.

---

1   Chelsey Glasson, "So You Want to Be A UX Manager?" *Boxes and Arrows*, March 12, 2019, http://boxesandarrows.com/so-you-want-to-be-a-ux-manager/

How I Knew I Was a Design Leader

by Monet Spells

Monet is a design leader who has simplified design processes, elevated the design voice, and encouraged collaboration at startups, agencies, and tech companies.

I approach product and UX design as an artist approaches their next masterpiece. An artist does not start in the corner of a blank canvas, perfecting inch-by-inch, until they have a finished piece. An artist works in layers. Before the whole is complete, the vision is present and evolving. I value this approach because every designer owns a piece of the design leadership.

I painted the fine details of a progressive canvas as a junior designer. I designed UX solutions to specific user problems, on top of established frameworks. I sketched rough, directionally sound, canvas drawings as a senior designer. I established ecosystems and frameworks to address existing problems and proactively avoid future pain points. At each level, I contributed to the canvas and demonstrated design leadership.

I know what you're thinking: If every level of a designer's career involves leadership, what is a design leader? A design leader is the voice and champion of the team.

As a design leader, I take the product inconsistencies raised by junior designers and communicate that to other functional teams, arguing that these inconsistencies require resources or company input. I leverage the frameworks built by senior designers to advocate for reusable components on engineering teams that will simplify the product

It's true that many facets of design management apply to any other management role. The attributes of effective design managers are similar to those who manage scientists, sales teams, and accountants. But companies know what to do with accountants—whom they report to, what accountants should earn, what good accounting looks like, and whether an accountant actually knows their stuff. Many workplace cultures don't stifle good accounting or look bewilderedly at the finance department, wondering why they're using so many spreadsheets or doing so much … math. Many companies are nowhere close to saying the same thing about their design team.

development process. I share the innovative solutions raised by my entire team to highlight business opportunities and increase competitive advantage. I glean these details, ideas, and solutions to elevate the needs, progress, and accomplishments of my team.

As the voice of design, my relationship with other functional team leaders is pivotal. Product and engineering managers expect me to have a detailed understanding, strong opinion, and informed perspective on problems. Senior leadership expects me to understand business priorities and utilize resources in service of those priorities. These relationships require that I trust and listen to my team.

In order to focus on the 10,000-foot company view, I have to trust that my team is making the right decisions at the 100-foot detail view. To demonstrate my trust, I articulate priorities, connect goals to the day-to-day work, empower the team to take principled risks, and ask questions to understand the details. To gain the team's trust, I invite them into solution brainstorms, encourage them to challenge decisions, and welcome feedback. This bidirectional trust and transparency is the crux of the team's success.

An artist mentality reframes the work as an iterative process, creating breathing room and space for meaningful collaboration. As a design leader, remember that the canvas will evolve from sketch to masterpiece. The deliverables aren't the power of the team—the space to experience the process is the team's power.

Individual contributors collaborate to create masterpieces. Team leaders curate those masterpieces into a cohesive exhibit. Companies build and market museums based on these exhibits.

Now What?

Companies of all sizes and industries can no longer rely on monopolistic or feudal-like relationships with their customers. New competitors can arrive from seemingly nowhere, or move laterally into markets where incumbents once enjoyed fat profits and little competition. The mission to grow revenue and shareholder value while providing a differentiating customer experience has never been more challenging or important.

Businesses that never hired designers will be staffing up design teams. Companies where designers worked on one product will have to expand their practice across the organization. Design teams will be expected to head off these challenges more than ever before. As a result, there will be a greater need for design managers to lead innovative teams to solve more challenging business problems than our predecessors did from only a few years ago. The problems are harder. There is more at stake. The seat at the table will be hot.

That means we'll need to rethink how we lead, promote, and grow our teams. We'll have to evaluate how we hire, as well as how we share our victories and measure our successes. We'll have to apply greater focus to our self-awareness—how we inspire, communicate, and perceive the world around us.

And as more organizations recognize the need for design and start adding designers to the payroll, there will be more opportunity for more first-time managers, and for the veteran leaders to groom them, than ever before.

Not every attempt will resonate. Some may even initially backfire. Much like how we preach iteration in our product cycles, we'll iterate on how we build trust, establish influence, and grow competent, curious designers for the future.

To some, these responsibilities are a burden. The old days may, in fact, seem easier. Less stressful. Fewer expectations. And it may take some time for those jobs to become completely obsolete. But eventually, even those companies will realize they should have been empowering design change agents all along.

Such an opportunity cannot be wasted or taken for granted. It's easy for practitioners to say "Well, it's about time!" when we really should be saying "Well, now what?"

CHAPTER 2

Designing Diversity and Inclusion in Your Teams

Successfully designing for an interconnected global marketplace will require more than rethinking your product development process or talking to customers more often. You'll have to rethink who makes up your entire design team.

This chapter isn't meant to be an all-encompassing playbook that, if followed to the letter, will immediately result in a diverse team where everyone feels included. Unfortunately, that's just unrealistic. Instead, this chapter is supposed to be a practical starting point where design managers can reflect on how they have been shaping their teams and where they can make changes for the better. There are far more experienced, educated voices[1] than ours who explore these complex workplace topics with greater scrutiny and analysis.

> **NOTE** SHOUT-OUTS, THANK YOUS, AND NODS OF RESPECT
>
> Special thanks to Michelle Y. Bess; Erin L. Thomas, Ph.D.; Lisa Welchman; Gail Swanson; Amy Johnson; and Eli Montgomery for their invaluable help shaping earlier drafts of this chapter.

The most effective design teams will be composed of individuals who can think differently from each other, see problems from different points of view, and reflect on their unique experiences as they imagine what's possible, together. In short, to improve your odds for success, design teams will have to be diverse teams.

As the manager or leader of a design team, you have the influence and responsibility to recognize the makeup of the design team and the environment in which the individuals on your team are welcomed, respected, trusted, confided in, and listened to.

Some people may think that's a tall order—or even out of the scope of their job description. On the other hand, managers are *very much* responsible for building and maintaining a high-performing team with low turnover and employees who are happy to come to work.

Staffing a design team with people who are different from one another, respect each other, and are able to be their best professional selves at work will be the foundation of performance. Diversity, then, in thought and experience will be paramount to building

---

1 Michelle Y. Bess, Director Global Diversity, Equity and Inclusion at Sprout Social and Erin L. Thomas, VP – Head of Diversity, Inclusion and Belonging at Upwork both reviewed this work voluntarily because they're amazing people.

high-performing, resilient teams that can handle the challenges of an increasingly complex, competitive business environment.

The 2015 McKinsey study *Why Diversity Matters* captures the benefits of team diversity by stating that "more diverse companies are better able to win top talent, and improve their customer orientation, employee satisfaction, and decision making, leading to a virtuous cycle of increasing returns."[2]

Other statistics in the same report are even more notable:

- Inclusive teams outperform their peers by 80%.
- Gender diverse companies outperform their peers by 15%.
- Ethnically diverse companies outperform their peers by 35%.

For those design managers who struggle with prioritizing diversity because it's not their job, the characteristics of diverse teams are similar to the attributes of high-performing teams. As such, if organizations expect their leaders to build high-performing design teams, they can start by building diverse design teams.

Blind Spots Plague Products and Homogeneous Teams

In 2016, *The Atlantic* sent a survey[3] to dozens of influential Silicon Valley executives, founders and technology leaders in an effort to better understand trends and perspectives of the industry. Among the results that stood out: men were three times as likely as women to say that Silicon Valley was a meritocracy, where the best and brightest were rewarded on their competence and contributions.

"We're hiring the best of the best!" many people could imagine them saying, and likely follow with "Besides, we don't see color or gender." However, these firms had spent years only hiring engineers and funding companies composed of homogeneous networks of privileged white men. They couldn't see a problem here. Then these companies were caught off guard when the platforms they built

---

2   Vivian Hunt, Dennis Layton, and Sara Prince, *Why Diversity Matters* (McKinsey & Company, January 2015), www.mckinsey.com/business-functions/organization /our-insights/why-diversity-matters

3   Adrienne Lafrance, "Is Silicon Valley a Meritocracy?" *The Atlantic*, October 13, 2016, www.theatlantic.com/technology/archive/2016/10/is-silicon-valley-a -meritocracy/503948/

didn't have protections in place when women, underrepresented minorities, or people of color were bullied or put in harm's way.

Such a lack of representation subjects your products, teams, and larger organization to unnecessary risk. There are many stories of companies backtracking after they realized that homogeneous teams resulted in embarrassing, preventable gaffes, or decisions that hurt people. For example, YouTube's iOS app didn't accommodate left-handed people who were uploading content, resulting in every video appearing upside down.[4] Apple left out menstrual cycle monitoring in its initial release of HealthKit, despite originally claiming to let its users "see your whole health picture."[5, 6] And far more seriously, women rideshare users had no way to call for help or indicate they were in danger when their drivers they trusted subjected them to abuse, harassment, or worse.

It's total conjecture to say that if these products had been designed by teams with diverse backgrounds and different experiences that there would have been any different outcome.

But it's plausible that a diverse team, working in a psychologically safe environment where teammates could call attention to an unconsidered possible outcome such as abuse or exclusion would have designed many of those safeguards from the start.

Blind spots creep into recognizing bias, too. Boston Consulting Group surveyed over 16,000 employees in 14 countries to learn more about what particular obstacles women, racial or ethnic minorities, and LGBTQ employees face in the workplace.[7] Straight white men, who overwhelmingly make up the majority of corporate leadership, were 13 percentage points more likely to say that the day-to-day employee experience and major decisions—such as who gets hired,

---

4 Sean Buckley, "Unconscious Bias Is Why We Don't Have a Diverse Workplace, says Google," Engadget, September 25, 2014, www.engadget.com/2014/09/25/unconscious-bias-is-why-we-dont-have-a-diverse-workplace-says/

5 Rose Eveleth, "How Self-Tracking Apps Exclude Women," *The Atlantic*, December 15, 2014, www.theatlantic.com/technology/archive/2014/12/how-self-tracking-apps-exclude-women/383673/

6 Sarah Perez, "Apple Stops Ignoring Women's Health with iOS 9 HealthKit Update, Now Featuring Period Tracking," *Techcrunch*, June 9, 2015, https://techcrunch.com/2015/06/09/apple-stops-ignoring-womens-health-with-ios-9-healthkit-update-now-featuring-period-tracking/

7 Matt Krentz, "Survey: What Diversity and Inclusion Policies Do Employees Actually Want?" *Harvard Business Review*, February 5, 2019, https://hbr.org/2019/02/survey-what-diversity-and-inclusion-policies-do-employees-actually-want

promoted, or asked to participate in stretch projects—were free from bias. On the other hand, *half* of women and underrepresented minorities responded that they felt such bias *did* exist. In short, left unchecked, people are unlikely to recognize their own bias to blind spots in their thinking and world-view.

These blind spots can cripple products, hurt morale, and expose the organization to risks that it never expected to have. Business as usual is no longer good enough for business.

Diversity in Design Teams

Building diverse teams of individuals unique from one another helps give teams different perspectives that it needs in order to success-fully design products and services in a diverse, complex marketplace. Diversity will reduce the likelihood that your teams and products will suffer from groupthink. Individuals will feel more engaged with their colleagues, their work, and their employer. And last, but certainly not least, you'll yield greater innovation, more effective problem-solving in complex situations, and improved changes in the products that you design and the environments in which you work.

The benefits of a diverse team don't stop at practicing designers, either. Research indicates that leaders with diverse backgrounds and experience can help companies innovate more. Diverse leadership teams are also more likely to foster an environment that leads to new ideas and unique or innovative approaches to problem solving.

Remember: Individuals are not diverse—groups are diverse.

Diverse Teams Signal a Positive Workplace

Numerous studies suggest that people prefer working in a diverse workplace.[8] In a survey of 1,000 respondents, the job site Glassdoor found that 67% of job seekers note the diversity of the workforce when considering a new job. Leading women candidates especially prioritize working for organizations with women in significant leadership positions. A recent survey found that 61% of women look at the number of women and their roles in a business when deciding

---

8   Stephen Turban, Dan Wu, Letian (LT) Zhang, "Research: When Gender Diversity Makes Firms More Productive," *Harvard Business Review*, February 11, 2019, https://hbr.org/2019/02/research-when-gender-diversity-makes-firms-more-productive

among offers. In other words, building a diverse team will also help you attract additional people who come from different backgrounds, thus creating a compounding positive cycle over time.

Improving the Pipeline

The hiring process is the first line of defense against homogeneous teams. Your approach to hiring should attract a broad range of candidates to build or reinforce a diverse team. We explore how to increase your pipeline of candidates to join your team beginning in Chapter 3, "Designing Your Hiring Process," but let's briefly cover a few approaches here:

- Write performance profiles that use gender-neutral language and don't include skills that are unnecessary for the position. (We cover this in depth in Chapter 4, "Performance Profiles and Interview Guides.")

- Post your job descriptions and performance profiles to internet sites that cater to diverse communities of practice (specific examples are cited in Chapter 3).

- Don't require years of experience as an anchor for qualification—in many cases, men apply for a job when they meet only 60% of the qualifications, but women apply only if they meet 100% of them.[9] Promote responsibilities that people may have accomplished, with less regard to tenure.

- Recruit at a wide range of colleges and universities, including women's colleges, historically black colleges and universities, minority-serving institutions, and community colleges.

- Conduct an audit of your website and other collateral to make sure that photography and language reflect a diverse environment.

- Establish a presence and sponsor events at meetups, conferences, and other events, and create relationships with these organizers and leaders. *But remember*—it's not the event organizer's job to be your recruiter.

---

9   Tara Sophia Mohr, "Why Women Don't Apply for Jobs Unless They're 100% Qualified," *Harvard Business Review*, August 25, 2014, https://hbr.org/2014/08 /why-women-dont-apply-for-jobs-unless-theyre-100-qualified

In addition, it's also up to you to apply a fair and comprehensive selection process that mitigates bias throughout the entire recruiting and hiring experience. We'll explore how to improve your chances of hiring great people from a diverse pipeline in Chapter 3, but in the meantime, it's never too early to rethink or apply the following qualifications:

- Use a diverse hiring committee that defines the needs of the position, the ideal candidate, and what traits are more important than others. These traits should include prioritizing specific technical skills and soft and social skills, such as presentation and communication aptitude, the ability to collaborate with others, and more.

- Establish how you will rank and score experience, skills, and answers prior to any interviews.

- Create flexible timing and scheduling of interviews.

- Have interviews that include exercises directly relevant to the position, rather than tests or whiteboarding sessions that aren't appropriate for some roles.

- Make fair offers based on market value for the role, which are independent of the candidate's prior salary.

Remind yourself that hiring a diverse team likely extends far beyond your sole responsibility. Talk to your Human Resources partners to learn what other efforts are planned or underway that you can put to work within your design team.

Retaining Diverse Talent

A diverse hiring pipeline and an interview process that reduces bias are the foundation for creating a diverse team, but it's not enough to sustain a diverse workforce. For many women and underrepresented minorities, their biggest challenges aren't necessarily found in landing the job, but in what happens once they are on the payroll.

The previously-mentioned Boston Consulting research concluded these factors all drive women and nonwhite men away from the job:

- Pervasive bias and microaggressions in the day-to-day work experience

- Lack of opportunity to advance a career within the company

- Little flexibility when juggling family responsibilities

Design managers, once aware that their colleagues are experiencing these obstacles, can put processes and other checks and balances in place to eliminate these behaviors and increase the likelihood these people will stick around.

We discuss how to mitigate or remove these obstacles in your design team by sponsoring colleagues instead of just mentoring (examined in Chapter 13, "Developing Designers"), through clear career ladders (also Chapter 13) and in how you prioritize inclusion in your design team activities (see "Team Building Activities That Don't Build Teams" later in this chapter).

Preparing for Friction

Design managers leading diverse teams may experience more conflict and friction than they may be accustomed to when they led homogeneous groups. That's the process at work, and it's to be celebrated, not extinguished. Remember, people who are generally similar will arrive at a consensus faster, consider fewer alternatives, and generally abandon the creative process sooner by fixating on an agreed-upon decision. And that's exactly what you *don't* want.

"Diverse teams are more likely to constantly reexamine facts and remain objective. They may also encourage greater scrutiny of each member's actions, keeping their joint cognitive resources sharp and vigilant. By breaking up workplace homogeneity, you can allow your employees to become more aware of their own potential biases— entrenched ways of thinking that can otherwise blind them to key information and even lead them to make errors in decision-making processes," David Rock and Heidi Grant said.[10]

Be prepared for these early-stage disagreements by establishing that respectful conflict is okay and to be expected. Establish constraints for when honest disagreement is encouraged, such as focusing on what is up for discussion and what has already been decided. Have methods in place to challenge other previously approved ideas so that you don't get derailed in crunch time, and make sure that everyone knows how to escalate risks or threats that get uncovered during the creative process.

---

10 David Rock and Heidi Grant, "Why Diverse Teams Are Smarter," *Harvard Business Review,* November 4, 2016, https://hbr.org/2016/11/why-diverse-teams -are-smarter

As the design leader, you'll still want to monitor conflict to make sure that it's productive and not personal, petty, or mean-spirited. "When that happens, it is often because team members are bringing different values, rather than different ideas, to the table. It's difficult to overcome differences in values, no matter how well-intentioned colleagues may be," said authors David Rock, Heidi Grant and Jacqui Grey.[11]

If such a situation occurs, you may need to cut short the meeting and talk individually with each of the participants. Reiterate the importance of people with different backgrounds and experience working together and why mutual respect is expected by and from all parties.

We discuss how to respectfully communicate disagreement and introduce new ideas in depth in Chapter 10, "Leading Continuous Critique."

Designing Inclusion Within Your Teams

Inclusion is not necessarily an extension of diversity, even though it's frequently paired with the term in many job titles, blog posts, and conference talks. Diverse teams are not automatically inclusive, and likewise, homogeneous teams can either be inclusive to each other or be just as fragmented and unwelcoming to their colleagues as any other team.

Defining Inclusive Teams

Inclusive teams are made up of individuals, management, and partners who trust and respect each other, both as people and as contributors to the company mission. People's differences are welcomed, not simply tolerated. Those people who may be different from the majority are not expected to assimilate or conform—they are empowered and able to work as themselves.

Inclusion isn't about everyone being best friends in and out of the office. It's not about making sure that everyone goes to lunch together or binge-watches the latest show that premiered over the weekend or live-Slacks the award shows. It's creating the space where it's okay if people *don't* go to lunch together, it's okay if you *don't* watch the same shows, and it's okay if you *don't* drink at the company happy hour. An inclusive environment may also mean setting aside how

---

11 David Rock, Heidi Grant, Jacqui Grey, "Diverse Teams Feel Less Comfortable—and That's Why They Perform Better," September 22, 2016, https://hbr.org/2016/09/diverse-teams-feel-less-comfortable-and-thats-why-they-perform-better

the person sitting next to you voted in the last election or spent their time on the weekend, too. It's where the individuals on your team are still welcome and expected to do their job, regardless if they don't partake in things that others on the team choose to do.

Inclusion is about creating a safe environment where people can be professionals and do their jobs in an environment where they are welcomed, heard, appreciated, and able to contribute positively to their projects and also their work environment.

Let's explore how to create that environment where these diverse teams can thrive.

Inclusion Is Easy to Screw Up and Hard to Repair

While building a diverse team can be challenging, developing a sense of inclusion within the entire team isn't something to be taken for granted either. It's even harder to achieve if the design manager isn't committed to creating an inclusive environment for everyone—not just their directs.

When you are looking back, it's simple and obvious to see what you might need to do differently. Perhaps more frequent skip-level one-on-one's could give additional insight into what others on the team are feeling. Or if you have a culture of avoiding conflict, instead of resolving it, it could lead to people not opening up about how they truly feel at work until long after they have left the organization. In short, fostering psychological safety, and holding yourself and others accountable for when you fall short, can make a difference in some people's lives for the better.

Much of the advice, topics, and points of view in this chapter are the result of listening, reading, and following underrepresented people—designers or otherwise—who have been in toxic environments themselves. These strategies and tactics hopefully will create an opportunity for progress and growth on your team, and hone your ability to recognize negative situations and how to correct them before they spiral out of control.

There should be a tight correlation between increasing the time spent learning about and empathizing more with others as your influence, power, and responsibilities also increase.

Creating and Sustaining an Inclusive Team

In many ways, hiring a diverse team is just the beginning of the work, as much of the effort will have been spent in creating and sustaining an inclusive work environment.

Inclusive teams should:

- Know and support the team's and company's mission and how their individual role contributes to that success.

- Understand how and why corporate decisions are made.

- Be empowered to act autonomously and to ask for help when needed.

- Regularly engage in a healthy critique of the team's work.

- Resolve conflicts directly and without personal attacks.

- Provide opportunities for individuals' ideas and concerns to be voiced and heard.

- Offer pay and advancement opportunities in a fair and equitable way.

- Ensure that boundaries between work and out-of-work responsibilities are well understood.

- Collaborate within and across teams.

- Have transparent, publicized reward systems in place that recognize both individual and team accomplishments.

- Know how to recognize teammates who may be feeling marginalized and how to recommend changes to correct behaviors that led to that marginalization.

- Have channels in place to notify you, senior management, human resources, or other outlets if something makes someone feel uncomfortable with the prevailing culture.

In other words, inclusive teams care about each other, so they can care about what matters to the business. If your team already exhibits a lot of these traits, you're probably fostering an environment that promotes inclusion. Be careful not to equate inclusion with assimilation or expecting the minority to conform to the majority.

But what if some characteristics stand out that aren't where you want them to be? There are several steps you can take to continue marching toward this environment, some of which you've probably done in the past, but perhaps may need revisiting with your team.

- Regularly schedule one-on-ones with your directs and skip-level one-on-ones with your directs' teams.

- Conduct all-hands meetings monthly or quarterly to share any updates or changes to corporate strategy, review and discuss financials, and revisit other news related to the larger organization.

- Schedule show-and-tells to ensure that everyone knows what teams are working on, particularly with larger and distributed teams.

- Set clear expectations and goals for projects and the contributions that individuals will be expected to make.

- Be clear that if someone makes a mistake—such as an unwelcome remark, sexist joke, or other offensive comment—that the offender must own the behavior, apologize, and recognize that doing it again will have further consequences.

Monitoring Language, Lingo, and Jargon

The language you use can also divide your teams into the in-crowd and the excluded. As the manager, you should be setting the tone for how your teams communicate with each other, both in formal expression and interoffice banter.

For instance, managers who fail to use gender-neutral language when addressing mixed groups of people risk alienating women in the group. Male managers may not recognize the microaggression by saying "Guys," but that doesn't mean the women won't notice.

Managers also risk alienating individuals on their team by overusing sports analogies, war metaphors, or only quoting the same movies or TV shows again and again. As much as some people love a well-timed *Dumb and Dumber* or a Billy Madison quote, you're directly excluding the people who have chosen to do other things than fill their heads with sophomoric mid-1990's filmmaking.

Keep in mind that you can have an inclusive team where everyone feels welcome and supported and still have a lively discussion about *The Bachelorette*, *The Crown*, or Game 6 of the NBA Finals. But be self-aware as a manager to see who consistently contributes to these conversations and who starts to back off as these topics get revisited over and over again.

Promoting Employee Resource Groups

Employee Resource Groups (ERGs) are voluntary, employee-led groups that serve as a support system—a safe space—for members and organizations by nurturing an environment that is directly tied to the organizational mission, values, goals, business practices, and objectives of the workplace.

Well-known ERGs include the Twitter @Blackbirds, supporting African-American employees of the messaging service, and the Gayglers group, comprised of gay, lesbian, bisexual, and transgender employees of Google. Other ERG's also support employees with disabilities, veterans, and working parents, to name a few.

As the manager of an inclusive, diverse design team you can help recommend these ERGs to employees who may be interested, or provide the support necessary for your team to create one directly. Also create or prioritize time so that you or the individuals on your team can participate or help contribute to their ERG.

Here's a hint—if you have people on your team who would likely benefit from an ERG, chances are they're already creating unofficial support networks through other means, even if it's as simple as private Slack channels. Provide your teammates with the means and support to make those unofficial ERGs sanctioned so that the rest of the company's employees can benefit as well. As the manager of a team starting an ERG, ask how you can apply your influence or position in the company to help.

Lastly, tie the mission or activities in the ERG back to your business priorities. Not doing so can make such ERGs seem disconnected from the rest of the business or just another choir preaching to itself. If that happens, it's only a matter of time before the ERG loses executive support.

Cultural Biases

by Maria Pereda

Maria is a veteran design leader who has led product, agency, and startup teams in three countries, and she'll always tell you the truth.

Throughout my career, I got the same feedback over and over. "Passionate, hard-working, but sometimes too blunt, perhaps harsh in her approach. Needs to work at softening the way she provides feedback." And I tried, year after year, but it kept coming back. Even recently, during negotiations for a new role, the hiring manager told me as he was offering me the position, "We love your candor, but tone it down."

My struggle is, I look white, I just don't sound or behave like I've lived in America my whole life. I'm Spanish, and Spain is a culture that relies on directness, honesty, and passionate dialogue to communicate. Growing up there shaped who I am today.

As the world becomes more connected, we benefit from working together with people who come from different places than we do. As design leaders, we, more than ever, need to be aware of cultural biases and how they affect our hiring and managing of diverse teams. Different cultures will bring a richness of perspectives and some welcome friction that results in better work.

Cultural bias, according to Tom E. Yingst III,[12] involves a prejudice or highlighted distinction in viewpoint that suggests a preference of one's culture over another. It introduces one group's accepted behavior as valued and distinguishable from another lesser valued societal

Identifying Marginalization

Despite efforts to create a transparent environment where people can open up if they're feeling marginalized, as the manager of your team, you will likely not be the first person whom individuals will confide in if they're concerned.

And as the team manager, your position of power likely means that the designers on your team, who may be feeling marginalized, won't directly tell you how they're feeling. If you don't personally witness

---

12 Tom Yingst III, "Cultural Bias," *Encyclopedia of Child Behavior and Development*, eds. S. Goldstein and J. A. Naglieri (Boston, MA: Springer, 2001), https://doi .org/10.1007/978-0-387-79061-9_749

group. These biases are not always conscious, and they can easily sneak up on us. Sometimes, it is an accent that makes someone hard to understand. Maybe they won't be good at managing a conversation with that sneaky PM. Or maybe the way they answered that question seems as if they defer too much. Will they be too pleasing?

These differences can present in many ways, and if not understood, create a set of boundaries that can divide us. According to Dr Erin Meyer,[13] as explained in her book The Culture Map, there are eight different contexts in which our cultural differences can create friction at work: general communication, providing feedback, leading, taking decisions, persuading, disagreeing, trusting, and scheduling. By understanding your culture relative to someone else's in that scale, you can avoid harmful assumptions and start shedding your own biases.

Going back to my feedback. Turns out that in Spain, being direct and frank when giving feedback just shows that you care. But when received by North American cultures, it can come across as too direct and harsh.

Becoming aware of our own cultural baggage and appreciating where the cultures you deal with sit on those scales will enable you to become the cultural glue of your team. Teach people how to understand those differences, and how to suspend judgments they might have had about those who behave differently. Have them make a map of where they sit relative to the other culture for each one of the eight attributes. In the end, less cultural homogeneity will result in friction, but will also create a stronger, better team.

team members being marginalized, it doesn't mean that it's not happening. You're probably not maliciously oblivious—rather, your perspective, privilege, or position may not expose you to what makes people feel that way. Similarly, if someone tells you everything is okay, you may need to look for other cues.

Use one-on-ones with your own directs and quarterly skip-one-on-one meetings to dig into or identify any early signs that the environment isn't what it should be.

---

13 Erin Meyer, *The Culture Map: Breaking Through the Invisible Boundaries of Global Business* (New York: PublicAffairs, 2014).

It can be problematic to try writing down the attributes of notice-able behavior of someone who feels marginalized. For example, one person may be entirely comfortable coming to work, putting on headphones, collaborating exclusively through Slack or Skype, eating lunch at his desk, and going home a few hours later. Instead, look for behavior change. Perhaps this same person was originally grabbing the whiteboard markers and driving meetings, sharing stories from his personal life, calling teams into the design studio, or going to lunch with a group of coworkers. In that case, the teammate's withdrawal and exclusion from activities he used to do warrants a discussion.

If you have a designer or researcher who is the only one working remotely, or working on a solo project while the rest of the team works together, create consistent situations to bring that worker back into the daily cadence of a team. Be sure they have time to share what they're working on with the larger team, or make sure that you create time for those designers working on other projects to become familiar with the work of the person working solo. Be sure these people still share what they've learned or what could be done differently in retros or stand-ups, even if others on the design team won't know every detail as if it were their own project. This isn't inclusion theater at all—rather, it shows that working independently on a project doesn't mean you're a lone wolf with no additional support system from a pack.

Be sure the pendulum doesn't swing too far the other way either and that because a person doesn't go to happy hour, they are disappointed they're *not* at happy hour.

Supporting Religious Inclusion

Religious freedom at work, to many, is a subject for employment law attorneys and human resources. But as the design manager, you can still take steps to make sure that designers who practice their religion understand they're a valued member of your work culture, even if the rest of the team is more secular or most of the team observes a similar faith. For instance, be sure that your meeting schedules, check-ins, demos, and other group events respect prayer time during work hours. You may need to work with HR and even facilities if your office doesn't currently have a prayer room. Instead of leaving your designer to navigate these waters, use your influence and seniority to do it for them.

Similarly, be cognizant of scheduling work travel and major delivery dates around religious holidays—do a bit of homework to learn about significant events that aren't recognized as federal holidays so that your team isn't stuck having to choose between their faith and their job.

As mentioned earlier, add some variety to your team-wide celebratory lunches. If pizza has been the team's standard group lunch for months, consider restaurants and catering companies that provide kosher and halal options.

Creating Space for Neurodiversity

Diverse teams are composed of more than just people of different races or cultures. A healthy, functioning team also enables a neurologically atypical team to thrive and be their best self at work. In most cases, neurodiverse or neuroatypical labels are used to include people who are diagnosed as dyslexic, somewhere on the spectrum of autism, show symptoms of attention deficit disorder, or learn and process information differently than typical people. It's important to keep in mind these traits aren't the result of mental illness, disease, or injury.

Similar to how creating accessible digital products usually means just creating more thoughtful products for everyone, creating an environment for neurodiverse colleagues is more about establishing a respectful space that will benefit everyone, typical or not.

For example, if you work in an open office, try to establish a more modular arrangement where people can be more heads down with noise-cancelling headphones on and away from distraction when the space isn't used for a specific collaborative activity.

See what options exist for wellness rooms, similar to Mothers' Rooms, where colleagues can recharge and recenter themselves. In many cases, these rooms or spaces can provide relief to someone who has extreme responses to light, sound, and touch, and after some time alone, they can return to the team ready to be productive.

In many cases, just ask the person on your team how best you can help them be successful at work—whether that means keeping your confidence if they have to excuse themselves from meetings, if certain activities or environments may trigger a reaction, or other ways that they'll need their manager to understand instead of leaving you to draw your own conclusions.

As the person in authority, you should also make sure that everyone knows that they can open up about these situations, because the thought of just leaving a meeting mid-presentation or going home to regroup may be terrifying to someone. They may feel they've put their jobs and livelihood at risk by trying to cope. Make sure they know they can come to you first. One such effective way is to address your whole team at once, as a group, to discuss how individuals can communicate with each other, and see if there are styles or approaches that work particularly well or should be avoided when designing together. Even in a team culture with strong psychological safety, individuals may not speak up, so you still have to talk to folks privately to see if you need to adjust anything.

And as a reminder, the second you feel underequipped to have these conversations, seek help from your own management and human resources team to get the advice you seek; don't think you have to go it alone.

MANAGING MENTAL ILLNESS

By far the worst moment of my career—and I hope nothing ever comes close to surpassing it—was when a designer on my team took her own life after suffering from severe depression in 2016.

Since then, I've questioned whether I did enough as a man-ager to try and give this incredibly talented but tormented designer the space to address her illness, which seems to be a common feeling among those who have lost friends or loved ones in this way.

If you see a team member starting to act in ways that indicate they might harm themselves, such as retreating from projects that they once found captivating, avoiding workplace relationships, or uncommon emotional out-bursts, go on high alert and stay there. If you have a hunch something could be going from bad to worse, please, *please* don't keep it inside. Get help. ■

Team Building Activities That Don't Build Teams

It's also possible that you may be inadvertently creating environ-ments where inclusivity *cannot* thrive by scheduling activities that cater only to a portion of the team. In some cases, these activities are intended to create camaraderie within the team, but can quickly create an us-versus-them environment if you're not careful.

Consider these situations when planning team activities:

- Be mindful of remote and distributed team members when planning events that only pertain to one office.

- If alcohol is involved, set limits on how long and how much will be provided by the company. Be aware of how many events include alcohol and measure against the larger organizational culture as well.

- Scheduling events after work, such as attending sporting events or even industry meetups, may strain coworkers with families or second jobs at home and create additional burdens—especially childcare. Physical activities such as road races, obstacle course events, or even bowling can also exclude members of your team.

- When ordering team lunches or going as a group to lunch, be aware of vegetarian options and allergic needs of your team so as not to alienate teammates.

- If you are doing activities that not everyone will participate in, be sure to tell the entire team that the event is optional and non-participating team members won't be penalized or suffer directly or indirectly if they don't attend.

- Understand the larger work culture in the organization to recognize if taking the team out (during or outside business hours) for team-building events will compromise your and your team's reputation. Seek approval, confirm approval, and document the outcome for senior management.

Remember, while some people enjoy merging their social life and their work life in one place, there are a lot of people who simply don't expect, or want, their employer to also be their source or provider of social activities.

Wrapping Up

Some design managers may say this is more than they signed up for, or that it's not their remit, that supporting diverse and inclusive teams is an HR problem, or that they're on the payroll only to ship great products. The last statement is certainly true—design managers are on the payroll to ship great products.

Great products will only be possible, however, with diverse teams that are empowered, trusted, and supported to design successful products. Don't let a culture of homogeneity and exclusivity impede your team's potential to be amazing together.

Work with your own management team and human resources department to make sure that the high-performing women and people of color have the opportunity in their daily work to become the leaders your future diverse design team will look up to.

The good and bad news about supporting diverse and inclusive teams is that your work as a manager and leader is never done. You can change homogeneous teams into diverse teams, but as people move onto other jobs, your once-diverse team can revert back into homogeneity. What was once an inclusive environment can become unwelcoming to individuals. Conversely, teammates' marginalizing behaviors can change and people can grow to support and foster inclusion.

As a result, it's your job to repeat a few steps over and over again:

- Continue honing your own self-awareness and monitor yourself and your team for bias or exclusionary behavior.

- Listen—and believe—what your team tells you. Be mindful and observant of the things the team doesn't say.

- Encourage a psychologically safe speak-up culture, where your team is comfortable voicing new ideas, suggestions, and reporting possible marginalizing behaviors to you and others on the team.

- Nurture a diverse pipeline of future candidates.

- Highlight the positive contributions and achievements of a range of individuals on your team, particularly those in the minority of your team.

- Reinforce your team's commitment to diversity and inclusion so that your team hears it from you, rather than only from outside groups.

Fostering a safe place for people of diverse backgrounds and promoting an environment where everyone feels included may never feel like it's on autopilot. That's exactly what you want. You want to be aware of how your team feels as individuals and as a unit trying to work to achieve a common goal over time, as well as when there are disruptions or disputes that threaten that environment. Regular consistent follow-through—day in, and day out—will show both your team and outsiders that you're committed to nurturing a positive, psychologically safe workplace culture where people of all backgrounds can thrive.

CHAPTER 3

Designing Your Hiring Process

Hiring designers *is* the most important part of the designer manager's job—*not* delivering amazing design work, *not* creating the culture in which design is practiced, *not* retaining the designers already on the payroll, and *not* scaling design throughout the company.

Hiring designers is the most important responsibility because the design manager creates a compounding cycle where hiring awesome, diverse designers is only possible because of the culture, the process, and the folks already on the team. And the new designers are there to help deliver more work. They'll also grow their leadership and management skills and even lead their own teams one day. Yet hiring designers is often treated as a chore, or worse, an inconvenience.

Design managers who have not crafted a strategic, repeatable hiring process can introduce significant and expensive risk to their team and organization. For example, they may hire homogeneous teams who think and act the same way. Hiring decisions might be plagued by bias, whether overt or unintentional. And hiring the wrong person could set their team back months in productivity and crush morale as they begin the search all over again for the right person (but with the same tactics and methods that brought the wrong person into the organization in the first place).

And as if that weren't enough to rethink how you do your hiring process, the demand for designers is always increasing. An InVision report[1] surveying design teams indicated that over 70% of more than 2,000 respondents would be increasing their team size in the next year. Only 7% were planning to reduce their design team.

All of this means that design leaders need to reflect on their hiring process as it stands and question where it can be improved. They need to find where questions can be standardized and scored consistently. They need to rethink whether or not design exercises deliver the outcomes they want to see. They should question how they review portfolios and if they are prioritizing the right experience relative to the candidate's potential to learn and grow within the team.

In some organizations, the design operations team designs the hiring process, while in others, it's the responsibility of the design manager.

---

1 *Design Trends Report: Talent* (InVision, June 2019), www.invisionapp.com/design -trends-report-talent

Regardless, they owe it to their organizations, their colleagues, and their candidates to design an equitable, humane hiring process.

It's not necessarily difficult, but it does require a diligence, awareness, and commitment to learning where to improve just how you hire designers onto your team.

Defining a Successful Hiring Experience

Articulating a successful hiring experience may be more challenging than you think. At first glance, some people may say that a successful hiring experience is simply finding a competent designer who sticks around for a while and is good at their job. Easy enough.

But that stance fails to consider many of the other perspectives that should influence a successful hiring experience. Formally establishing what a successful hiring experience looks like is the first step toward designing such an experience, instead of settling for whatever the default experience may be.

While any two organizations may define a successful hiring experience differently from each other, there are several factors that should underpin any effective hiring process. Consider how important these factors are to your organization and where you think your process stands today.

- **Equitable:** Is your hiring process actively trying to reduce bias, sexism, and racism via such steps as blind screening, diverse hiring committees, and predetermined questions and response scoring?

- **Transparent:** Are the team and candidate aware of the steps in the hiring process and where they are in that process? Does everyone have a clear understanding of how long the process may take and what's expected of them?

- **Productive:** Does everything the candidate does as part of the hiring process help move the company to a decision?

- **Consistent:** Do you ask every candidate the same questions and score their responses the same way every time?

- **Communicative:** Is there a schedule that outlines when the candidate and hiring committees are notified of where they all are in the hiring experience? Are there gaps of time when someone may not know what's going on?

Honestly answering these questions is a useful about-face to learn where you may need to make changes in how you hire new people on your team. Let's zoom in more closely and see what a successful experience looks like for specific participants in the hiring experience as well.

The Candidate Experience

Designing the candidate experience usually starts with understanding the touchpoints of when the company will interact with the candidate. These communications may be as simple as emails or as complex as full-day interviews. Mapping the frequency of these interactions, and how near or distant they are to other milestones such as submitting the résumé or appearing onsite, will reveal where you may decide what to explore deeper. For instance, you may find patterns indicating that candidates were not advised they wouldn't be getting an offer until weeks after they had interviewed. Perhaps that's just because they interviewed early in the process—but that doesn't mean there couldn't have been an additional touchpoint to notify them that the decision might take an extra month.

In many cases, it's not enough just to ask yourself how you would like to be treated, simply because your own experiences probably don't represent the broad spectrum of possible applicants who will be sending their résumés into the applicant tracking system. Instead of basing a hiring experience around your own history, try turning the experience into a collaborative discussion.

Ask a cross-section of your team—perhaps someone recently hired, someone who interviews candidates, or a product manager who hires other product managers—to complete a simple fill-in-the-blank statement individually in less than two minutes.

A prompt similar to this one is easy enough:

> We want candidates who apply to join our design team to feel
> _____, _____, and _____ throughout
> the recruitment and interview process. To do this, our team will
> promise our candidates they'll be _____ and
> _____ while avoiding _____
> or _____. This approach will help us
> stand out from the competition, while showing that we value
> _____ and _____.

That sets an ideal state. Now try to uncover more about the current state. Ask the same folks—again, people recently hired to your team and those who have hired others—another series of questions about what actually happened when they were interviewing candidates or were candidates themselves. To get a more complete understanding of the experience and additional insights, you can include people whom you extended offers to who declined, or people you rejected, but you probably shouldn't expect a response from everyone.

These questions can rely on a Likert scale of 1–5 with 1 being in strong *disagreement* with the statement and 5 corresponding with strong *agreement* with the statement.

- Overall, the interview experience was positive.

- Recruiter communication was always clear, responsive, and actionable.

- My interviewers were well-prepared.

- I had regular updates about my progress throughout the interview process.

- I felt I had a good understanding of the open position.

Asking your team members to complete this simple exercise individually reassures you that you don't inadvertently risk groupthink or someone dominating the conversation and leaving some ideas left unshared.

With the current state assessment and a candidate experience vision in place, you can look at the candidate's journey and see whether or not you're fulfilling this promise or where to dig a little deeper to learn why not.

Designing a successful candidate experience pays off more than just in the people you hire. You'll also stand out in the minds of the people who don't fit your needs now but may later. Plus, you'll probably be well-regarded by the people to whom you offer the position, but who may decline for their own reasons, but might want to work with you in the future.

A recurring theme throughout much of the next few chapters is establishing consistency in your hiring process. *Structured interviews* go a long way toward building that foundation of consistency. All candidates are screened the same way, are asked the same questions in the same order, and are judged by the same criteria as everyone else. Applying structured interviews to your screening and hiring process helps you and the hiring committee create objectivity during the interviews and will dramatically improve your odds of hiring the right candidate.

Rethinking Hiring Committees

Many companies use hiring committees to interview candidates. But many of these committees aren't effective because they're often just composed of whoever doesn't have a meeting when the candidate is being interviewed. Staffing *roles* versus *people* is the first step to rethinking how you should develop your hiring committee. Strategically deciding what roles should participate in the committee, and how the committee will make decisions, will improve the outcomes and the overall hiring experience for the candidate and the organization.

Be crystal clear about what is expected of being on the hiring committee. If you're asking someone from another department to join the panel, you may find that your expectations are different than how they hire. For example, decide what you want them to focus on specifically, or how you need the committee to structure their notes on each candidate.

Decide ahead of time if the hiring committee is looking for majority of approval (meaning three people out of five vote yes or no to hiring the candidate) or if you expect consensus (all five members of the hiring committee must approve an offer). Since research suggests small groups of odd numbers of people make better decisions via consensus,[2] we recommend only extending offers after *everyone* on the hiring committee has voted to extend an offer.

Diversify your hiring committees as well. Resist the urge to keep asking the same person to participate because you think they're a

---

2 Brian H. Bornstein and Edie Greene, "Jury Decision Making: Implications for and from Psychology," *Association for Psychological Science*, February 4, 2011, https://journals.sagepub.com/doi/abs/10.1177/0963721410397282

good interviewer. Instead, look for others who could become great interviewers if given the chance. Scheduling practice sessions where colleagues role-play the candidate and the interviewer, followed by feedback, can strengthen less-experienced interview skills. If your own schedule is too full to see this through, work with your partners in DesignOps or seek out a colleague on your team who has expressed interest in developing their leadership skills and delegate the responsibility to them, and make time to check in to monitor progress. It's that important.

Diverse hiring committees also improve the likelihood of hiring more women and people of color. "Implementing diverse hiring panels has enabled us to cast a wider net at the outset of the hiring process and systematically help reduce unconscious bias in our hiring," says Danielle Brown, a human resources executive at Gusto and previously Google and Intel.[3]

Diverse panels of women and people of color benefit the candidate's experience as well. These interviewees see people who look like them thriving in the company and show that they could be successful there, too.

3   Katherine Reynolds Lewis, "Diverse Interview Panels May Be a Key to Workplace Diversity," *Working Mother*, June–July 2017, www.workingmother.com /diverse-interview-panels-may-be-key-to-workplace-diversity

These diverse panels even play a role in weeding out bad apples who aren't capable of working with a diverse team. For example, if candidates only address a man in the room, particularly when a woman on the hiring panel asks a question, you may have seen all you need to see to make a hard pass on that candidate.

Interviewing Design Leaders

If you're hiring design leadership such as a Director of User Experience, Design Manager, or another senior position, you'll need to focus on stories more than portfolios and prioritize examples of inspiring people over compelling artifacts. Such a situation calls for asking the candidate to discuss examples from the past and what difference their work made to the design team and other departments and teams across the company.

Most of your questions should focus on how the leader created change across the organization and how they prepared their junior reports to grow.

For instance, what types of mentorship and coaching did the candidate implement or foster in prior positions? Can they describe what the result was of one or more of their junior staff who grew to contribute beyond original expectations?

Design leaders also need to use their perspective across the team to see what needs to change and make it happen. Look for stories where candidates adjusted process or created a new effort to address a shortcoming, weakness, or opportunity.

For example, don't settle for a simple story about how the participant overhauled the way in which teams reported status to management. Probe the candidate to discuss symptoms of the original problem, the underlying issue (mistrust, lack of understanding, etc.), and how their change in procedure addressed the problem.

Many senior design positions also require significant time and effort evangelizing design further throughout the organization, or at least cultivating relationships outside the design team. Ask for specific examples of how the candidate directly changed how different teams now work together and sustained that new partnership over time. Hopefully, the candidate will also describe why that net change was positive and institutionalized. If not, continue probing for an adequate *so what?*

DESIGN LEADER PORTFOLIO

A quick check of your favorite job postings resource will show you that it's not uncommon to see a request for a portfolio in a design leader role description. It's paramount to understand just what *portfolio* really means here. To some hiring managers, a portfolio represents a body of work that a person has performed themselves. They expect case studies describing the contributions the designer made to the project, the tools they used, and the impact and outcomes of their design decisions. But to other hiring managers, a portfolio may mean a presentation summarizing the candidate's responsibilities, challenges, and successes, regardless if they did the work or nurtured the environment for the work to get done. They may be less interested in screenshots and more interested in what story is told and how it's delivered to an in-person and remote audience.

This presents an interesting dilemma for the candidate and the hiring manager.

From the hiring side, decide if you're asking for a portfolio to gauge the candidate's design skills.

If you're hiring a senior leader with several years of experience leading teams, how much time would you have expected them to spend working hands-on with project-related work that generated artifacts? Is that time you would consider to be well spent on tactical-level work instead of time spent investing in the operational and cultural aspects of setting a design team up for success?

Is there something different that you could ask for to showcase how candidates performed leadership duties? Would a case study, or case studies, help highlight or provide additional details that allowed you to assess a candidate and their ability to do the role that you're hiring them for?

From the candidate side, ask the company or recruiter which definition of *portfolio* they are expecting to see.

You might want to consider creating a presentation that showcases your career achievements and standout accomplishments, whether you're actively seeking a new role, or you're perfectly comfortable where you are. Design a combination of case studies, data points, and highlights that will showcase your value as a design leader over 5, 10, or 20 minutes that could appeal to hiring managers who may not have ever been designers. You could even include how you hired design leaders in your previous organizations and highlight the contrasts in approaches.

It's easy to understand how an employer could ask to see a portfolio for a leadership role. It may be a standard bullet point for a different level role that got carried over and then overlooked in a review process. It might be that the type of work requested is hands-on, as well as leadership-level activities, which may be influenced or determined by the type, size, or maturity of the organization. Or perhaps the hiring manager just wants to *see* your story, versus *hear* you tell it, which may not be too much to ask.

Regardless of what you decide, a little empathy goes a long way. People are on both sides of the hiring process, and they are trying to make the most informed decision with the information they have. A hiring process isn't free to anyone and restarting it can have a significant impact for hiring managers and candidates alike.

Things to consider when you're asking a design leader for a portfolio:

- If you're hiring an experienced leader, what are you expecting in a portfolio?

- What do you hope that a portfolio from a leader will show you or prove to you?

- Could you do something different in your hiring process to give you the same information?

Things to consider if you're being asked for a portfolio for a design leader role:

- Do you have a recent portfolio of work you've done? Consider sharing it.

- Could you create a few slides to highlight your leadership accomplishments?

- When reading over your own résumé, are there bullets that would be more effective if shown as an image, photograph, or chart?

- What would you like to have others learn about you that might not be covered in an interview situation, or that could drive or lead to a good interview discussion? ∎

Defining Consistent Scoring Practices

Deciding upfront how you want to score skills, experience, and other attributes helps you compare candidates against each other.

Before you even read one résumé, let alone discuss the opening with a candidate, establish priorities and thresholds in a comprehensive interview guide (see Chapter 4, "Performance Profiles and Interview Guides"). These guides will be the foundation for posing the same questions to everyone in your candidate pool and scoring their responses, once you begin screening and interviewing.

It's been said that the interview script should be like a math test— every student in a 20-person class gets the same exam, so the teacher has an accurate means of determining who understood the material.

Much like math teachers don't hand out 20 different math tests, be sure to use the same script and questions for each candidate.

This consistency levels the playing field. Many online applicant tracking systems, such as Greenhouse, provide scoring tools in their interview kits, such as in Figure 3.1. By relying on the structured interviewing format and standardizing the scoring and the script, you remove the likelihood that an especially charismatic candidate can wow you, or one anecdote can convince you that a person is right for the job. You also reduce the chance that one candidate sounds inherently more like you or your team, lest you inadvertently find yourself drawn to the candidate who may not be the best, but the most familiar.

Scoring guides don't require using third-party services either—you can create your own easily enough by including the question or prompt, what to look for in a response, and how to score what responses you may find valuable to learning if the candidate is a fit. See Figure 3.2 as an example.

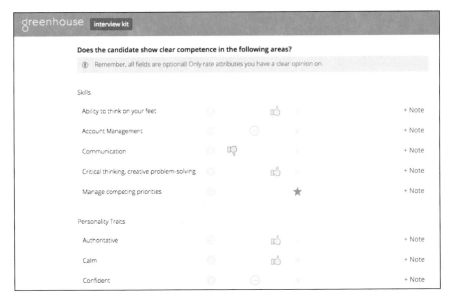

FIGURE 3.1

Greenhouse.io's talent acquisition and applicant tracking system's scorecard.

Prompt				Notes
"Tell me about a time when a lead or manager disagreed with the direction you were taking a design, even though you thought your approach was the best—what did you do, and how was it resolved?"				*Don't focus on if the designer "won" the disagreement in direction, listen for how they learned why there was disagreement*
Response				
Candidate does not provide any response to this question	Candidate cannot speak to conflict resolution or articulate how they learned more about why the other person felt that way	Candidate mentions ways to appease the disagreement in direction without exploring why there was disagreement in the first place; may suggest tactics leading to a "vote" like just prototyping 2 things to be selected	Candidate discusses how they learned more about disagreement, suggests research, and/or mentions what they need to learn to make a decision	
0	**1**	**2**	**3**	

FIGURE 3.2
Create your own scoring rubric with the interview prompt or question and show how you'll score what responses are useful in making a decision.

Likewise, such a scoring foundation makes sure that even candidates who have great experience and skills, but don't create a strong connection or rapport with the committee, can still earn a face-to-face interview. By reducing the opportunity for bias to influence your decisions, you increase your chances of interviewing a stronger field and finding that best candidate.

Facilitating Hiring Decisions

Earlier in this chapter, we recommended that hiring decisions should be made after reaching consensus, not a majority, as people vote on a candidate.

When designing your hiring process, you're establishing guidelines, not painting yourself into a corner before you've even spoken to a candidate. That means you want to set ground rules: *Is a strong yes different than a yes? Does a person outside the design team have an equal vote compared to the hiring committee?* These are just a few questions you'll want to address before you find yourself needing an answer in the moment.

Be sure to have a plan in place if someone is uncomfortable with placing their vote for a candidate. Your hiring committee should have a process where they can get more clarification or additional information to get them closer to a decision (whatever that decision may be). This may involve setting up another phone call or even requesting that the candidate come back to the office, depending on the necessity of getting the information you need to make a decision. Do your best to respect the time of the candidate and your colleagues before asking the candidate to visit your office an additional time.

We also explore how to arrive at a hiring decision in Chapter 7, "Offers, Negotiating, and Onboarding."

Hiring for Culture Add *and* Culture Fit

It's easy to fall into another hiring trap when interviewing candidates—specifically, seeking out and extending offers to designers who seem to be just like the rest of the team. Often, this is chalked up to hiring people for culture fit, and many teams wear hiring for culture fit as proudly as a badge on their chest.

Cultural fit is the likelihood that someone will reflect and adapt to the core norms, beliefs, attitudes, and behaviors that make up your immediate team and the larger organization. It's now generally accepted that employees who fit well with their organization, colleagues, and manager have greater job satisfaction, have higher retention rates, and are recognized as superior performers.

But if you're not careful, hiring for culture fit can mean hiring more people who are just like most of the current team, and who will think and behave exactly like the rest of the team.

We've discussed how diverse teams directly improve the quality of the products or services that the team creates, as well as making happier, more engaged employees (see Chapter 2, "Designing Diversity and Inclusion in Your Teams"). But in many cases, organizations unwittingly incentivize growing homogeneous teams through referral programs and recruiting at the same colleges and universities as the rest of the organization and even the competition. What's even worse is that these teams of similar, like-minded people are hired based on how well they get along with the rest of the team.

The hiring manager concerned with "Would I want to hang out with this person? Will they be fun at happy hour?" is prioritizing arguably the least significant or fundamental attributes of their candidates and likely downplaying stronger candidates who may not give the impression they're a killer at karaoke on Thursday nights.

Such workplace culture is much more complicated and stretches much further than how small teams decompress or how their norms and practices mesh (or don't) with the larger organization. You can construct some of your interview questions to reveal clues as to how your candidates may assimilate or opt out of your workplace culture. Then you can better determine the risks and rewards for hiring for culture fit.

For instance, the degree in which your team collaborates and shares information is a bona fide element of your workplace culture. Some organizations (inadvertently or not) encourage teams and people to work as individuals and share information only when necessary. If a candidate isn't familiar or comfortable in that cultural environment, they may not thrive in such a culture where sharing work early and often is not encouraged.

NOTE CULTURE FIT IN PRACTICE

Positive examples of culture fit include the following characteristics:[4]

- Shared enthusiasm about a company's mission or purpose
- A common approach to working—together or individually
- A mutual understanding of how to make decisions and assess risk

Culture fit is *not*:

- A shared educational, cultural, or career background
- A sense of comfort and familiarity among coworkers where colleagues are friends
- Mutual enjoyment of such perks as ping pong, video games, or craft beer

Likewise, some organizations are much more focused on the result and not necessarily the journey to get there. If the candidate is

---

4   Sue Shellenbarger, "The Dangers of Hiring for Cultural Fit," *The Wall Street Journal,* September 23, 2019, www.wsj.com/articles/the-dangers-of-hiring-for -cultural-fit-11569231000

adamant about how they adhere to the process, they may also find themselves uncomfortable working in an environment that rewards the sum and not the parts.

You could even ask a candidate if they've worked in an environment where they didn't think they fit in with the culture and explore why, if, and how they tried to rectify it, and what they're looking for in their next environment where they can be more productive and happier. If they felt like they belonged, on the other hand, what are they looking to find again in their next move?

In many ways, an astute candidate will notice many external traits of your culture during the interview. The applicant can learn about the work culture by observing your own behavior and your office dress code (including how you and your team dress relative to the rest of the organization). Be sure to show the candidate the design team's office area, because the actual work environment signals much about the culture of the team.

Culture fit should be one more gauge that factors into your decision-making—not a deciding factor one way or the other. Weigh its importance in how you score candidates in advance so that you and the hiring committee are prepared when interviews are underway.

Creating a Partnership with HR and Recruiting

A surefire way to make an adversary out of your HR or recruiting team is to put yourself in a position where it looks like you are circumventing them because you think you know how to do their jobs better than they do.

Instead, ask how you can do more of the legwork that usually falls to them—whether that means posting the job description to their distribution channels (that they likely have a bulk subscription account to use, whereas you may be expensing it yourself) or writing the job description or performance profile itself.

Ask when they should get involved—if they need or want to interview any candidates, or if they need to advise on compensation. (Hint: they do.)

In short, make it look like you're helping them, but as a result, you'll be improving your own chances of landing a successful new addition to your team.

By addressing culture fit throughout the recruiting process, you set up yourself and your team to hire designers who will flourish in their new roles and contribute to a healthy, productive work environment. You'll increase both your own and their odds for success in your organization, and ultimately save yourself the time, money, and challenges of recruiting all over again.

Designing the Pipeline

It's a pretty safe bet that your employer has probably hired people before. (You're on the payroll, right?) That means, for better or for worse, there are practices and procedures already in place that you can follow by default. However, many organizations today allow teams to source and interview their own candidates, which may mean more work for you in the short term, but also will likely lead to better candidates and an improved hiring process.

Ideally, you'll be augmenting HR's standard recruiting procedures to fill open positions with your own detective work to identify people from elsewhere—including your networks, the larger design community, and through practices that appeal more closely to designers than perhaps other departments.

More importantly, though, is moving away from a just-in-time, hair-on-fire approach to hiring in which you're entirely reliant on whoever is responding to your performance profile that they found on the internet. Instead, nurturing a pipeline of designers and product development professionals with varying levels of experience, specialization, and background can help you and your team be more resilient when you need help, and be more accommodating to interested parties when you don't.

Diversify Where You Look

The HR team will likely post the job opening to the usual suspects of job boards—such as LinkedIn, Indeed, and Glassdoor. Here you really just want to make sure that the HR team is using your performance profile and allowing you to screen whatever applicants you receive. It's worth posting your performance profile to other sites that cater more specifically to designers and product development professionals as well, such as Authentic Jobs and Dribbble.

But there are still some more interesting places to either post design openings or browse through directories of diverse designers who may be interested in discussing your firm's open positions. Let's look at a few sites and how they describe themselves:

- **College and university career sites:**

  If you're looking for entry level to early career design positions and a degree is required, you can have a lot of success identifying undiscovered candidates here. Often, the posting is free, and you can also conduct individual candidate searches by major and year of graduation.

- **Latinxs Who Design:** www.latinxswhodesign.com/

  "Latinxs Who Design is a living directory of thriving Latinxs in the design industry. Their mission is to provide a space to find outstanding people to follow, look for a mentor, make new friends, or discover talented individuals to join your team."

- **Blacks Who Design:** https://blackswho.design

  "Blacks Who Design highlights all of the inspiring Black designers in the industry. The goal is to inspire new designers, encourage people to diversify their feeds, and discover amazing individuals to join your team."

- **Women Who Design:** https://womenwho.design

  "Women Who Design is a Twitter directory of accomplished women in the design industry. It aims to help people find notable and relevant voices to follow on Twitter by parsing Twitter bios for popular keywords."

- **Queer Design Club:** https://queerdesign.club/

  "Queer Design Club's mission is to promote and celebrate all the amazing work that happens at the intersection of queer identity and design worldwide—from LGBTQ+ designers' contributions to the industry to design's role in queer activism throughout history."

These directories provide an effective method of introducing you to people you may otherwise have never crossed paths with. But just blasting directories of people—whether from LinkedIn or one of the above community-focused services—won't work if you're not communicating the right message and tone to get people interested in learning more.

How to Get the Best Candidates from a Design Recruiter

by Joanne Weaver, President of The Joanne Weaver Group,
a NYC-based boutique talent agency.

As a manager, you should understand at the outset that this process will require an investment of your time and energy. It's time-sensitive, too, as candidates are moving through other companies' interview processes concurrently with yours. (I can't count the number of times a candidate has gone from "just starting to look" to "fielding three offers"!) So just embrace it and commit to it up front.

When you first start working with a recruiting firm, setting up a weekly standing call can be a good way of keeping everyone on track, with email/phone check-ins as needed along the way.

Within 24–48 hours after each candidate touchpoint (initial submission and after each interview), give the recruiter thorough, useful feedback about the candidate, both positive and negative, and indicate your next steps. Timely feedback ensures that the candidate feels "seen," which keeps them engaged with you, so you have a better chance of ensuring that you've got them as a choice. It also helps the recruiter quickly understand if they are getting it right or need to switch it up.

On Day 1 of the search, provide the recruiter with a job description, a pre-approved salary band from HR/Finance, a bonus % and equity range where applicable, and a checklist of benefits: health plans + price breakdowns, PTO policy, WFH/flexible working policy (this is increasingly becoming more attractive these days), 401K (matching %?). Other perks and selling points might be: a design-driven culture or a place where design has a real seat at the table. Or opportunities for growth/management? Catered lunches? Sane hours (for realsies)? Education reimbursement? This information helps the recruiter qualify the right candidates for you, and also helps them verbally "sell" the role to folks out there and generate interest, so that you get more choices.

Also, make sure that you outline the interview process up front. How many rounds are there? How long is each round, who's there, and what is the format/focus of each one?

Make sure that you realize that no one candidate is going to check off every single box. Delineate the musts-haves vs. nice-to-haves early on, and if you think your top choice could grow into the role, decide if you're willing to train them or perhaps keep the role open for a little (or a lot) longer. Those "areas to grow in" may indeed turn out to be selling points to your candidates—good designers always want to grow and learn—so that can be a win/win!

Show Off the Design Practice

Design teams can also work with the broader marketing department and corporate communications team to design their own website to promote who they are, how they work, and what they actually work on together.

Many times, these sites will also include brief bios of the design team, links to blog articles they've authored and presentations they've delivered, and the open positions on the team. While not necessarily a new idea, companies such as Lyft, Airbnb, Shopify, SAP, and Facebook all continue actively contributing to their design team websites to craft their stories about how they design at work.

The customer-messaging platform, Intercom, launched a new website (see Figure 3.3) using the .design top-level domain name to help their recruiting efforts, and they saw second-order positive impact as well.

FIGURE 3.3

Intercom.design's home page helps interested candidates know more about the team and their work.

"Our goal for intercom.design was to give people an inside look at what it's like to work at Intercom. We did this by sharing our values, processes, levels, and expectations publicly so that designers can clearly see what we're like and what we hire for. We've seen a spike in inbound applications after launching, but we're just as excited about the positive response from the community. Sharing high quality resources transparently helps product designers and teams everywhere learn from our practice," said Jasmine Friedl, Director of Product Design at Intercom.

If your team is interested in producing a website to promote your organization and your work, be careful not to go too crazy and try to build the entire site without some sort of corporate approval. Have a clear vision and goals that you want the site to accomplish, and treat the effort with the same diligence you would a regular, business-as-usual project. Make sure that it doesn't become a never-ending project that delivers no upside or value to the company.

Wrapping Up

Designing your hiring process is a lot of work—and you haven't even emailed a candidate, read one résumé, or leafed through a single portfolio yet.

This work, however, makes all the difference when building your team and how your candidates feel about your organization—sometimes for a lifetime. That means it's worth evangelizing how you hire throughout the company.

Contact your human resources team and walk them through your performance profiles and interview guides. They may see if they can adapt it into their own approaches. HR may even ask if you can make time to help other parts of the organization with the workshops you conducted with your teams to help them craft a more equitable and effective hiring process.

But don't stop there—promote your process outside the company as well. Describe your team's values, how you interview candidates, and how your committees decide to extend offers. If candidates recognize that they'll be treated fairly and with respect, you'll get better candidates who are more eager to be part of your team.

Designing your hiring process isn't just about who will be doing the interviews and what questions you'll ask. The InVision 2019 Product Design Hiring Report cited that the number one criteria for job-seekers is a strong design culture—rather than working for a well-known company or designing a product they personally use.

Your hiring process should reflect that design culture where curiosity is encouraged, people work together as allies, and diverse ideas and approaches are valued.

Performance Profiles and Interview Guides

A *job description* is a documented format that defines the expectations for an individual who fills a role at an organization. These descriptions include super important details, like the type of degree a person has, how many years of experience they possess, what kind of tools they use, and a bunch of other bullet points that make it easy for candidates to qualify or disqualify themselves quickly.

Performance profiles take a different approach to the job description by informing candidates what their success will look like. Performance profiles are focused on the job, which makes it really easy for a good candidate to determine whether or not they've got the skills and experience to succeed in it. When candidates can align themselves to achieving the success you're looking for, you'll have people applying who can achieve the outcomes you're seeking, instead of those who have alleged knowledge of a listing of tools or skills that don't always have a lot to do with the needs of your team.

The *best* candidates respond to the *best* job descriptions, which we're arguing are performance-based and called *performance profiles*, so be sure to invest time and effort in crafting what you expect from and promise to potential candidates. A performance profile is often the first view into your organization. You owe candidates an understanding of what they can expect when working with you.

Why Do We Use Job Descriptions?

The obvious explanation for using a job description is that it is good for attracting talent to open opportunities within your organization. However, if the job description isn't given the appropriate attention and care that it deserves, it can also turn people away instead of drawing them to you. Job descriptions are experienced-based, and it's difficult to show that they are any good at all at predicting the future success of the people that you hire into your organization.

Some job descriptions read as if they're seeking every bullet point of skill and capability under the sun. The description seeks someone who does UX/UI, or perhaps someone who can manage a client, create project plans, write user stories, lead user research, write front-end and back-end code, filet a tuna, make homemade donuts, and organize, write, and edit content like a one-person McSweeney's. Sometimes job descriptions contain such heinous references as "rock star" or "unicorn" or "ninja," or some other deplorable batch of words that may cause the best talent to quickly do an about-face from your organization. Other times, job descriptions seem to be a checklist of items that tell people "this isn't for you," and that's hardly a great impression to make.

That's probably not what you're going for, and yet, this is what a lot of job descriptions can look like. Job descriptions are a two-way street—you're seeking talented candidates to become the next great individuals to join your organization, who can elevate the output of your team. Candidates are also seeking organizations where they can be challenged to grow and learn, and also to bring their skills to strengthen and mature your team.

It's your responsibility to ensure that you live up to the promise of your position description—make sure it's a good one, and do your best to exceed the promise you put into writing. As Victor Lipman (author of *The Type B Manager: Leading Successfully in a Type A World*) reminds us: "People leave managers, not companies." The best way to set people up for success on the way into your organization is to let them know what success looks like (performance profiles) and then provide them with the support they need to achieve it.

Performance Profiles: A Different Approach

There are essentially two different ways to write job descriptions, and the one many of us are familiar with is possibly the "laziest, don't-give-a-crap activity" around.

You're familiar with this one: you type the role you want to hire into your favorite search engine/job site/professional networking social media site and find the role that's closest to the one you're looking for.

Then you take advantage of your word processor's handy "search and replace" functionality to swap out company names, adjust your bullet points to meet your slightly more specific needs, update everything to make sure that you're following your company's/HR's guidelines and format for job descriptions, and then you add the company introduction and standard legalese and compliance information. You forward your new job description to a couple of people who will skim it quickly and send back a "looks good!" addition, and then off it goes to all the places it needs to be posted.

Crafty job seekers know how to take the first line of seemingly anonymous job descriptions and drop it into their favorite search engine to see if the position is posted elsewhere, or if the description really is just copied and pasted from others on the web.

While this is a gray area ethically, you also risk looking lazy and disinterested in the hiring process, which will likely reduce the quality of applicants responding to your post. Savvy job seekers also know that they're not being set up for success, and that the hiring manager is more interested in adding bodies to an already stressed team instead of building the right type of team inside the organization.

There's a variant of this one where you only borrow the headings and completely make up your own bullets to make sure that you feel confident in the structure and organization of the information you pull together.

The other version is a lot more involved, because you dedicate yourself to creating the job description from scratch, and you need to create the best one possible to bring in the best candidates. There are various templates that will help get you started, hopefully within your organization or out on the internet in a variety of articles by a wide array of experts.

There are even less impressive, less helpful options, too. Sometimes, job posting websites or the less advanced applicant tracking systems (ATSs) have guided forms that allow for very little creativity or flexibility. They may offer rigid, form-based approaches to filling in a position description, based upon requirements from a hiring era that has long-since passed.

These are good places to start—in absence of better options. A template only shows you how to fit a few requirements into a pre-existing mold and doesn't help you actually generate the important content that you need.

This is why performance profiles—performance-based job descriptions—can work to your advantage. They are defined to help the candidate *know* what their success will look like, and the candidate who applies will *know* (in most cases) that they can meet or exceed the expectations, how to deliver upon them, and how to explain how to achieve their success to you and your team.

Performance Profiles Set Candidates Up for Success

by William Rooney, Director of Strategy and Operations at U.Group

As Simon Sinek[1] teaches, *what* and *how* are nowhere near as important as *why*, and this philosophy is no different in the war to find talent. You're trying to attract the best, and the best people are going to be driven by purpose.

Organizations make huge investments in branding that communicates their mission, but often fail to carry through that branding to the job description, which is their primary mechanism for attracting the talent that's required to deliver on that mission in the first place.

The standard job description is almost entirely focused on describing, in painstaking detail, what things a person would do in a role, which is then followed up by a long list of tools, techniques, or experiences that somebody thinks are required to be able to do those things. This approach leaves it totally to the reader to guess at the impact they'll have and how their work will matter to the organization.

A performance profile leads with the impact that a person will have in the role they are filling. It provides specifics on what the reader should expect to achieve when they're imagining themselves in the role. This approach helps candidates view the opportunity through the lens of their experiences, in order to decide if it's something they are interested in and if they will be successful in the role.

Performance profiles increase candidate quality and engagement, but more importantly, diversity, since they focus on outcomes instead of simply describing a narrow set of requirements.

---

1   Simon Sinek is an author and motivational speaker. Learn more at https://en.wikipedia.org/wiki/Simon_Sinek

As an added bonus, if you're working with recruiters, your performance profiles allow them to have an understanding of the real requirements and prevent them from being accidental gatekeepers to strong candidates who may not have that illustrious DreamWeaver tool you accidentally left on the skills list.

Workshopping the Performance Profile

Lou Adler, author of *Hire with Your Head: Using Performance-Based Hiring to Build Great Teams,* has been promoting performance profiles for years. While a limited few well-known folks in the design industry may also be fans of the performance profile, they definitely aren't in wide implementation. The challenge, of course, is that in an unscientific survey of about 20 different design leaders and managers, none of them thought that creating any type of job description was fun (and more than one may have used the word "torture" to describe the process).

In addition to Jen's advice, we've found a way to create performance profiles that involve sticky notes and markers (or your favorite digital alternative such as Mural, Miro, etc. and a document) and a few timed activities to boot.

A quick way to get started is to get into "workshop mode" to create a performance profile for bringing in the best talent to your team. The added benefit of a workshop: you get to involve other people in

Performance Profiles: A Converted Believer

by Jen Tress, HR/talent leader

I was first introduced to performance profiles when I was the talent director for 18F and working with the U.S. Digital Service on collaborative hiring. For me, what's useful about using profiles vs. job descriptions is the focus on performance. What performance does the organization need from the individual who will fill that role? The profile should clearly describe what success looks like and the experience/skills a candidate would need to be considered. This generally pulls in a smaller number of candidates, but that's a good thing. It's a waste of time for the organization to wade through résumés that are not a good match for the role. With traditional job descriptions, organizations often telegraph messages that turn off the talent they're seeking, resulting in a high volume of applicants who aren't a strong match for the job. By listing too many duties, qualified candidates can infer that the workload appears overwhelming or surmise that they can perform, for example, 5 of the 20 duties, so they must not be qualified (this is especially true for women). I've used both methods. Performance profiles deliver the best return.

While at 18F, I led and attended these workshops, and they were helpful. This approach is also best suited for organizations that invest meaningfully in HR/People Operations, meaning that the people who are responsible for hiring have the time and space to devote to this effort, just like any other important project or initiative. If you're a busy hiring manager or a lean operation, don't fear. Use these key takeaways as your North Star: focus on the three to five top objectives that a person will need to accomplish to be successful in the role. Get specific. Design and test with SMEs who are in the role (even better, with the people who will be interviewing and making selections). Take that profile and use it as the basis for evaluating applicants. What should you look for in a résumé/portfolio? What questions should you ask to assess a candidate's ability to perform the objectives? What does a good answer look like? How will you score the candidates? As a person who has often facilitated this process, I've been able to deliver the goods in three to four hours, from profile development to interview guides to documenting how it will run. This gets the hiring team excited and engaged, which is not something you often hear when thinking about HR, but that's how it should be.

the creation of the performance profile—it's team-generated, which means that the people doing the work are involved in outlining the needs and the performance. This helps ensure that the right content is generated, and if it doesn't add a little joy to your process, it perhaps at least spreads the misery around a little bit.

Go ahead and gather those supplies and review Figure 4.1 for a sample agenda for the performance profile workshop.

Timing	Task	Notes
15 minutes	Introductions / Welcome	High-level overview of the agenda and what's happening in the workshop.
10 minutes	**Activity** Why would a new hire quit?	
10 minutes	**Activity** Why would a new hire get fired?	
10 minutes	**Activity** Why would a new hire get promoted?	
10 minutes	**Exercise** Vote/Prioritize the top reasons why people in the role were promoted.	Dot-vote to determine the top reasons a person would get promoted.
10 minutes	**Activity** What type of work would this person do in their first year? What kind of exposure to work could they expect?	
10 minutes	**Exercise** Vote/prioritize the top types of work and work exposure.	Another opportunity to dot-vote!
15 minutes	**Discussion** Explore and validate the top 5 reasons someone would be promoted and merge with the types of work that would be done, or that would be exposed to the new hire.	
30 minutes	**Activity** Write detailed descriptions of the top 5 reasons people were promoted. Each reason should transition to an *objective*.	Think of this in the form of position objectives. It's okay to merge and morph what you've created that aren't in the top 5s, if they overlap.

FIGURE 4.1

Sample agenda for a performance profile creation workshop.

Performance profiles should be treated like the team charter that is created with your team (see Chapter 8, "Unifying the Team Culture with Charters"). The team generally has a good sense of what types of skills are needed, as well as the experience that an employee will have while working with the team.

Of course, you may also be the only person on the team, and if that's the case, see if you can wrangle someone from another discipline (or your Talent/Recruiting/HR equivalent) to join you in the activities.

The activities are all relatively short (in minutes, not hours) with the goal to get as much information as you can in as little time as possible so that you don't spend too much time dwelling on extra fluff that is unnecessary. After you've generated the information, it will be easier to go back and refine and revise it, and make your words form coherent sentences.

Round 1: Learn About Role Success and Failure

First, you'll want to get everyone thinking about what it's like to work for your organization and how people thrive or find their demise during their first year (or so, depending upon when opportunities for promotion may exist) of working with your team.

Get the team set up with Post-its (one idea per Post-it, please), or paper with predefined columns, or the online collaboration tool of your choosing, and ask them to answer the following questions:

- **What would cause this person to get fired?** (10 minutes)

  Quickly describe as many of the reasons you can come up with for what would cause this employee to be fired from their role. You'll use this information to help you think about how you'll want to set up the employee for success, both in the job description and in the role moving forward.

- **What would cause this person to quit?** (10 minutes)

  Write as many of the reasons that you can think of why an employee would leave your organization. Be descriptive and clear; it's okay to think in terms of processes, lack of access to tools, or even individuals, as long as they're valid reasons why someone might join your team only to end up leaving.

- **What would cause this person to get promoted?** (10 minutes)

  Now that you've expelled the negative aspects of the potential employee's future, rapidly describe all the things that could be done to help trigger a promotion. Include actions and behaviors that would make you view the person as exemplary, or think of them as accomplishments.

- **What type of work would this person do in their first year? What kind of exposure to work could they expect?** (10 minutes)

  It's time to break out your sticky notes! Write one idea/outcome per sticky note and set them aside. This is more challenging with agency-model organizations; the work a person does may frequently be dependent upon the work that has been sold or is readily available. However, you should be able to identify some of the key types of work or environments in which the employee will work. For product-focused organizations, write explicitly about the type of work that will be focused on and what you expect to be accomplished.

After you've completed these tasks, it's probably a pretty good time to take a quick break. You've just been putting your mind through some sprinting exercises, and a little rest will help you get ready to tackle what's ahead.

Round 2: Content Grouping and Prioritization

If you've been working as a team, review all of the information that has been written down. You might notice that by writing and discussing the negative reasons for people to leave your organization, it becomes easier to bring out the positive elements.

Take all of the sticky notes and put them on a table, a wall, an easel pad, or whatever area you have available to you where you can see them all together. If you're a design-minded person, you already know what's happening next:

- Sort the sticky notes into logical groupings to identify the key areas of success indicators for your employee.

- Let the discussion around the groupings happen naturally.

- Create clear and sensible labels for each primary grouping.

Hopefully, you'll have somewhere between 6–20 groupings to work with and prioritize. You may choose to dot-vote or use any other method for providing the team with the ability to assign priority and importance. If you decide to dot-vote, give each person five votes and have them apply them to the different groupings. You can decide if you want to give people the opportunity to vote more than once on each set of groupings as well. (For more information on the dot-voting method, you can learn more in the book *Gamestorming*[2] by Dave Gray, Sunni Brown, and James Macanufo.)

When you've completed the dot-voting, tally up the votes to determine the top four to six key objectives that describe what the performance expected of the new position looks like. These four to six objectives now need to be rewritten into sentence form for your primary audience—the potential candidates who will read the performance profile.

The sticky notes within the objective grouping are the basis for the supporting bullet points you'll include with your objective. These will help candidates learn more about the objective and what success looks like while fulfilling it on your team. Keep in mind that this doesn't have to be full-on, formal paragraphs—a simple sentence or two can get the point across nicely and help your potential candidates see themselves in the role.

---

2   *Gamestorming* is also available for free online (and with updates) at gamestorming.com

A good target is between four to seven strong bullet points to support the objective you've written. The amount of detail will depend upon the position, as well as the type of organization in which you work.

After you've completed these, you should have a good sense of what the expectations are of someone whom you want to fill—and be successful in—the position that you're hiring for, and as an added bonus, some criteria to gauge candidates against.

The workshop portion of the activity is complete, however, you're not done yet.

Round 3: *Now* Write the Position Summary

Be sure to include a position summary at the beginning of your performance profile. The summary is much easier to write after you've completed the objectives that you're hiring for. The position summary is going to be a brief synopsis of what the job is about, and you should probably have your best persuasive writing hat on while you create it. Your primary audience, again, is the potential candidate who will read this. A sample summary could resemble this one, only much more tailored for your specific organization, of course:

> The UX designer is one of the most important—if not *the* most important—role on the organization design team. Our UX designer will help us establish a new culture and practice of design within our organization that will improve the way we deliver our services to our partners.
>
> We're creating our UX design team in a way that ensures that we're preparing our team for success in the future. While the team is new and evolving, the UX designer will be responsible for defining team processes and ensuring that they proliferate across the organization. The UX design team builds coalitions and brings the entire organization together through a strong and shared language of design and a passion for learning more about the technical aspects of UX design.

After you've completed your position summary, make sure that it's the first piece the candidate reads (or try to make it as close to that as possible) after any of the required content from the organization you work for. If you've got editorial support on your team, make sure that they take a couple passes of your summary to correct any grammar or plain language issues.

Words matter—a lot. If you've listened to any motivational speeches, you've likely been drawn to specific words, phrases, sentences, or entire passages that have been carefully crafted to make sure they have the right impact with as much of an audience as possible. The same goes with your performance profiles—when you're careful with the words that you choose, you can help ensure their success with the most diverse audience possible.

This task may feel daunting, and it truly can be. Adjusting the language and the tone of voice that you're accustomed to isn't always a simple accomplishment. You have built up a history of the "way you speak and write" that may seem like "normal, conversational words"; however, those same words may also have inferred biases that can come across as negative to groups of people.

It may seem innocuous to say that you want a teammate who works hard and plays hard, or who is extremely flexible or works independently, but these phrases can all suggest a workplace that prioritizes long hours and intertwining of personal and professional relationships, unclear expectations, and little coaching or mentorship.

Adjusting your language also helps ensure that you're seeking people who are a cultural addition to your organization and not just a cultural fit. Fitting into the way the organization works certainly helps; however, adding different perspectives happens when you ensure that you're bringing people into the organization who have different perspectives and exposure to different experiences than your own.

If you don't have access to editorial support, invest some of your budget in hiring a temporary resource to help polish the work that you've already done. Remember: you're hiring someone who will be part of the future of your organization. They, and the organization, are worth the expenditure.

After you've wrapped this part up, you should consider a service like Textio[3] to take one more pass at making sure that your language is inviting and inclusive and will help you bring in the best-qualified candidates. Textio will review your job descriptions and provide alternate suggestions to some of the common language used, while also providing you with statistics to reinforce the choice. Here are some great examples from their website:

---

3   Textio is available online at https://textio.com/products/

"In this position, outside the box thinking is a must."—Replace *"outside the box"* with *"creative"* to help you fill the position twice as fast.

"Do you want to manage customer relationships?"—Replace *"manage"* with *"nurture"* to attract more women to the position.

"You're interested in continuing to learn."—Replace *"interested in"* with *"passionate about"* to raise the qualified applicants by 12%.

Remember: you're also sending a strong signal about your organization's diversity and culture. Whether or not you intend to send these messages is a bit irrelevant; the interpretation by your users—amazing potential employees—is what matters most.

You've now got a well-formed, performance-based hiring tool—your very own performance profile. Put this into practice and map it to well-defined interview guides and a consistent, structured interview approach, and see what kind of impact your team and organization receives from these measures.

Designing Your Interview Guides

The interview guide is the next step toward ensuring a structured, equitable, repeatable hiring process when hiring designers. These documents capture what happens before, during, and even after the interview. They're not overly complicated, but to be most effective, every interview guide should include the following for each candidate who will be screened or interviewed:

- The open position
- Hiring manager
- Hiring committee members
- Candidate name
- Date
- Rating or scoring scale
- Interview script
- Additional questions for the hiring committee members to complete

Each guide should also have a paper copy of the performance profile and the candidate's résumé.

Some interview guides will also provide additional notes for the committee, such as preparation tips, reminders, or even what not to ask during the interview.

QUALITY IN, QUALITY OUT

I've found that a good interview guide will provide a good, consistent framework for interviewing. The best way to do that is to align your interview questions to the performance profile objectives you defined.

Additionally, an interview guide can provide insight into strong answers and the warning signs that the responses received by the candidate may not be at the level that is required for the role.

Here's a sample mapping:

Objective: You will participate or lead in research for every project—internal or external—that you work on, in order to drive a user-centered focus for your partners.

- Participate in the planning of and leading of ethical user research.

- Seek opportunities to grow and expand the research knowledge of the UX team and the teams of your client partners.

- Clearly articulate and promote user-centered methods to teammates and client partners.

- Incorporate research findings into a report that is easily understood.

- Provide actionable next steps based upon insights gained from user research.

Map the objective to the interview question:

Question: *How have you determined the best research approach and methods that allow clients to also learn and grow their own capability?*

Good Signs:

- Provide clear examples around being informed about limitations and opportunities.

- Show decision-making based upon understanding of clients.

- Identify challenges and also recognize solutions and opportunities.

Warnings:

- Doesn't have previous examples of determining a research approach.

- Is unfamiliar with common research techniques.

- Does not see value in sharing expertise with client partners.

Spend the time making sure that you're asking questions of your candidates that map to the performance profile. You've invested the time and energy to create a very thoughtful, success-based approach for someone. Make sure that you're helping them be successful in the interview, as well.

This approach shows your candidates that you're invested in the future of the role. Avoid setting unrealistic expectations by deviating from the performance profile—you defined it for a reason, and the right candidates will be prepared to answer questions related to it. ■

Make sure that each person on the hiring committee has the complete interview guide for each individual interview. Having a completed guide for each candidate after you've interviewed everyone makes it much easier for you and your committee to recall the details of the first few interviews you conducted if the process has stretched into multiple weeks, if not longer.

> **NOTE** NEED A TEMPLATE?
>
> The Society for Human Resource Management has an effective template for an interview guide at **www.shrm.org/LearningAnd Career/learning/Documents/Template_InterviewGuide.pdf**

Interview Questions

It's important to make sure that your script advances you to that decision-making goal and does not get mired in cutesy or philosophical pontification. You can, however, bend some general or high-reaching questions into determining how those answers will identify the right person for the job.

For instance, it's easy to imagine an underprepared hiring manager relying on any of these topics:

- Tell me how you define UX versus UI.

- What's your favorite or best-designed product or website?

- Should designers code?

- Describe your ideal design process.

Unfortunately, these conversations won't tell you if the person across from you is the right fit or could grow into a significant contributor to the team.

These vapid questions may seem to open a unique window into the candidate's mind, but they fail on several fronts:

- The candidate's responses aren't grounded in any previous experience that could suggest the candidate should be offered a job—in fact, most could be addressed by reading a few blog posts or even tweets.

- The questions don't give the candidate any insight into your own team, company, or design practice.

- There's little ability to know if the candidate is just talking a good game in case you're wowed by their articulate, mind-bending responses.

However, it's possible to tweak some of those questions into a dialogue that may help paint a better picture to see if the candidate could be a fit.

Consider instead:

- How does your organization understand any differences between UX and UI design? Has that changed over time? Did you have any role in educating the organization?

- Discuss what project you are most proud of and specify your contributions to its success.

- Describe the role of designers in your organization and what skills make them successful. What's the relationship with your engineering or development teams? Could it be better? How?

- Draw your ideal design process and overlay it with your most recently completed project's approach. How did that happen?

Notice how in these modified versions the candidate is relating the crux of the earlier questions to their actual lived experience. Likewise, it's perfectly reasonable to discuss your own organization's experiences as a follow-up to the candidate's responses, instead of simply bantering about what you think could be an ideal design process yourself.

And while many design researchers will avoid asking questions about the future, you as the interviewer have a bit more leeway to determine how a candidate may behave in future situations.

Try these future-focused questions:

- How would you redesign this interview process?

- If I said we had an antagonistic relationship with our development organization, what would you do to try to make it more collaborative?

- How would you develop the skills of a design intern we brought onto the team?

Wrapping Up

This effort may seem like a lot of work just to create a performance profile. It is, but this is the type of investment and effort that your candidates and your organization deserve. This exercise helps you create a job description that is based upon performance, which means that candidates will know right away what they're going to be expected to achieve and what they'll be measured against. You're immediately setting the candidates up for success—so don't reuse the same job description for every role that you hire. Invest the time required in making sure that all of your roles have a fitting performance profile, and you'll make sure that your employees understand your expectations of them when they join the team, and that helps them get adjusted quicker. In the long run, this time investment will result in cost-savings for the company because you'll be hiring the right people for the right roles.

CHAPTER 5

Screening Designers

Designers are clearly in high demand, but it's still a competitive, rapidly evolving job market. Despite having effective performance profiles and publishing open positions on job sites that are visited by high-performing designers, you'll still likely receive a lot of résumés from people who just don't have the right mix of skills or experience to meet the needs of your team and organization.

As a result, you need a structured, repeatable process to identify the most promising résumés from the pile. At the same time, you still have to be careful you don't become so overly selective that you find yourself with homogeneous teams from the same schools, same experiences, and same approach to problem solving.

In many cases when you're working with an internal HR team or external recruiting firm, find out how the applicant tracking system is configured to screen résumés. Many of these commercial systems allow you to hone or weight aspects of the incoming résumés, so take the time to figure out how they're configured to screen the résumés before you realize you've been missing out on some great people. You may even want to see if you can spot-check a few résumés that have been denied further consideration to make sure that your automated screening settings are working as intended.

Ultimately, screening designers requires prioritizing minimum and preferred qualifications, in both the résumé and portfolio. Finding a balance between the two gives your hiring committee a wide enough net to cast to ensure a diverse range of candidates of people who could be your next great colleague.

Almost all of the material here can be applied to situations where you'll be screening all inbound résumés yourself or if you have a dedicated team and ATS who are screening the initial wave of résumés for you to review.

Deciding What You Need to See from Candidates

So you've got your job description, and you're prepared to post it across the internet and start getting names of potential candidates. Make sure that the HR team is aware you're out in the world hustling for leads.

It almost sounds like you're ready to go, but there's one more important task to think through that may initially sound simple, but can yield a significant difference in the quality and quantity of the respondents.

What are you asking interested candidates to do, specifically, to indicate that they're interested? Let's consider some of the qualifiers we frequently see today.

- "Apply via LinkedIn."

- "Send a cover letter, résumé, and portfolio."

- "Send your résumé, portfolio, links to publicly available work, and three recommendations."

- "Send the link to your website, tell us about your favorite apps and why, and solve this design problem in order to be considered."

There is a natural tension between wanting to know enough about a candidate to warrant further consideration and limiting your talent pool by too much and too soon.

You can tailor what you need from candidates by several factors. Consider the following information when determining what is minimally required, if anything, from candidates responding to the job opening.

- **Your own experience at hiring designers:** If you've successfully hired designers in the past, you should be aware of what to key on, such as the firms and schools they're coming from and what skills they choose to prioritize (tactical software-based skills vs. presenting to leadership, for example).

- **Your own experience in the open position's domain:** How well you know the field and discipline will also determine how selective you should be in the early stages of recruiting. If you're hiring designers for your first Internet of Things or artificial intelligence foray, you probably don't want to be overly restrictive with whether you start the conversation or not.

Simply put, you may not know enough about whom you need to hire to be building barriers before you've even called anyone back.

Perhaps more importantly, some positions or disciplines within the design industry won't lend themselves to portfolios or recommendations yet, so make sure that your minimum requirements are realistic.

- **The seniority of the open position:** Treat hiring a junior designer differently than hiring a general manager of a design organization. Would a junior designer really have the robust portfolio that some employers may require in order to apply? If they did, why would they be applying for a junior role in the first place? However, perhaps asking a prescreening question to discuss how managers have scaled teams across organizations in an introductory email can winnow down your pool to a few better-prepared candidates.

- **Average response rate from previous open positions:** This is relatively simple: if you regularly get a ton of responses to similar positions, tighten the qualifying factors at the start. Ultimately, you need to focus your time on the best candidates, not every person who is looking for a job.

- **The expected phone and face-to-face interview process to come later:** Recognize that the interview process begins far sooner than the first face-to-face handshake. It begins with the interested designer deciding whether to play ball with your initial requirements and how stringently you'll adhere to those expectations. With that in mind, look at the bigger picture of what the phone interview and onsite interviews will entail. If your phone script doesn't investigate references or dig into the candidate's favorite apps, why bother asking her to jump through such a hoop?

NOTE USING WHAT YOU ASK FOR

Anything submitted by the candidate should directly make a difference in moving toward a hire/no-hire decision.

Don't play games with such tactics as "I just want to see how the candidate thinks," or "I heard Google asks questions like these, and I want to see what the candidate will come up with." If the information expected by the hiring organization is too time-consuming, egregious, or comprehensive before the hiring manager has even talked to the candidate, you risk earning a reputation where it's not worth it to even bother responding to your job ad, regardless of the job description or performance profile.

Blind Screening

To further reduce bias in the screening process, organizations are implementing methods to hide or mask biographical information from each candidate's résumé, such as their name, names of employers, and the schools the candidates attended. By hiding these attributes, you or the screening committee have fewer details that may lead to inadvertently assuming someone is less qualified than others because they lacked a perceived pedigree.

One of the first and well-known examples of blind hiring occurred when the Boston Symphony Orchestra began blind auditions when interviewing musicians. With the candidates performing behind screens to hide their race and gender, researchers from Harvard and Princeton found that the blind auditions increased the likelihood that a woman would be hired by between 25 and 46%.[1]

Blind résumé screening is even more important regarding race. Researchers from M.I.T. and the University of Chicago created fake résumés with identical qualifications where half of them featured black-sounding names (such as Lakisha Washington and Jamal Jones) and the other half used white-sounding names (Emily Walsh and Greg Baker, for example).[2] The résumés with the "white" names received 50% more callbacks for interviews than those résumés with "black" names. There are a few methods to make sure this doesn't happen to your design team.

While some software can automatically hide identifying information, you can take matters into your own hands with just a Sharpie and a spreadsheet.

First, throw out the résumés that don't stand a chance of being considered. Then collect the résumés that seem worthy of evaluating for the phone screen.

Create a spreadsheet that will act as your answer key to what will become of the blinded résumés. So if Row #1 is Chris Avore in the spreadsheet, then take your Sharpie and cross out the name on the

---

1   Claire Cain Miller, "Is Blind Hiring the Best Hiring?," *New York Times*, February 25, 2016, www.nytimes.com/2016/02/28/magazine/is-blind -hiring-the-best-hiring.html

2   Marianne Bertrand Sendhil Mullainathan, "Are Emily and Greg More Employable Than Lakisha and Jamal? A Field Experiment on Labor Market Discrimination," *National Bureau of Economic Research Working Paper Series,* Working Paper 9873 (July 2003), www.nber.org/papers/w9873.pdf

résumé and write a #1. To continue the example, the second row would be #2 and Russ Unger, and you'd scratch out Russ's name and write a #2 on his résumé. Do this throughout the résumés up for consideration, and you'll end up with a stack of résumés with no names—just numbers.

You may also decide to scratch out the specific schools that candidates attended and clubs, activities, or other information that could imply each candidate's race, gender, or other protected or privileged status.

With your résumés blinded, you can begin the process of systematically scanning your lot to find who will be asked to interview over the phone.

Screening Résumés

Any interested applicant—even friends, former colleagues, or classmates—should provide a résumé to initiate the hiring process. Even if *you* know the candidate personally, your hiring committee will still need to agree that the person is qualified. Plus, chances are that your organization will need a résumé for its records.

You need an approach to quickly scan a designer's résumé that can scale to dozens of responses. Let's review what to look for—and perhaps more importantly, what not to use as an automatic disqualifier.

What About Getting the Basics Right?

A designer's résumé does not have to look like it was cut and pasted from the CV of a certified public account. Any designer should take the opportunity, when appropriate, to improve information hierarchy, prioritize relative experience, or to accommodate speaking at conferences, authoring guest blog posts, or podcasting contributions.

But if the designer forsakes the primary information to show quirky pie charts to represent how much they know about user research, or completion bars filled in to demonstrate how much they know about HTML (if you only know 75% of HTML, isn't that only HTM?), the design choices are distracting you from your goal—determining if this résumé deserves a callback.

Focus your time on scanning for the employers these candidates have worked for and what they've done for them. Don't be distracted by professional objectives, extracurricular activities, or lists of software titles.

What About Providing Adequate Context?

Scan the résumé for material change you can tie directly to the candidate's actions in each project or prior job. While many people may be leery to claim a concrete return on investment, deft designers can also show their net contribution in other ways, such as these examples:

- Overhauled user research practice, which led to increasing number of customer interviews from 15 in 2017 to over 50 interviews as of July 2019.

- Mentored two then-junior designers who were promoted to team leads overseeing other new junior designers.

- Organized quarterly lunch-and-learns with business stakeholders to show demos of work, review customer research findings, and show how final designs evolved since the last quarter.

Also, look for designers who recognize that their efforts are part of a wider team (unless, of course, you're reviewing the résumé of a lone founder). Even freelance, independent consultants looking to join a team should indicate who implemented their recommendations, when they joined a project, and when their roles typically ended.

What About Conflating Skills with Software or Deliverables?

Sketch, wireframes, and HTML are tools to accomplish tasks, and yes, being proficient in one tool over another may be a core component to be successful at the job. But it's better for candidates to explain how they use the tools they have at their disposal to solve design problems rather than simply claiming they're adept at using one particular software product, language, or common deliverable.

For example, if the résumé has a laundry-list of software titles, do a quick scan to see if the accomplishments reference these tools they're listing. If they mention *personas* right before *Photoshop*, do they also mention conducting user research anywhere? Or visual design? If not, you may have a person who is trying to stuff keywords into their résumé or does not fully understand why or when to use such tools.

What About Multiple Employers?

Long gone are the days of designers spending years at one company. If a designer has a lot of jobs as her experience indicates, don't assume she can't hold a job. Instead, use the phone screen to learn how many of those jobs she saw to completion or through a release or launch. Chances are you're looking at a designer who can adapt to new, complex environments, pick up new domains and audiences, juggle overlapping deadlines, and dedicate herself to hustling for her work.

While it's certainly possible the job-hopper really can't productively function in one place for over a year, you can't rely on dates on a résumé when screening a stack of interested applicants.

What About Title Mismatch?

Job titles in the design industry are anything but standardized, let alone at the more senior levels in organizations. Be hesitant to reject a candidate just because their current job title is Product Manager, because perhaps this person talks to customers and prototypes possible solutions. Rejecting candidates based on lack of seniority in job titles is even more risky. What makes a senior designer in one organization may be the same as a nonqualified designer title in another, or a Director of User Experience may not be as lofty in practice as it is in other organizations.

As we discussed, when exploring job descriptions, you risk alienating possible applicants by saying these specific titles are required to apply. Don't drain your talent pool with artificial restrictions that aren't going to net you better candidates.

What About Years of Experience?

Similar to job titles, "years of experience" is too amorphous from company to company to be a concrete factor when comparing two résumés. Instead of requiring five years of experience to apply, think about what you need for a candidate to have accomplished in those five years.

There's a chance that the applicant has been doing those exact things, but perhaps not as long as initially preferred. Besides, keep in mind that you're *scanning* these résumés. If you start doing the math to add up total years spent interviewing customers—which may be an arbitrary number anyway—you'll never get to the bottom of that pile.

It's important enough to write again: *Claiming a number of years are required in the job description means groups of talented people will think they are unqualified.*

What About Education?

Don't be seduced by names of famous schools or turned off by degrees that may seem irrelevant. Yet again, you run the risk of eliminating quality applicants—or, in other cases, awarding too much credit to a candidate—by overtly emphasizing education one way or the other.

You'll also likely see more applicants with various education "boot-camps" on their résumés. Upstart education providers such as General Assembly claim to prepare students for roles in design and development in as little as eight weeks. If the open position requires significant contributions from a skill the candidate only learned recently at such a bootcamp, don't throw the résumé into the rejection pile, but be sure to probe more heavily on the phone screen to learn how the program's curriculum prepared the applicant to join your team.

Be careful not to assign too much weight to GPA, majors, or programs, regardless of the university. Overweighting a technical or design degree over a traditional liberal arts degree such as English or history—particularly when the candidate's recent experience indicates they have the chops to deliver, can also leave good talent off your team. Unless you're recruiting for an early career position where most of your applicants just graduated from college in the past two years, you risk placing too much weight on factors that occurred long ago and not enough emphasis on the details that could indicate a productive candidate.

It's also important to consider candidates who have no formal education, provided you go into the vetting process with both eyes wide open. Candidates may be able to acquire the day-to-day skills through eight-week bootcamps or through their own commitment to teaching themselves. However, logging hours in a coffee shop or library might not prepare the candidate for the social expectations of working in a corporate environment. If a candidate is self-taught and seems legit, don't project your own assumptions about their maturity—address it on the phone screen.

When building the team at Nasdaq, we didn't make education a deal-breaker to get an interview. Designers came from all ends of the spectrum of higher education, including General Assembly and Tree-house certificates to MFAs from the best of the best private colleges. How you weigh education when building your team is yet another factor upon which you can diversify your team for the better.

What About Time Off Between Jobs?

While many people are quick to say the technology field moves so fast that what is important today is old news tomorrow, many aspects of the design industry simply have a far greater shelf-life. If you see a candidate with a great résumé who meets the criteria of your personal profile but hasn't held a design-related job in a few years, don't immediately reject the candidate. Many qualified people leave the workforce for a number of reasons: from caring for a sick family member, to starting a family, or to just experience something different while they have that personal flexibility. In some cases, it may make for an even more well-rounded contribution to your current culture. And as stated previously, you'll kill your efficiency at screening the good résumés from the not-so-good if you're spending your time doing math calculating how long people have been out of work.

Screening Portfolios

There has been some debate recently about whether designers—particularly user experience designers, researchers, information architects, and service designers—should be required to compile a portfolio of their work.

Whereas some design leaders argue that portfolios shouldn't be required to apply for a position, many design managers who are responsible for building teams said that at some point in the interview process, a portfolio of work—be it screenshots, video clips, articles, reviews, or other artifacts—must be furnished to continue the interview process. This doesn't necessarily have to happen for a candidate to just get a callback from you, the hiring manager, but you shouldn't feel unreasonable for expecting a candidate to have to show a portfolio at some point.

In some cases, having a portfolio as a qualifier means that you can immediately have one more filter to screen clients against—much like how location can disqualify the London-based designer applying for a full-time onsite position in New London, Connecticut.

Initially, screening candidates via a portfolio requires much less diligence than reviewing a candidate's portfolio in the interview with the nervous designer sitting across the table. That means don't drive yourself crazy overanalyzing every wireframe, comp, screenshot, or workflow included in the portfolio, and instead look at enough evidence that the candidate warrants a further discussion via a phone interview.

You're only looking for enough information to determine if the candidate should advance or not.

Weigh the portfolio alongside the résumé to ground your expectations. Does the résumé indicate the candidate has worked for a few years in an advertising agency? Then the portfolio will likely look very different from that of the sole UX designer at a half-dozen startups over that same time period.

You may find more polished screenshots representing the final state of the effort in the agency portfolio than the journeyman, which means it's up to you to decide if you should probe deeper into process and measures of success (hint: you should).

Look for the following information:

- **Measures of success in each project:** Even during the first, high-level glance at the portfolio, you should find whether or not the project was successful and why; designers should recognize and highlight such primary information in summarizing their work.

- **Clear, defined roles and contributions to each project:** Effective portfolios communicate what the designer's role was throughout the project. Perhaps a user researcher contributed to facilitating interviews and moderating usability tests at the onset and toward the end of a project, whereas an interaction designer may have been most effective throughout the design and development phase.

- **Variety of artifacts comprising each project:** Usually, designers turn to a variety of artifacts and methods to achieve their goals. Do these portfolios include sketches, photos of design exercises, or wireframes and visual design comps evolving with the project? You should be able to spot such diversity of resources quickly in a few seconds.

- **Concise, direct ties to the candidate's résumé:** The featured works in the portfolio should strongly tie to the résumé; for instance, the most recent work experience in the résumé should ideally be in the first section or two of the portfolio.

Red flags:

- **Only showing the end-state of each project instead of how the project developed over time:** Designers must often facilitate how a project evolved based on user feedback, business needs, unintended constraints, and other variables. If a portfolio only shows one slice of time, you may risk interviewing a designer who doesn't understand the importance of such a facilitation of the process and the trade-offs and opportunities that define a project.

- **Few details describing each project's goals:** It's easy to pull together beautiful pictures in a clean layout, but it's much more challenging to show how those pictures directly influenced the goals of a project.

- **Dated work that's not relevant to the current position:** It's easy for people to assume the more, the better, but portfolio-stuffing with old, irrelevant work only distracts you as the hiring manager from your core goal of seeing just enough work to know whether to schedule a phone screen.

Preparing the First Round of Callbacks

At this point in the hiring process, it's important to revisit the team you've assembled to act as your checks and balances against any latent biases or blind spots you may bring to the decision-making stage as the hiring manager.

It's not an effective use of anyone's time to have a hiring committee review every single résumé submitted if you're getting dozens of résumés. (However, if you have fewer than a dozen applicants, you can fully engage your committee to review every one.)

In the case of a situation with dozens of résumés, engage your committee to identify whom they want to talk to, based on the criteria you've already prioritized. Here's how to ensure that you're reducing bias in your hiring and using your colleagues' time effectively.

As the primary hiring manager, you should highlight which résumés you're convinced should be called back and create an additional list of candidates you're unclear on and want the support of your colleagues to weigh in on.

But now you need to eliminate the bias that your committee might have in order to appease you (as the boss or hiring manager) and simply agree with everyone you nominated. Make a list that only you have access to and give the full list of must-interviews and maybe-interviews to your committee to review and see how their list maps to yours. If there are galling differences, such as the committee recommended not calling multiple candidates you had identified as must-interview, regroup and make sure that you're all aligned on the performance profile and how you're ranking each candidate's experience.

Keep the list of how you and the committee have ranked skills, education, and experience close at hand as everyone reviews the résumés. That way, you don't inadvertently suddenly want a CS degree from someone who has relevant work experience but only studied design over a few community college courses.

Likewise, imagine that your committee has agreed that the successful applicant has managed teams of more than five designers over the course of several projects. The initial stack of résumés includes all résumés that mentioned just managing a team. In this instance, you may need to begin more legwork, which could include writing each candidate to find out the size of the teams they managed.

PROVIDE A PRESENTATION FOR CANDIDATES

At Nasdaq, we had better conversations with more qualified candidates after we began emailing a deck of a few
highlights about our design team prior to scheduling the
phone screen. This deck included how big the team was at
the time, who the design leadership was, conferences we
had or were scheduled to speak at that year, photographs
of the design team working with a variety of stakeholders,
and links to articles and press releases about our design
work and process.

Because we provided this info ourselves, naturally we expected more
thoughtful, compelling questions than what a candidate might have found
by just reviewing the corporate website. ■

After you have your list of phone-screen candidates, do yourself a
favor and when you begin scheduling the interviews, identify any
logistical deal-breakers, such as location, start date, or huge differences in expected or target compensation.

Phone Screens

Conducting a phone screen can be a bigger challenge for some people
than leading a face-to-face interview. It can be all too easy to just think
that the phone interview is an opportunity to see if you can get along
with the applicant before they advance further in the interview process.

Remember that the goal of the phone screen is to acquire enough
information in 30 minutes to determine if you should bring the person into your office or set up more comprehensive interviews where
you can then make the go or no-go decision (which will likely take at
least 90 minutes and more people).

But those offer-on-the-line interviews are such critical and time-
consuming events for all parties that it's your responsibility to make
sure that you're only bringing in the right people, and the best way to
find out efficiently who those folks are is through a concise, effective
phone screen.

Set the expectation that everyone who participates should do just
that—participate and pay attention. Of course, participation may
mean copious note-taking and not speaking during the interview.
Resist allowing folks to just drop into the phone interview to see if
they have any thoughts. They won't be familiar with the interview
guide, and they won't know what criteria you're evaluating.

Steps to a Successful Phone Screen

It's too easy to assume that you can wing a phone screen by getting the candidate to talk about his or her experiences that are outlined on the résumé. *Consider this quite possibly the worst thing you could do at this stage of the game.* You just invited the candidate to guide the entire interview with information he or she has provided you, and you'll only hear glowing things about those experiences.

Don't assume that just getting the candidate talking about their experiences is effective or will lead you to the best person to invite to later stages. Instead, be assertive with the direction of the interview, have a plan in place, and establish what questions need to be answered before advancing further.

Here are some additional steps to prepare you to lead an effective phone screen:

1. **Prepare your team.**

   Be sure everyone on your hiring committee knows their role and what's expected of them during the phone screen. They should have the latest version of the interview guide (discussed in Chapter 4, "Performance Profiles and Interview Guides"), the candidate's résumé, and the scoring rubric. If just one person is conducting the phone screen, make sure that the rest of the hiring committee knows where to access your notes and the interview guide.

2. **Know the résumé.**

   Read the résumé three more times—top to bottom and bottom to top. You'll be amazed at what you (and maybe even your committee) skipped over when you were trying to separate the pretenders from the hopefuls. Pay attention to dates, software titles, any management or leadership responsibility, and anything else. If it's written by the candidate, make sure that you've read it.

3. **Know the context.**

   Visit the websites of the employers or jobs (and don't judge). Familiarize yourself and your phone screen committee with the domains in which the candidate has worked. Keep in mind that the résumé may not explicitly say if that person worked on the public website, so don't be quick to judge the candidate negatively before the phone call has begun.

4. **Follow your script.**

   The phone screen is a valuable opportunity to share who you are and why you're hiring new designers. Start the interview with a background of the design team, such as size, where it sits in the business unit, or what types of clients you specialize in, and how design decisions are made as a team. You want your candidate to be able to frame their answers relative to your world, not necessarily back to everything he or she has done previously.

5. **Focus on useful questions.**

   Don't just rehash the résumé—ask related questions that pertain to the open position. One of the biggest layups—either on the phone or in person—is to have a résumé of a candidate in the interviewer's hands, and that interviewer asks the candidate, "So, tell me about your role as a UX Designer at ACME." This lazy request for information is problematic because much of those details are already right in front of the interviewer, and because the candidate's response may not have anything to do with what the committee needs to hear to drive a decision. Focus your questions on what you need to know that are based on the résumé, not spelled out in the résumé.

   Don't say, "Hmm, I see you were a lead UX designer at ACME. Can you tell me about your design process there?" when directly under their heading of working at ACME reads: "Led and executed Lean and Agile UX design process to implement a Build/Measure/Learn methodology across the design and product teams."

   Yes, that can be interesting. Yes, it could be very telling *if* the candidate expands on the topic. But why risk hearing about what Lean is for 10 minutes? Instead, relate the question to your work environment so the candidate also can determine if they'll be a good fit, too.

   For instance: "I see you've led Lean and Agile design process at ACME. Here at Winco, we've created a culture of discovery, learning, and then iterating on what we design based on those findings, and this Lead UX Designer position is expected to continue supporting that culture. How is that similar or different than what you have accomplished?"

   Now you've framed the question to how it related to the environment you're hiring for, instead of simply hearing about what they did in the past as a stand-alone data point.

6. **Monitor the candidate's questions.**

Monitor what types of questions the candidate asks about you, the position, and the company. The types of questions a designer asks you about are strong indicators of what types of questions the designer should likely ask a client or a stakeholder. After all, effective designers are curious and prepared to address a variety of unknowns and unplanned variables that can unexpectedly appear mid-project.

NOTE CANDIDATE QUESTIONS MATTER

In a phone interview that could mean a new job for the candidate, have they done any pre-interview research on you as the hiring manager, your design team, the open position, or the company itself? Perhaps your corporate website doesn't explicitly cover the team or the primary product the candidate may work on. But that shouldn't stop the candidate from asking about a conference talk you've given, blog posts that others from the team have authored, or if this position is for the design team that worked on a prominent app or another part of the business. During the interview, write down the questions each candidate asks you and your team as another pre-weighted data point to consider.

7. **Keep the dialogue at the appropriate level.**

Keep expectations tailored to the seniority and complexity of the position as well. Junior designers may ask questions around process and approach: "Does your organization perform contextual inquiry?" "What happens to the code the design team writes when dev begins their work?" More senior candidates may be more interested in where funding is derived, what position the highest ranking designer in the organization holds, or what the maturity of design as a practice in the organization is.

Phone Screen Format

Relying on a consistent format for conducting phone screens means that you have less to worry about every time you are hiring, and it gives your team and colleagues some expectation about how you conduct hiring for your team.

While the specific questions may be unique from position to position, we've found that most of the phone screens are quite similar, regardless of the actual open position.

First, strike a balance between what you need to hear about a candidate and what a candidate needs to understand about the team and the company.

Usually, you identify what you need to learn in less than 30 minutes with the following outline:

1. What the company does and why it has a design team.

2. What types of work the design team does in the company.

3. Discuss the specifics of the open position, including whom this role will work closely with, the types of deliverables and outcomes expected of the candidate, and where you see this position growing.

4. Preplanned questions identified by committee:

   - How does any of the above map to your goals?

   - Describe how your experience prepares you for the position.

   - Discuss a time when you were successful at a current or previous position that addressed a challenge that you've mentioned.

5. Candidate questions to group.

6. Logistics of the face-to-face interview, expected time frame to hire, salary and other compensation questions to be addressed over email or on a separate call.

7. Thank candidate for their time.

Such a structure arrives at a few goals discussed earlier. You don't just talk through every line of the candidate's résumé, and it keeps you in control of gathering what you need to learn from the candidate in as repeatable and efficient a manner as possible. Furthermore, the candidate has the chance to learn about the company and team dynamic, and the hiring committee learns how the candidate ties their experience to what they just heard shared by the interviewer.

Phone screens aren't about tricking the candidate with witty questions, just as much as they shouldn't be a dramatic reading of a résumé. Instead, create a format to gather the right information quickly to learn if you should invite the applicant into the next stage of the interview process.

Evaluating the Phone Screen

At the conclusion of the phone screen, give your hiring committee the chance to ask any other additional questions or request clarification about what they heard. Once the candidate is off the phone, collect the score sheets and additional notes from each of your committee members. Then consider handing out Mad Lib–like prompts to give your hiring committee the chance to frame their opinions of the candidates in addition to the numeric scoring guides.

Much like the score sheets, these prompts reduce the variety of biases and hunches that are so prevalent in hiring as you ask each person on the committee to articulate why they support a candidate or not. Consider these examples that may be in a post-interview summary:

- What surprised you about the candidate?

- What is unique about this candidate?

- How did the candidate distinguish himself or herself from their résumé? From the rest of the applicants?

- What would be your biggest concern about this applicant if they were to be interviewed?

These questions don't so much reference the numeric scoring of each candidate but rather they show what people on your committee feel about each candidate.

With all the artifacts and materials in hand, store them in an easily findable and shared workspace for later when you compare all the screened candidates at once to determine who gets invited to the next step.

Wrapping Up

Identifying a hirable candidate from the phone screen is an exercise in preparation and expectations. By reducing how much you can be surprised by a candidate and their responses, you build a better foundation upon which to measure the candidates against each other and determine who gets the invite to the next step.

Congratulations! You've finally got your pool of candidates to invite to interview. Now the real fun begins.

CHAPTER 6

Interviewing Potential Team Members

Now that the phone interviews are complete, you're finally able to tally up the scores, review the notes, and identify whom you want to invite to the office for a face-to-face interview (although more and more firms with entirely distributed workforces will never have face-to-face interviews).

Remember that your scoring system should lead to a more exclusive round of invites than your résumé pool led to your phone interviews. The face-to-face interviews are a significant amount of time—even if they're an hour or less—for both you, your committee, and the candidate, so it's important to invite only the people whom you think you may want to work with and those who would want to work with you.

Don't continue the interview process with anyone who wouldn't take the position anyway. If you haven't done it yet, now is the time to email each face-to-face candidate about their timing to accept and start a new job, and most importantly, compensation expectations. It's not unreasonable to provide a realistic window into the base compensation package for the position—even if the actual offer may exceed what you initially quoted. While some companies may have human resources policies in place that prohibit you from discussing salary in the interview stage, it's worth it to know—one way or another—if you can afford the people with whom you're talking.

You also don't want to put candidates into a position where they're expected to negotiate against themselves. You risk turning away great candidates if you require them to disclose their salary history or what they're currently earning at their current employer.

Being forthright with a candidate can be as simple as "The minimum base compensation for this position, without bonus or equity, is $75,000, which includes benefits, three weeks of vacation, sick time, holidays, and other perks we can discuss after an offer has been extended. The actual offer will be determined by Human Resources and the compensation committee and presented following the interview process."

This statement shows that you respect the candidate and aren't trying to lowball good talent. You also reinforce that the discussion is just beginning—it's not over already before the candidate has even entered the room. You're also clearly establishing that there are other stakeholders at play here. You're not trying to look like you hold all the cards and can just write checks at will.

Depending on where you work, you may be prohibited by law from even asking the question about previous salaries. Most importantly, by negotiating from the company's base salary and up, rather than what the candidate has earned, you reduce the risk of paying lower salaries to women and people of color by paying designers what the position is worth.

When conducting design research or emailing an executive, every word, phrase, and sentence should have a specific outcome or goal you're trying to accomplish. Communicating with your final candidate pool is no different. If your organization does not have a dedicated design operations manager, specifically identify who will be responsible for preparing the candidate and the interviewing team so that they all know where to be and when it's showtime.

Preparing the Candidate

As you email the candidates whom you want to interview in person (or whatever the final interview step may be), be sure to include a number of details that may go unnoticed or left to chance. Failure to do so just increases the possible stress on you or the candidate, which could easily be prevented ahead of time.

It may seem basic to some folks, but nevertheless be sure to share the following information prior to the day of the interview:

- Specific location, including any nearby public transit stations or where to park (also advise if your company validates or reimburses parking expenses)

- The name and phone number (preferably a mobile device to enable texting) of the primary point of contact in case something goes sideways

- How to access the building, floor, or suite where you work

- Duration of the interview

- Expected dress code for the interview

- General format of the interview—the candidate should know if they'll be reviewing their portfolio for about an hour, doing a design exercise, or if the format is more conversational

- Names of the primary interviewers—this not only gives the candidate the opportunity to do some minor background research on these folks, but also gives old-school candidates a ballpark number of résumés to print

- Links to any websites or blog posts that will help prepare the candidate

- The technical environment in the interview room, including specifics such as:

  - Guest WiFi capabilities

  - Available dongles

  - Types of displays to show or discuss work

These specifics will likely be unchanged for every interview, so consider maintaining one document that you can cut and paste or attach to the email.

Preparing Your Hiring Committee

Likewise, you also need to have a checklist for your own team so that nothing on your side slips through the cracks. This list likely includes:

- Who the primary point of contact is for the candidate

- General agenda with time and dates and a complete interview guide prepared and circulated to the team

- Remind nondesigner stakeholders they are interviewing a design candidate

- Supplies and materials for any exercises, including markers, paper, supporting documents, WiFi guest account details, and necessary dongles

- Conference room booked and any and all squatters removed from the space

These details may seem trivial or simple common sense, but they provide a foundation for preparation that gets the interview off to a safe start without undue stress on anyone. They also establish a sense of professionalism for the candidate that you, your team, and your organization take the interview process seriously and respect the candidate's time and attention.

The Interview

The conversation between the candidate and the hiring manager will likely outweigh the portfolio review or any design exercise. This dialogue should reveal how candidates present themselves, what statements trigger additional questions, and how the responses can drive the decision to make an offer or not.

But just because this is a conversation doesn't mean it's a free-for-all—after all, the format we're recommending is called *structured* interviewing. Rely on the script in your interview guide (discussed in Chapter 4, "Performance Profiles and Interview Guides") to make sure that you're asking the same questions of each candidate, for every interview.

Equally important to an effective, informative dialogue with the candidate is your own behavior—including what you *don't* say.

Be sure to give the candidate the respect they deserve and put away your cell phone or other devices to focus on the discussion at hand. If the interview includes a dedicated notetaker, introduce that person to the candidate as such so the candidate knows why that person is typing or writing the whole time.

Be aware of your own and your team's body language—sit up or lean forward toward the candidate, especially when they're speaking. Resist the urge to frown, even if that's how you usually imply understanding—it's easy to misconstrue as disagreement. Monitor your arm and leg positions as well. Folding your arms across your chest and crossing your legs will likely suggest that you're not open to listening or understanding the candidate.

And once again, the traits of a good design research interviewer (or any human with generally refined social skills) will serve you well here:

- **Don't interrupt.**

  Always easier said than done, but you have to let the candidate finish, even if they're going down a different path than you intended.

- **Don't make the response all about you.**

  Be sure that you listen and internalize the candidate's response without finding a way to turn the answer immediately into something about your team or the open position.

- **Don't put the answer in the question.**

  Make sure that you let the candidate answer with their own responses based on their experience and perspective. See the difference between:

  - **Bad:** "So it says here you led user research! Great, did you do face-to-face interviews? Usability testing? Surveys? Observations? Or …"

  - **Good:** "You said in your phone screen that you currently lead user research. Can you talk a little more about what that means at your job, including how research is prioritized and what methods you most frequently use?"

> **NOTE** SILENCE IS GOLDEN
>
> As the primary interviewer, silence can be a significant tool to get the candidate to open up more. If you're afraid you may appear socially awkward by just staring at the candidate hoping they'll talk more, try this tip from user experience veteran Boon Sheridan: Beg the pardon of the candidate and say that you need to finish up your notes. After a few seconds of writing, you can wave

the candidate to continue elaborating. Even if the candidate thought they were finished, it's likely they'll pick back up where they left off, and you'll officially be in the bonus round.

As the interview continues, remember that it's critical to make the questions and answers as quantifiable and consistent as possible when you review your notes and those of the committee later. Asking each person the same questions as the rest of the candidate pool will create a baseline of responses so that you can compare every answer to the other candidates.

Portfolio Review

Screening portfolios when you're looking for someone to call back is very different than reviewing portfolios with a candidate during the actual interview.

It's yet another activity that needs a plan and constraints to be most effective and move you closer to a hiring decision. Much like the résumé and even the dialogue, you risk being either wowed or turned off by a candidate who does one thing well (or poorly) that may not make a big difference to their later success.

The portfolio review shouldn't feel like a whole new segment of the interview with different people, in a different room, with an entirely different demeanor. If you and the team are prepared, you can transition from the dialogue into the review as easily as just saying "So let's check out some of your work and see how it fits with where we're going." Why is it that easy? Simple. You've already done all the work.

In addition to writing the script and weighting possible responses, there are further steps to take to make the portfolio review as focused and efficient as possible. After all, the portfolio isn't the résumé, and you should have different goals and outcomes from the portfolio than the résumé.

For instance, the portfolio can offer:

- Another glimpse into how the candidate organizes and prioritizes information, particularly without formal supervision or direction (since most résumés will rely on reverse chronological order)

- What artifacts and projects the candidate believes make a compelling story

- Opportunities to elaborate on perceived gaps in experience or delivery based on the résumé

- The preparedness and presence of a candidate talking about their work—particularly if the position requires the designer to present works to other teams and stakeholders

Do your best to make sure that everyone who will be in the portfolio review has at least seen the candidate's portfolio and understands the questions you want the review to address. This is the time when you want to dig into what's on the résumé and what's in the portfolio— and ask for clarification if you see something in one that may not jibe with what's in the other.

For instance, if a candidate's résumé has mentioned that they've shipped a lot of mobile work, but the portfolio is primarily desktop systems, ask where to find the mobile interfaces, screenshots, or prototypes on a device. If a designer emphasizes they're not a visual designer, but the portfolio is primarily just rich, high-fidelity comps, probe deeper into what their exact contribution was to the project, and likewise ask why that information isn't in the portfolio itself.

Adjust your standards accordingly with the position and the experience required for the job. Junior designers may not include everyone on a project team because they simply didn't have the exposure to business or commercial stakeholders. Their presentation skills when talking to you and the interviewing committee may be less polished since more senior leads pitch all work to clients. But that said, there are several resources available to designers of all levels of experience that make a disorganized, incoherent portfolio unacceptable for a candidate who is serious about securing a new job.

When reviewing mid-to-senior level designers, raise your expectations of both the participant and the interviewing committee. Effective portfolios will reveal insights and nuances of the applicant's experience, but in some cases, it's up to the interviewing team to draw out those stories that may not immediately present themselves in the actual portfolio.

For instance, effective portfolios draw a process map from start to finish of the most important and successful projects, and show where those paths diverge from client to client or through different projects. But your interview committee may need to explicitly ask what challenged the applicant most, or which environment the applicant performed best in and why.

It's also expected that a design portfolio highlights artifacts, but divulging the teams and stakeholders who were responsible for other aspects of the project can reveal the level of significance that the designer had to the company. If the designer mentions the work was for the CEO, it's fair game to ask if the designer presented work to the CEO directly or conducted research with members of the C-suite.

Likewise, effective portfolios go beyond showing artifacts to also showing the activities that led to those design decisions. If the portfolio shows photographs of sticky notes, explore what the purpose of the activity was, what teams participated in the exercise, and how the outcomes directly impacted the work. It may be compelling to ask the applicant just how they managed the sign-off to conduct the activity—did it require political capital to get approval, or was the designer established enough that they didn't need to jump through hoops to get something done? Such insights can be valuable and revealing to you and the committee, but only if you go the extra mile to explore beyond what's in front of you.

Much like how there are no perfect interview questions, there are no real magic questions around the portfolio that will separate the best candidates from the pretenders. But prompting the candidate to compare experiences—both across projects, channels, and time—is a trusted method to elucidate insight that may not be readily available from page to page in the portfolio.

Consider these questions when evaluating projects in the candidate's portfolio:

- How did your specific deliverables change from two of your recent projects?

- Was that your decision and why?

- Describe any differences in how you handled impasses in your last three projects.

- What lessons did you learn from one project to another that we can see in the portfolio?

- Walk us through how you made those decisions and show us the cause and effect of applying what you learned elsewhere.

The best portfolios will not only show the outcome of design decisions, but they'll also clearly demonstrate the problem that was solved and the value and effectiveness of the design decisions that addressed that problem. This doesn't have to be excruciatingly difficult—if a candidate's portfolio states that the shopping cart abandonment rate was too high, they can show how they consolidated steps and eliminated unnecessary hurdles. Clearly communicating how the designer addressed the business and user problem is the crux of the portfolio review, not necessarily how complex the actual problem may have been.

Candidate Portfolio Presentations

How the candidate shares the portfolio with the interview committee is also another data point to measure, particularly if the open position calls for presenting work to senior stakeholders and clients.

Introverts and extroverts alike should be expected to walk through their work with conviction and confidence. The comfortable, prepared presenter will experiment with how much backstory to share for each project and confirm with the room and anyone on the phone if they have any questions before moving on. They may flip the script and even ask you and the committee if this or that project is particularly relevant or appropriate, based on the research they've done on the company and your team.

Body language, posture, eye contact, and the vocal projection can also indicate someone who is polished or a nervous wreck. It's up to you to determine if the candidate captivating the room is all talk, or conversely, just someone who works better at presenting to those people they're comfortable with. Don't be fooled with style over substance—but if that presence is a required part of the job, don't dismiss it, either.

Getting Informed About Design Exercises

One of the more polarizing topics among design teams is whether or not to use time-boxed design exercises, such as sketching on a whiteboard, design studio, or even wireframing or visually designing something on the spot, as part of the interview. Some organizations assign projects to be completed at home and presented back to the hiring committee as part of the interview process.

In one camp, proponents of the design exercise claim that they need to see how a candidate thinks on the fly, what questions they will ask about something they don't know, and how their mind works through solving the problem.

Opponents of design exercises—either in the office or exercises to be completed at home—say the whole thing is theater—simply a crude simulation of how design work actually gets done. Others say that asking designers to perform an exercise in front of the group or to present a project they worked on at home are loaded with biases that favor only one group of people—the folks who can think fast on their feet when the pressure is on, or those who had enough time and materials to work on what you asked for.

Like many things in the design field, there are likely ways you can strike a balance between both camps.

If you're going to use a design exercise, create a challenge that will get you the insights you need to observe to make a hiring decision and will show you how the candidate addresses design problems that aren't reflected in the portfolio.

Find a Useful Exercise

The best designer will likely struggle with a design challenge that's half-baked, unclear, or difficult to surface what you need to see. Consider these attributes of an effective design challenge, whether you are considering an in-office exercise or a take-home exercise (explored more specifically in this chapter):

- **All candidates should be able to understand the challenge.**

  ATMs, kiosks, alarm clocks, email, ticketing, and task management systems can be useful challenges. Don't create a challenge based on your domain or industry, if for no other reason than to avoid the impression that you're looking for free work.

- **Your design challenge needs a clear problem to solve.**

  Easily state what you need to have designed and remember to structure the challenge as solving a problem.

- **Provide multiple ways to solve the problem.**

  Don't just expect a finished sketch of a thing. Storyboards, multiple sketches, and a journey can all reveal the insights you need to make a hiring decision.

Talking Hiring with Randy Ellis

by Randy Ellis

Ellis is the founder of the creative agency 5ivehat in Chicago. He is currently Global Director of DesignOPS at Mokriya, and has taught user experience at General Assembly.

Q: *As a design leader with enterprise experience from your days at Alight Solutions and an instructor at General Assembly in Chicago, you must have some interesting perspectives about hiring designers and also helping your students get hired. Is your approach for interviewing candidates for enterprise roles different than how some of your teaching colleagues try to help their students get hired?*

A: My hiring style is more about understanding the student's learning style and how it impacts the energy they inject into their portfolio's case studies. I advocate building success out of failure. I would say that for some of my teaching colleagues, my approach might be uncomfortable. It's natural in some design communities to be a perfectionist. Perfectionism can lure a designer into a false sense of security. Just showing your final production/high-fidelity prototype designs and trashing your "back of the napkin" drawing process doesn't truly show your thinking. Showcasing the final result instead of the iterations continues to be a problem. I want to know more about the adversity they may have encountered when their first ideas weren't their best.

- **Reveal constraints, goals, and other relevant information at the start of the challenge, not on the fly.**

  Clearly state how much time the candidate has to complete the challenge, any information about a user or customer base, and what, if anything, is off limits to the challenge.

- **State how you'll be scoring the exercise.**

  The candidate must know how you'll be judging their work in advance. Don't be vague by stating "We just want to see how you work." Instead, specifically say if you want to see what questions are asked, how they will work through different ideas, or when they may pivot from one idea to another.

Q: *Is how a designer handles adversity important to their career?*

A: If your career has been filled with nothing but wins, then I'll have little interest in bringing you onto my team because you haven't been battle-tested. As a UX professional, you have to know that your role is met with skepticism from the accountants to the C-suite. The world has been under the control of the ego-driven to make sure their voice was heard loud enough to get their way. Now you have this "UX Person," who claims they use "the data" to design and can improve our market penetration by some exponential amount.

On the other hand, candidates think because they get the offer letter, the firm must have a solid understanding of user experience (since they're hiring UX designers). However, their job has only begun. They have the responsibility to convince peers, managers, executives, and ultimately the market they're designing for.

Q: *Why is how a designer handles adversity important to you as the manager of the team?*

A: Not simply taking the answer "No, this can't work" as a final answer is what makes a designer better. Creative problem solving is about finding multiple possible solutions for a complex challenge. Hearing terms such as "this is the way we have always done it" is not the way a company innovates. Forcing your business to step into uncharted territory is the approach that businesses have to embrace to remain ahead of their competition.

- **Don't require extensive imagination or role-playing.**

  Some organizations have tried conducting mock one-on-ones or performance evaluations a year into the future, as if the candidate was already on the payroll. There's likely little actionable value you can glean from these conversations since the candidate has no realistic basis for what they would be discussing. Stick with things they can talk about—lived experiences and behaviors.

In many cases, there are a number of exercises that are anything but useful, most often because candidates won't know enough about the domain, or it's dangerously close to seeming like actual project work.

For instance, don't ask candidates to redesign your home page, your primary navigation system, or a feature or workflow. The same also goes for asking candidates to redesign anything of your competition. It's just not worth seeming sketchy asking for free work before you've got the candidate on the payroll.

Know Why You're Having an Exercise

By now, this should stand out as a common thread: know what you want out of this exercise, much like a résumé, portfolio, phone screen, and face-to-face interview. Set the parameters with your hiring committee about what you hope to see and how important it is to the position. You should also be able to articulate specifically why you need a design exercise in the first place. Describe what a design exercise will reveal that you cannot extract through portfolio reviews, résumés, and the rest of the artifacts you've already reviewed.

Reflect on your own work environment to map out the exercise. If you rarely have to whip up design solutions out of thin air, you may not benefit much from watching a candidate do exactly that. On the other hand, if you regularly must confront changes to requirements late in your development process, don't ask a designer to whiteboard something from scratch; instead, have your exercise explore how to make unexpected or unplanned changes to a spec within time or other constraints.

Most importantly, monitor how the designer goes about exploring the possible solutions in your design challenge.

Observe if the candidate asks a lot of questions about whom they're designing for and what their goals are, project constraints, and perhaps how success could be measured. (A note to you and your committee—you better have those answers!)

Be sure to take note of the *types* of questions the candidate asks as well. Perhaps they focus more on the customer, or the business needs, or perhaps competing services. These can be useful data points you want to monitor when making your decisions.

Additionally, record how the designer discusses their possible solution to your challenge. Many designers will realize they have other ideas after you start discussing their decisions. This could reflect an open mind about solving challenges, not taking feedback personally, or a comfort with iteration. It could also just mean they talk a lot when they're nervous. Interviewing is hard, ain't it?

Also pay attention if they sketch or propose a full solution or individual parts of a broader thing, be it a website, product, service, or otherwise. If you conduct a design studio–like exercise, you can see if candidates start with a wider, broader approach at finding a solution or dive into disparate features that address the challenge. While neither approach is wrong or right, it's your job as the interviewer to explore why the designer chose that path.

Don't Hope for Free Labor

Design exercises are supposed to help you and your hiring committee see how the candidate works through design challenges—not to augment your design team for an hour of work.

Find a problem that either you've already solved, or better yet, make up a problem that is easily understood by most people, even if it's well outside of your domain. In fact, some hiring managers intentionally stray far from their domain or industry so they don't become overly critical or hinged to too much detail that could cloud the effectiveness of the exercise.

Don't Expect Greatness

Your hiring committee should keep their expectations in check and monitor what you all are looking for as the candidate completes the design exercise. Don't necessarily overemphasize the final product against how the candidate got there—this is one example where process should outweigh the result. If the designer quickly draws up a proto-persona, a quadrant of needs, goals, pain points, and constraints, an imaginary journey, or a SWOT analysis, but the wireframe doesn't show much detail, you could be looking at a great designer who will understand the problem before diving into finding solutions to it.

TAKING A STAND ON TAKE-HOME ASSIGNMENTS

Back in 2007, I was interviewing for a Director of User Experience position, and the corporate recruiter asked me to review the company's website home page and share some comments in an email.

After sending back a few high-level points on the hierarchy and prioritization of the page, not to mention some questions around navigation labels, the recruiter wrote back asking for more specifics and recommendations about how to address the shortcomings I pointed out. At this point, I was now at a crossroads: I could play ball and comply with the request, essentially doing some free work that the company could put into action, or I could stand up to say I wasn't comfortable with the request.

I chose to explain to the recruiter my position—that the work he was requesting was exactly what I did for a living, and that for a more comprehensive heuristic review and recommendation, it should be a legitimate gig with legitimate pay. The recruiter found the money, and I had a new client. Incidentally, a few weeks later I landed the job. ■

Take-Home Projects

Some organizations feel that take-home assignments are a better opportunity to understand how people could work with the design team rather than in-office design challenges.

Participants can apply more time to think through what they are trying to solve, review additional documentation or artifacts, and you, as the hiring manager, may even expect more output than just a quick sketch. However, much like in-office design challenges, take-home assignments are rife with pitfalls if you're not careful.

You should absolutely compensate any participant you send home with a work assignment—regardless if they get an offer or not. For larger companies, that means you still have to have that money readily accessible to pay out—don't make a candidate become a registered vendor and wait to be paid net-30. Cut a check on delivery. If you can't hand over compensation on the spot, then don't assign take-home design exercises.

Also, be careful about assuming that your candidates have the capacity to undertake your exercise. Asking a candidate to work on a side project for a few hours over the next week may seem innocuous to you, but it may create some real hardship for your interviewees. For example, you're basically assuming this candidate now has a working computer readily available, internet access, and the time to work on your exercise.

Perhaps this person is solely responsible for ensuring that their children get home from after-school care before 6 p.m., or helping them with homework after preparing dinner, and still has two freelance gigs to complete prior to getting up for work the next day and doing it all over again.

In addition, take-home assignments must be written clearly so the candidate won't need to contact you for follow-up questions. You don't want to burden the candidate any more by adding a sense of uneasiness that you're also evaluating their communication skills and the rate at which they ask questions. Everything the candidate needs to know to complete the challenge must be in the document outlining the challenge itself.

Wrapping Up

Interviewing people doesn't have to be a stressful activity that takes time away from your "real job." Effective interviewing is your job, as is making sure your teammates understand what's expected of them throughout the interviewing process.

It's too important to wing it when the candidate is waiting in the office lobby. Simply trying to have a conversation and relying on your gut just doesn't cut it anymore—either for your organization or the candidates themselves.

With the right practice, performance profiles, interview guides, and clear expectations, you can stay true to your vision of your hiring process. You'll find your team conducting more concise interviews with consistent scoring to make sure that you can compare candidates on the merits of themselves and the demands of the job. With an accurate picture of each candidate's experience and abilities, you can fairly and equitably begin the process of making your decisions to see which person will receive the offer.

CHAPTER 7

Offers, Negotiations, and Onboarding

You're almost there. You've seen example after example of candidates' work, you've listened to the responses to the same questions across candidates, and you've been scoring who has performed highest in your scoring rubric—and not necessarily against each other. Now is a good time to notify HR that you will be narrowing down your list to one primary target so they can be prepared for how and when they re-engage with the process.

Checking References

When checking in with HR, ask them to revisit the company's policy on checking references. Some organizations simply will ask for confirmation of employment. Other firms will expect candidates to provide contact information for direct managers, direct reports, and other colleagues to ask for a reference. In other cases, your organization will outsource the reference check entirely so that you may not have anything to do with it at all.

If you, as the hiring manager, will be conducting the references check, follow a similar playbook as you did with the candidate and ask the same questions of each reference the candidate provides, for each candidate you check.

Effective questions include the following:

- Did you see the candidate grow or evolve over time when you were working together?

- What should I know about the candidate to make working together be more successful?

- What was one of the candidate's biggest accomplishments when you were working together?

Many of these questions are more useful than questions asking if the reference would work with the candidate again or about their strengths and weaknesses for a simple reason: the candidate knows they're going to say positive things about them, since they furnished the contact information. Instead, the above questions should give you the opportunity to hear stories about the candidate that the reference can authoritatively speak to (versus asking the reference if they think the candidate would be a good fit at your new job, for instance).

Also, keep in mind that much like the interview process itself, you are likely legally bound *not* to ask about the candidate's personal life, age, marital status, etc.

It's been said that the design community is small and looks out for each other. There's a good chance that many people in your hiring pool are also in larger communities you participate in, too. And with tools like LinkedIn, Slack, or Twitter, you may realize that someone you know has worked with one of your candidates, even if that person wasn't included as a reference. Content strategist Margot Bloomstein refers to asking your network about working with someone as the *Slackground Check*.

Asking these people what it was like working with your candidate can yield an eye-opening, unvarnished experience.

You may also find out information that you would be hard-pressed to uncover in the interview process we've outlined here—information that could lead to immediately dispelling the candidate from consideration in many cases.

Before you start asking others about a candidate, ask yourself just how reliable these folks you're asking are—did they work with that person? Or are they repeating the same story you've already heard? How unbiased is that group of people you're asking?

Ultimately, if you hear something that concerns you via someone who worked with the candidate, assume their best intentions in sharing their experiences with you.

Try to triangulate their experience with others so that you have a thorough perspective of whom you're about to hire. If you've heard something that gives you pause, try to investigate further from different people to see if a pattern of questionable behavior or work actually exists, and be glad you caught it early.

Document Your Reference Checks

When conducting reference checks, track your interactions with the people your candidate provided, similar to how you were scoring your interviews. In other words, in addition to your qualitative notes, also keep a scoring rubric that reflects the questions you ask—what could be a negative, positive, or neutral response. Factor in any need to apply weighting to your rubric and then total your score. If multiple people listen to the reference check or check references on your behalf, have them complete a scoring rubric as well. Provide all rubrics with scores and notes to the hiring committee.

Scoring and tracking your responses accomplishes similar outcomes to conducting the interviews for positions. You'll find that your reference checks are less likely to be influenced by recency bias, confirmation bias, or opinions formed with little standardized record of what was asked and answered.

Making the Decision

Deciding who among your candidates will get the offer is a high-stress exercise. You may be expected to achieve hiring targets or risk falling behind. Preferred candidates may have alluded to being in the final stages of interviewing with other companies, too. Or perhaps you feel that not making an offer will just seem like weeks of interviewing wasted when you could have been doing something else. By having a plan in place throughout the hiring process, you reduce some of those in-the-moment pressures you could possibly feel creeping into your decision-making process with your hiring committee.

After the last interview is complete, call another meeting with the hiring committee (which includes everyone who interviewed the candidates, as well as the appropriate HR/Recruiting representative to help facilitate the decision-making) to evaluate the candidates. To reduce the risk of recency bias where the committee may be overly positively or negatively influenced by the last candidate, try to schedule the decision meeting at least a day after the last interview is complete.

The agenda is fairly simple: review the candidates, discuss the merits or risks of each person, determine if you have enough information needed to make a vote, and if so, commit to extending an offer to that person.

To successfully review the candidates and discuss the qualities of each candidate, prepare and distribute the following materials in advance:

- The performance profile or job description for the open position

- Interview guide

- Candidate résumé/CV

- Scoring matrix and interview notes for each candidate

- Photographs or original sketches of any of the candidate's work they created in the interview (possibly of the design exercise or if the candidate used a whiteboard to illustrate any concept)

- Employee referrals, references, and any other external notes

- Recruiter comments

Give the hiring committee enough time to review the documents for each candidate so that the meeting can be thorough, concise, and efficient—at least 24 hours before the decision meeting. As a group, review the performance profile of the position, the interview script (including any design exercises issued to the candidates), and the scoring matrix.

Then discuss each candidate for no more than five minutes and ask each person on the hiring committee if they have enough information to vote (but not yet voting). If after five minutes anyone on the committee isn't prepared to vote, identify what the committee member needs and determine how they can get that information. Then agree to move on to the next candidate.

Reviewing all candidates prior to voting ensures that the committee doesn't prematurely vote on *a* candidate prior to reviewing *every* candidate. After all candidates (or finalists) have been reviewed and everyone is comfortable to vote for or against each person, vote *to hire* or *no hire* for each candidate.

Relying on the performance profile or job description and the matrix scores with notes ensures that you have the original foundation of what the committee deemed important, alongside how the candidate communicated their experience and potential during the interview. This combination of artifacts should provide the hiring committee with enough details and context to move to a unanimous decision of whether to extend an offer, while reducing biases that lead to homogeneous teams or ineffective new hires.

NOTE GOOGLE RE:WORK

There are a lot of stories about how Google interviews and hires, but to get their practices straight from the source, check out re:Work, a "collection of practices, research, and ideas from Google and others to help you put people first." **https://rework.withgoogle.com/**

Providing Feedback

One of the worst outcomes a candidate may experience is unfortunately far too common when interviewing for a new job: the dreaded *ghosting*.

Once you and the hiring committee recognize that a candidate isn't going to get an offer, provide closure informing them that the process won't be continuing. Your organization may have specific language you should or should not use, so be aware of what's considered acceptable.

But if your company does not have specific language outlining what's acceptable to tell unsuccessful candidates, consider the following structure of providing feedback to the candidate (see Figure 7.1).

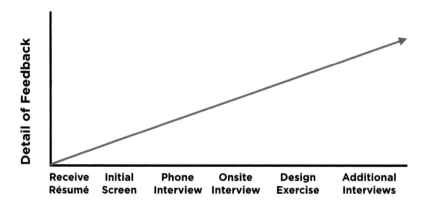

FIGURE 7.1

Strive to provide more detailed feedback as the candidate progresses further in the interview process.

If a candidate comes to your office, they deserve feedback. If a candidate puts in the time to entertain a design exercise, they definitely deserve feedback. And if a candidate has been to your office multiple times, there's basically no way the candidate shouldn't get some legitimate reason they won't be getting the job.

Feedback doesn't have to be exhaustive. It may be as simple as saying that another candidate was more qualified. But the difference between saying someone else was a better fit because of their specific experience within the industry is very different from a form email wishing the candidate the best of luck in the future despite the hours, if not weeks, of time invested in the interview process.

You risk tarnishing your design team's and your broader organization's reputation in the industry if you treat your unsuccessful candidates as people unworthy of your time.

Hold yourself and your team to the vision you outlined when designing your candidate's experience and provide appropriate feedback to those who won't be joining your team.

Extending the Offer

After your hiring committee has decided which candidate will receive an offer following the reference check, it's time to confirm with HR who presents the offer to the candidate. In some cases, it may be you, as the hiring manager, while in other organizations, HR will do it on your behalf for the company.

When you're preparing the compensation package, don't rely on pinning your offer to what the candidate earned in prior jobs. Not only are some states making it illegal to ask for salary history, but you also risk perpetuating unjust compensation patterns of paying men more than women or people of color less money for the same work. It's often difficult to right these wrongs after people are already employed.

To make sure that you can offer a fair compensation package to your candidate, be aware of how other roles or titles are currently compensated—and who is doing those roles. If three other men are earning $100K for a design role, don't offer a female candidate $85K so that you have a ceiling if and when she negotiates her offer. Offer her $100K and go from there.

Even if you present the offer over the telephone, send a follow-up email that includes the following information for your candidate to review:

- Start date
- Job title
- Supervisor/manager
- Team/organization
- Expected responsibilities
- Compensation
- Benefits summary

Some organizations will also include specifics, such as the location where the new hire will work and who the direct manager will be. If you're not sure what to specify in the offer letter, just consult your HR team to make sure that you that don't accidentally neglect to include anything important.

Negotiating Compensation

Candidates today have far more data and access to information and channels that they can use to negotiate their offers, regardless of how awesome or incredible an offer may be. Negotiating is challenging—you may have been uncomfortable negotiating your compensation when you were hired, and now, in the absence of an HR/Recruiting counterpart, you may need to negotiate the salary of someone who is joining your team. Be careful to be aware of your negotiation bias and don't hold those against a potential member of your team. Look at this situation as an opportunity to showcase how you work from the perspective of an advocate and in terms of how transparently you operate.

Research indicates that more women avoid negotiating compensation compared to men, and those who attempt to negotiate their compensation packages are seen as ungrateful, demanding, or worse—finding themselves behind the eight-ball before they even find their desk.[1, 2] Make sure that your own, and more importantly your organization's, systemic policies don't continue this trend. Instead, treat negotiations as a dialogue between two interested parties trying to secure what's best for both of them.

Some candidates may make a counteroffer with a number that you could never afford, a number higher than your own compensation package, or perhaps something different than what they mentioned during their initial interviews (which is worse). You'll need to position the compensation package as a total paycheck—salary, potential bonus(es), benefits, and other investments that the company makes in people (such as paid time off, continuing education budgets, a variety of retirement and insurance packages, and so on) so that your

---

1 Andreas Leibbrandt and John A. List, "Do Women Avoid Salary Negotiations? Evidence from a Large Scale Natural Field Experiment," *Management Science*, (September 2014): 1–9, http://gap.hks.harvard.edu/do-women-avoid-salary-negotiations-evidence-large-scale-natural-field-experiment

2 Madeline Heilman and Tyler Okimoto, "Why Are Women Penalized for Success at Male Tasks?: The Implied Communality Deficit," *Journal of Applied Psychology*, 92(1), (2007): 81–92. https://doi.org/10.1037/0021-9010.92.1.81

candidate can have the best understanding of what is on the table, and they can accurately compare and contrast against other offers that they may have. It never hurts to share the opportunity to grow and learn with your team and as part of the organization, as well.

When negotiating a salary, any number of outcomes might occur. You may find yourself dealing with some of these more common scenarios:

- You may choose to do your best to get the candidate to accept a number they don't like or don't want.

- The candidate may make a counteroffer with a number that you are unable to approve because it's outside of your budget for the role in your organization.

- The candidate may make a counteroffer and negotiate a different bonus structure or nonmonetary items, such as more paid time off, additional continuing education budget, etc.

- The candidate might accept your offer and keep the process moving!

For example, look at the hypothetical offer and subsequent counteroffer shown in Figure 7.2.

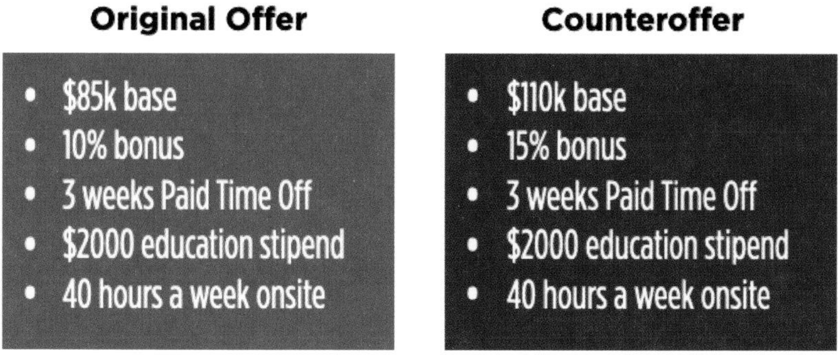

Original Offer

- $85k base
- 10% bonus
- 3 weeks Paid Time Off
- $2000 education stipend
- 40 hours a week onsite

Counteroffer

- $110k base
- 15% bonus
- 3 weeks Paid Time Off
- $2000 education stipend
- 40 hours a week onsite

FIGURE 7.2
Original offer and the candidate's counteroffer.

At first glance, these offers seem far apart. Negotiating seems hopeless.

Depending upon your organization practices, consider offering three slightly different packages all at one time that your candidate can choose from, such as these examples in Figure 7.3. (Since you've made it this far, you should have already made sure that you're at least in similar ranges together.)

Option 1	Option 2	Option 3
• $100k base • 10% bonus • 3 weeks Paid Time Off • $2000 education stipend • 40 hours a week onsite	• $95k base • 15% bonus • 4 weeks Paid Time Off • $4000 education stipend • 40 hours a week onsite	• $95k base • 12% bonus • 3 weeks Paid Time Off • $5000 education stipend • 32 hours onsite / 8 remote

FIGURE 7.3

Present three additional packages that the candidate can choose from and move on.

When you provide options for the candidate to choose from, you're also helping yourself avoid an extended negotiation process. By presenting three options, you're showing your willingness to be accommodating, even if you can't meet their initial counteroffer. You're also creating more autonomy and control for the candidate to choose from multiple options. They'll feel like they have more say in how they want to be compensated, such as risking a higher bonus with a slightly lower base or a more conservative high base, low bonus package.

And lastly, you can more easily say, "These are the packages we can offer—select what you're comfortable with, but we can't negotiate further from here." Of course, that's up to you how long you want to negotiate. But you've acted in good faith to negotiate by providing three similar packages, and it's not unreasonable to expect that you and the candidate will arrive at a compensation package and move on.

Onboarding

It's time to acknowledge that onboarding is not just specific Mondays in the month, and it's an ongoing process that starts before your employee comes to work on the first day and ends several weeks later. When you've written strong performance profiles and created consistent interview processes through your guides and evaluation processes, you're starting to show your candidates how your organization works, what it values, and just how important setting them up for success is.

There are a lot of pieces and a lot of touchpoints for onboarding a new employee into your organization. Designing an onboarding experience is an investment with few upfront costs in time with a big payoff when a new teammate starts, and it continues to pay dividends long after your colleague's first day.

It's easy to just rely on how you've onboarded new designers into your team in the past. Or perhaps HR has always handled the early interactions between your colleague and the company. However, it's worth the time up front to research these steps and discover what you've assumed to be the case versus what is reality.

Design an experience map of every single touchpoint for your new hire, such as in Figure 7.4. You'll probably be surprised at what you uncover and the opportunities in front of you. You'll also probably be surprised at how great a distance there is between the points where your candidates are communicated with, and that's a great place to identify easy wins for improving your ecosystem, and the connected ecosystems you may integrate with.

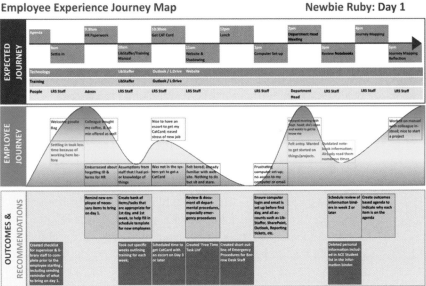

FIGURE 7.4
This employee experience journey map captures the first day at work.[3]

---

3   Hannah McKelvey and Jacqueline L. Frank, "Improving Onboarding with Employee Experience Journey Mapping: A Fresh Take on a Traditional UX Technique," *Weave: Journal of Library User Experience* 1, no. 9 (2018), https://quod.lib.umich.edu/w/weave/12535642.0001.903?view=text;rgn=main

It's not uncommon to perceive the necessary steps for bringing new people into the organization as just a process to move paperwork from one place to another, to create a new account here, and turn on access there. However, new teammates are people. And intentionally designing an onboarding experience centered on the new teammate means these folks will feel welcome, valued, and optimistic. It's a great way to start a new job, and you'll also get the benefit of your new teammates delivering value to your team and the company sooner.

Each of the following aspects should be considered in the onboarding process:

- **Performance Profiles:** Performance profiles are essential to make sure that you're interviewing the right people. (You can learn more in Chapter 4, "Performance Profiles and Interview Guides.")

- **Interview Guide:** This guide encompasses not only the questions, but also the goals/outcomes that you're seeking, and how they map to the performance profile someone is interviewing for.

- **Interviewing Candidates:** Using the guide consistently, you'll map the various interviewers to the types of things you're looking for (skills, mission, etc.).

- **Pre-Boarding:** Get in touch and help people land softly—prepared, informed, and empowered—for their first day.

- **Day 1:** Even though you and your team may not "own" this day, all the work you've done before today can help you "win" this day.

- **The Buddy System:** Teammates helping teammates find their way, navigate the new environment, and answer the burning questions about the crazy things you do in order to get the work done will facilitate the welcoming process.

- **The Internal Project(s):** These are safe spaces to fail, while learning how to work with a new team and helping your part of the organization continue to improve. Wins all around!

- **The First Project/Job:** This is really the big end game—by now, everything that's happened should make this day about understanding how to interact with new players and achieve a healthy work velocity quickly, not about trying to find out where the files are.

- **Additional Options:** There are a few other things that can be additive and helpful—and again, your mileage may vary.

- **Feedback:** You know who can tell you great things about your onboarding process? People who just went through it.

There is a lot of work just to get your new teammate working effectively and efficiently on your team. Be sure to bring new employees into your organization in a humane and welcoming manner where they can adjust to the new environment at their pace.

Know HR's Role in the Handoff

Almost every bad onboarding experience starts with good intentions, the assumption that "someone else is handling it" (whatever "it" might be), and that people are going about their day-to-day routines. However, just because someone else is the primary point for this phase of the process doesn't mean that you shouldn't be involved—people are, after all, joining your team, and the impression that they get through all the phases of the hiring process will reflect on you. "Insert yourself and key contacts into the process to compensate for others in the process who may not be as candidate-centered," according to Amanda Schonfeld, talent acquisition professional.

Review your employee onboarding experience journey. If you've got a gap between the interviewing and the offer, and the offer and the start date, work with your recruitment staff, HR, legal, and whomever else you need to work with to understand what the appropriate ways are to contact the candidates, as well as what content you can share with them.

Remember, sometimes the recruitment staff is overwhelmed, too. Your part of the organization likely isn't the only part that they're hiring for. That means there are a lot of candidates, a lot of scheduling, and a lot of juggling of everything for everyone in order to help grow the organization. One of the best things you can do is to position yourself and your team in a way so that you can ensure a certain type of experience for your new teammates. Work with the recruitment staff and see how you can be a partner and if there are ways to alleviate some of the gaps in connectivity in the process.

Essentially, don't just hand off your future teammate to someone else, entirely.

Keeping in Touch When the Interview Is Over and the Offer Is Accepted

by Amanda Schonfeld, talent acquisition professional

Here are some ideas for keeping in touch while the HR handles paperwork, background processes, and all of the other things they need to do that ensure an employee is ready to start work:

- Provide all the necessary points of contact so they can stay in touch and ask questions.

- Give permission to the candidate to reach out to you or the team.

- Share relevant news and communication about the team and its accomplishments and about the company.

- Remain available and approachable through it all.

Keep future teammates feeling good and knowing that they're valued. Restate that you cannot wait to have them on your team. Share information with them whenever you can—from blog posts to company news to updates on their first project—or just reach out to let them know that things are still moving along.

As the late, great Mr. Tom Petty says, "The Waiting Is the Hardest Part." Do your part to make sure their waiting doesn't seem so lonely and without contact.

The Pre-Boarding Call

It may be surprising to learn that not all organizations call their new employees before their start date. However, it's a great way to welcome them and help them understand what their first day/first week(s) will be like and what some of the team and organizational norms are. Once you've got a start date, and it's less than two weeks away, schedule a call (over video chat if you can or on the phone, if you must) with your soon-to-be employee. It's good to cover anything important about the work environment and share any news that may have happened between when you interviewed them and before they start.

This is in addition to whatever standard, possibly form-letter instructions that they will receive. You'll want to introduce them to their support team (who they report to, who their buddy is, etc.), explain to them about what to expect on their first day or week, and answer any additional questions they have. Keep it light and make starting easy for them.

All meetings deserve agendas, and here's a good starting point for this one:

- **Introduce the people on the call.**

  Explain why they're there.

- **Share your experiences about their first day.**

  Help the new teammate understand what to expect, who will be there, and who will be the point of contact after "organizational onboarding" is complete (i.e., who on the team to reach out to or who will be reaching out to them).

- **Highlight what the "working hours" are and what the expectations are for leaving on the first day.**

  For example, is it okay to leave after orientation? Should they stay and meet the team? Also, make sure to show them how to find their way around.

- **Identify their systems of support.**

  For example, is it an intranet, humans, HR, the support chain of command, or what?

- **Share things about the culture.**

  For example: You don't swear in Slack, general communication behaviors, pronoun usage, etc.

- **Answer all of their questions.**

  Make sure to let others on the call answer the questions as well so that more perspectives come through.

Also, make sure to share contact information as it is relevant or necessary to the person's first day and onboarding experience so they can follow up with anyone, as needed.

Day 1: Commencement

This is that happy day everyone's been waiting for!

You finally get to move your candidate officially to the "employee" category. They've graduated through all of the previous steps, and now this commencement is the first new step of their new journey in their career at your organization.

There aren't a lot of things you have control over on the first day, at least in larger organizations. The smaller the organization is, the more likely you will be able to make the experience a bit more personalized.

Here are some suggestions for handling the first day:

- Let the natural order of HR-planned events take place as scheduled.

- Triple-check new employee items are where they should be (computers, phones, office supplies, etc.). Make sure that things are also *not* where they should be—like the person's stuff who previously sat in their space, if you had a "seating chart" organization.

- Make time to welcome them to the team.

- Make it easy for the new teammate to leave when they've wrapped up the HR-planned events.

This, too, can be a little bit of an HR gray area. The day most likely starts with "Whatever an HR representative scheduled" in most/many cases. It also likely involves a lot of company history, which has probably already been consumed on the About pages of your website as the excitement before start date was building. Some organizations have mandatory training, project or team orientation information, explicit policies and procedures for types of access, and so on.

What happens after that?

It could be IT or someone who handles the acquisition of locations (where to sit), systems (computer, phones, devices, etc.), or the new employee could be released into the wild, which is where you come into play! Make sure that new hires feel welcome, besides the potential for a cafeteria lunch with everyone who started on the same day (YMMV with company size).

Your candidate has graduated to employee, and it's time to show them the type of organization you are.

The Buddy System

The "buddy system" helps you make sure that your new employee has someone they can depend on to provide them with insight, input, direction—that doesn't come from their direct supervisors. If there isn't a guide or handbook to help people know what they should be doing, the first buddy pairing is a great opportunity to start documenting what takes place and what works so that people know what's expected of the buddy role every time a new person joins the team.

The buddy is the primary point of contact for questions about your team and the broader organization. A good timeline for a buddy to be involved is the week before a new teammate starts and through the first two to three weeks—or more, as needed. Buddies can go longer, informally, of course, and that's up to the individuals.

A buddy will perform their duties by doing a lot of "being helpful" and "sharing information," which may include:

- Emailing the new teammate and making themselves available

- Collecting information for an internal announcement

- Orienting the teammate to the team—org chart and support structure, etc.

- Explaining all the tough-to-just-know things, like systems/files, what meetings are important/relevant and what they mean, helping with acronyms

- Checking in daily, or more, if needed

- Explaining systems like time keeping, travel, etc.

- Explaining company-required trainings

- Introducing the teammate to the rest of the team, as available

- Introducing to the buddy handbook or guide, etc.

New York University has an online Buddy Guidelines document that is a great place to get started (see Figures 7.5 and 7.6).

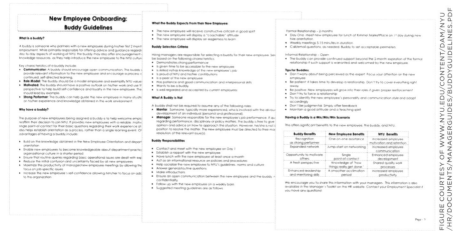

FIGURE 7.5

New York University's New Employee Onboarding: Buddy Guidelines.

Having a Buddy is a Win/Win/Win Scenario

This offers significant benefits to the new employee, the buddy, and NYU:

Buddy Benefits	New Employee Benefits	NYU Benefits
Recognition as strong performer	One-on-one assistance	Increased employee motivation and retention
Expanded network	Jump-start on networking	Increased employee communication
Opportunity to motivate others	Single point-of-contact	Enhanced employee development
A fresh perspective	Knowledge of "how things really get done."	Shared quality work processes
Enhanced leadership and mentoring skills	A smoother acclimation period	Increased employee productivity

FIGURE 7.6

Benefits of an onboarding buddy from the New York University New Employee Onboarding: Buddy Guidelines document.

One of the bonus aspects of "Having a Buddy Is a Win/Win/Win Scenario" is because it describes the benefits for everyone involved. You shouldn't shy away from showing the new employee what's happening behind the curtain, either—show them your Buddy Guide right away! This documentation helps them ask better questions and provides real-time feedback for how the buddy system is working for them, and gives them the opportunity to move at their own pace if the prescribed timelines aren't moving like they'd prefer.

As an added benefit, buddy opportunities are leadership opportunities for people on your team, especially when the org chart or HR may not have the opportunities available. You'll be able to see how buddies perform throughout the process and work with them to find additional opportunities as it makes sense.

Additionally, recent additions to your team also make great buddies. They've got a lot of recent and relevant experience that they can share to help people get past confusion, hurdles, and challenges in the workplace.

Internal Projects

Pretty much every team and organization has a backlog of things that need to get done in order to make the organization operate better and more efficiently. If you don't, generate some with your team, as well as with the new employees, and offer them as a backlog of projects for the team to work on—in their spare time.

Internal projects help new teammates acclimate to your team by helping them:

- Meet other people on the team

- Learn how the team works together

- Identify project and working norms

- Get up to speed with where everything is located—including files, software, shared drives, tools and services logins, and more

These internal projects also help your new teammate instantly provide value by helping to improve how the team operates.

Additionally, an internal project is a great opportunity to check in with your new coworker. You can learn what they're learning, what information they're missing, and how they handle the workload and direction (or lack thereof, to either). You can and should also learn how they produce their work product and artifacts, as well as how they communicate these, and use this time as a chance to coach them toward the way the team works. This can really help people find their way much more easily and in a safe space.

As an added bonus, internal projects also allow you to provide leadership and growth opportunities on low-to-medium risk projects, which also helps you understand ways to shape the growth of people on your team.

First Project

This is the real target—the big goal! It should also be a nonevent. By now, new employees should be able to find their place on a new product or project with minimal effort, largely due to their familiarity of onboarding with a buddy and working with others on an internal project. The first project will hopefully only require a little bit of directional support—from you or from the buddy—and most of the time will be spent familiarizing the teammate with their project team and this particular project's norms.

After normal product/project team onboarding occurs, a buddy and the new team will be able to provide project-level guidance and support. Recent experiences working with the internal team can help provide context that enables the new employee to ask better-directed questions and have them understand some of the working norms.

First projects are also a great opportunity to re-check in with your new coworker. Internal projects are convenient and a bit comfortable, but real "this is why we get paid" projects have a bit more stress and a bit more responsibility to them. This is your opportunity to remind teammates that raising their hand for support is a sign of strength and that you want to make sure they're feeling set up for success. It's much better to learn as much as you can about how they're working and what they're needing now than when a deadline is rushing at you.

Feedback

After you've completed the candidate-to-new-hire process—and at time/event-specific opportunities along the way—gather feedback from everyone involved in the process, especially the new employee. It's important for new employees to feel safe and to understand the value that they bring to help you improve the process for the next person.

Continually update how you are bringing candidates into the organization and how you transition them from candidate to new employee. It's important to remember that the process shouldn't ever gather moss—so keep it rolling.

Additional Options and Ideas to Consider

Here are some other suggestions that you may want to try to help round out your hiring-to-onboarding process:

- **Classes:** Semi-regular information sharing and AMAs about the various teams/departments.

- **Chatbots:** 18F created a Slack chatbot named "Dolores Landingham" (from *The West Wing*) that would send out acclimation DMs in Slack to help new teammates learn more about where things were, etc. (https://github.com/18F/dolores-landingham-bot)

- **Donut:** Another Slack-based app, Donut helps facilitate onboarding, pulse-checks, mentoring, and creating connections throughout the company. (www.donut.com/pricing/)

- **Intranets, etc.:** Nearly every company should have some sort of an intranet or online handbook that is easy to search and easy to use so that people can quickly find, or be shown, answers to questions, policy, etc.

- **Onboarding calendar:** Gabby Hon (@gabbyhon) suggests that companies should send a calendar, kind of like an agenda, with what the first couple of weeks will look like.

Finally, your team, especially recent additions to your team, should have a bunch of ideas for ways to make onboarding a positive experience. Be sure to share what you're learning and trying, and check with other teams across the organization to see what they've tried.

Wrapping Up

The final stages of bringing new people into your organization don't go out with a whimper but a bang—as in fireworks—celebrating an experience that is well designed, or as a series of ad-hoc or unintentional steps that should be blown up.

Negotiations will always be a delicate balance between finding what makes your candidate excited to work for you, but still adheres to the budgets within which you have to operate. Treat negotiations with the gravitas and respect they deserve—and remember to do your best to advocate transparently for your potential new teammate, as well as your organization.

You need to design a hiring experience where new employees feel that they have some control over their total compensation. Then you should pair it with an onboarding process that recognizes them as significant contributors to the organization as quickly as possible. This will help create productive, motivated, and happy employees ready to add value.

All the excitement and goodwill of starting a new job can dissipate quickly if the onboarding experience leaves the new hire feeling lost, confused, or like any other employee with a photo ID and a badge number.

Instead, research, design, and plan, and then iterate on the full experience by monitoring the steps you've been assuming were getting done by someone else. Interview the new hires to constantly understand the process from their perspective and improve upon it so that every person who starts on your team gets the latest-and-greatest experience possible.

CHAPTER 8

Unifying the Team Culture with Charters

The label "team" can be applied to many different things, but without a shared North Star and focus, well, you haven't really got a team at all. It's not uncommon that a group of people will be placed on a team together, yet the team itself represents a group of spokes that don't quite know how to make a wheel.

A team charter will help a team get aligned around its purpose for existence and core operational expectations. In addition, when a team invests the time in understanding itself and, perhaps more importantly, a shared understanding how it wants others to perceive it, the charter can be a touchstone to determine how well it is living up to its own definition.

That is, once the spokes understand that they're all a part of the same system together, they become a well-balanced wheel.

Companies may say they want to create or improve their culture on the design team—that it currently feels like a bunch of individuals who all do kind of the same thing for similar projects. The Team Charter is one of the first approaches we recommend to articulate who the team is and how to talk about it—to each other, and across the organization.

What Is a Team Charter?

A team charter is a living document that helps a team understand its understanding of itself. The team charter helps a team fully comprehend the following information:

- The team's purpose
- The team member commitments of behaviors and expectations
- The team's focus areas in the types of work that it does
- How the team needs to grow and improve

As a team leader, these may feel like things that you can articulate quickly to anyone who asks. However, if you ask the individual members of your team, you may be surprised at the lack of a shared message, or even the lack of the same language being used. And if a team's members aren't unified in their understanding of what the team is, how is it supposed to operate, figure out its goals and objectives, and hope to achieve much of anything? Give yourself, and the team, time to move into a true shared understanding and not just high-level comprehension.

Your team charter may also seem a bit like a persona for the team, as shown in Figure 8.1. It will help you and your team identify and acknowledge the existing behaviors and the perceptions of the team by itself and others externally. Then the team can establish how it wants to be perceived in the future, and finally, it will define the steps and behaviors that it needs to have in order to achieve that future perception, which will allow it to track its progress against the goal.

FIGURE 8.1
Team charter—the persona for your team.

Moreover, it will provide the agreed-upon language that represents the entire team when you meet with influential stakeholders or executive management throughout the organization.

Conducting the Team Charter Workshop

The following is a step-by-step method to craft your team charter with your team. The team charter will help paint a clear picture of the current state of the team and its path to its best future.

The Advantages of a Team Charter

by Dr. Steve Julius, President and CEO of HRCG/ Workplace Solutions

The team charter is a commitment infused with a purpose complete with objectives, clear roles, accountabilities, and rules of engagement. A team charter is simply a document to hang on the wall unless the signers actively incorporate the commitments into their daily work behavior and the stakeholders also take the time to monitor their actions.

When people actively align around their team charter, there is less interpersonal friction, more trust and camaraderie, more efficient decision-making, and improved speed to productive work outputs. Plus, when employees see their leaders living up to the tenants of the charter, this behavior becomes contagious throughout the organization.

The Setup

Creating your team charter requires a few things that shouldn't be too difficult for you to get your hands on:

- Easel pads
- Sticky notes
- Markers

You'll also need a couple of things that may not be as easy for you to find:

- Private working and collaboration space, including breakout space, depending upon the size of your team
- A dedicated full day of time (give or take—it can also depend upon the size of your team)
- An additional handful of hours to create your document

If your team is larger than six or so people, you should break the team into smaller working groups so that they can work independently of each other and then come back together and present their findings. When the groups present their report, then you can validate, remove, or merge their findings into a consolidated set of information.

(Re)Define the Team Purpose

One of the best ways to find out what a team believes it is supposed to achieve is to simply ask them and listen to their answers.

That said, it's not always easy to ask this question in a way that resonates with your team, and there may be more than one question to ask to get to the correct and best answers for your team. If you have researchers on your team or you've done user research, you're already nodding your head in agreement at this point.

First, arm your team with sticky notes and markers and provide them with these questions:

- What does this team do for the organization (and our clients/customers, etc.)?

- How are we successful? What do we excel at as a team and as individual performers in what we do for the organization (and our clients/customers, etc.)?

- What should our team be known for to others in the organization (and our clients/customers, etc.)?

You can spend about 45–60 minutes on this portion of the workshop. Consider having the individuals spend the first few minutes of time spent on each question generating ideas by themselves—one idea per sticky note. Then have each member share, explain, and put their sticky notes on the easel pad so the group can cluster and minimize or reduce their results into something a bit more concise. A general rule of thumb is to spend about 15 minutes per question in order to timebox the activity and keep the team from losing its focus.

This part of the team charter activity helps your team come together with an understanding of *what they are*, *what they do*, and *why they do it*. When the team has finished answering the questions, bring them together and have them share and explain the thinking behind their outcomes. You may see something along the lines of the following:

- We are experts about our users.

- We ask questions that challenge current models/thinking.

- We are critical thinkers with a strategic vision.

- We create the tangible outcomes from often vague requirements.

You're just beginning, so set these aside. You'll come back to them and put them to good use later.

The Work: What the Team Does, Does Not Do

There's a pretty good chance that if you ask your team about the types of work that they want to do, and the work they *don't* want to do, you'll get some really good, clear, and direct answers. There's also a chance that there are things that the team isn't doing—yet—because the skill either doesn't exist on the team, the opportunity to do the work hasn't materialized yet, or worse, both scenarios.

This exercise is pretty straightforward and easy to do, regardless of your team size. If the team is fewer than five or six people, have everyone work together on the activity. If the team has more than six people, break them into groups of 2–4 people, and have them collaborate on providing feedback for the team charter.

Ask the following questions:

- What are the types of work that this team does *not* do and does *not want* to do?

- What are the types of work that this team *does* do and *wants* to do?

- What are the areas where the team needs more experience?

- What are the opportunities for your team's growth? (This is largely about skills on the team that could be put to use with the work this team does and wants to do.)

This exercise can take around 30–60 minutes, depending upon how your team works through each question. The first two questions are tactical in their nature, and should be the easiest and quickest to get through, barring any major disagreements or discussions to work through.

When you start asking your team about where they need more experience and opportunities to grow, it's important to frame those questions as a positive exploration. It's not difficult for individuals to consider questions about what they don't know as measurements for themselves, which can sometimes stir up negative emotions. Additional exposure to new domains are what healthy organizations constantly want to see happening, and it may be helpful to frame this as looking for areas to bring in additional talent that can expand the team's overall skills. Additionally, it may be useful to explain that areas of growth and experience can be seen as a good way to identify training opportunities.

You may see answers like the following:

- We don't do graphic/print design.

- We don't do production work.

- We don't want to create presentations for others.

- We do user research, information architecture, interaction design, visual design, and front-end design.

- We would like to do more service design.

- We would like to learn about customer journey maps.

These answers help to paint a rather clear and definitive picture of what the team does and doesn't do, and how it wants to grow. The discussion that happens around getting to the agreed-upon answers also helps you and your teammates explain and understand why the decisions were made and how to defend them. This approach can be unifying and also build cohesion with the team while instilling a confidence that comes from having a shared understanding about the work the team does.

Team Commitment: Member-to-Member Behaviors and Expectations

For the next 30–60 minutes, you'll want to focus on answering the following questions:

- How do we want to work together?

- What are our expectations of each other?

- How do we review our work with each other?

- How do we support each other?

- How do we provide updates about our status and our work to each other?

- How do we create a safe space to work together?

When you ask the members of your team to declare how they want and expect to work together, make sure that their responses are focused on an ideal reality. This doesn't need to be peppered with flowery prose nor perfect-world Medium posts; however, it should be grounded in an achievable reality that everyone can agree on.

These questions can move beyond just saying that the team should be honest with each other or be ready to help when asked. Instead, you want more specific descriptions of how to work with each other and the behaviors to express.

If you're seeking starter material or reference content to help your team identify their behaviors and expectations, look no further than Amazon's 14 Leadership Principles.[1] These leadership principles are a useful example of the behaviors that the company expects its leaders, managers, and teams to apply when working together.

> **NOTE** AMAZON LEADERSHIP PRINCIPLE #13
> HAVE BACKBONE; DISAGREE AND COMMIT
>
> Leaders are obligated to respectfully challenge decisions when they disagree, even when doing so is uncomfortable or exhausting. Leaders have conviction and are tenacious. They do not compromise for the sake of social cohesion. Once a decision is determined, they commit wholly.

Agreeing to these norms and expectations creates a foundation for how the team will function—both by articulating what is okay and what behavior will need to be corrected if it falls outside of what is agreed upon. While the company may have its overarching set of values, its mission, vision, and any other type of statement, a team charter is specific to this team—your team.

How the Team Will Conduct Its Business

How your team conducts its business is all about how it decides to function from an operational perspective and in an ideal state. This process is about the "desired norms" of conducting business, and it may require a bit of forward thinking or forecasting to get to where the team *should* be and not where they currently are. For this activity, spend another 30–60 minutes exploring:

- What is our role in the broader organization?

- How do we work with our customers (internal and external)?

- How do we work together as we fulfill our business objectives?

- What *must* we ensure that we do in every engagement?

Review the results of the activity with the team—it may be beneficial to have each group share their own outputs. Spend time with the

---

1   Amazon's 14 Leadership Principles, which they use to help make decisions and solve problems. www.amazon.jobs/en/principles

team grouping and prioritizing the desired norms, and if necessary, writing brief descriptions for each. Select the top 4–7 desired norms to work on as a team; this number is arbitrary and is going to vary depending upon your team and what your team can tackle in any given period of time.

Next, spend another 30–60 minutes exploring what success looks like for each of the ways the team will conduct its business and what it takes in order to achieve each. These are a bit like an extended OKR session, in that you'll be asking people to answer the following for each of the desired norms:

- What is the behavioral evidence that the norm is present on the team?

- What are the actions for creating the norm?

This process will have you and your team defining what a future state of the organization looks like and how you're all going to get there together. It also provides a clear understanding of what success looks like so the team can track its progress against the goals, revisiting your prioritized list to add new norms to your list as you achieve them. This activity can also be helpful when you evaluate your design operations practice, or if you plan on investing time and resources into design operations. (We'll discuss design operations in greater detail in Chapter 14, "Scaling Design.")

Areas to Grow and Improve

Finally, for the next 30–60 minutes, focus on answering the following questions:

- What are the areas that the team needs to grow and improve in order to continue to be successful in our organization?

- What is the rationale that supports the areas of growth and experience?

- How will these skills and opportunities better support the goal of the broader organization?

As the team answers these questions, it helps focus the growth areas into a business case and justification for the need. For example, if your team believes it would be better served by learning more about service design, they'll also be responsible for explaining why they believe that, and how it will have a positive impact on the design organization. This exercise will help you and your team, as well as your stakeholders, see the value that will be returned in exchange for an investment.

The areas of growth and improvement aren't just about identifying training needs and seeking funds—they are also about the team understanding its own needs, how to recognize opportunities to get involved in helping the team meet the growth and improvement need, and sharing that across the team. The focus areas for growth and improvement will help the team stay continually focused on ways to continue to learn and share knowledge.

When the team acknowledges where and how it wants to improve, it implicitly creates a vision for what the future of the team should be. Not doing so risks complacency—an outcome that happens to many teams which don't set a North Star for where they want to go together.

Turn Your Findings into the Charter Document

You and your team have done a lot of work at this part, and the next part focuses on distilling that hard work into a clarifying document that is both actionable and measurable.

At this point, you will have tackled a lot of mentally exhausting work for you and your team. You *could* forge ahead and wrap everything up with a team charter that carries across the core findings from the day while it's fresh in everyone's minds.

You may want to consider having the team volunteer or vote on representatives who can finalize the document, over the course of a couple of weeks, and then share it back with the team for edits and revisions. Figure 8.2 shows what the outputs from a team charter exercise can look like.

If you choose to continue, move forward with getting your team to high-level definitions centered around these areas:

- **Team purpose:** Write a succinct paragraph that describes what the team does, what it excels at, and what others in the organization should know it for.

- **Commitments of the team:** Brief paragraphs describing how the team will work together, treat each other, and how they will behave toward each other.

- **Focus areas:** This can be a bulleted list of the types of work your team does (research, interaction design, etc.).

- **Areas of growth and improvement:** Document each area of growth with details around what will be gained by growing and improvement, and when the team will know it has achieved a new level of growth.

- **How the team conducts business:** Document and define the desired norms, what it takes to build the norm across the team and organization, and the behavioral evidence that the norm is present on the team.

The charter is part of your team, and a reminder of the commitment and focus your team has toward its goals and objectives. It's worth the time from you and your team to invest in making sure that it's a reflection of your efforts by formally documenting it.

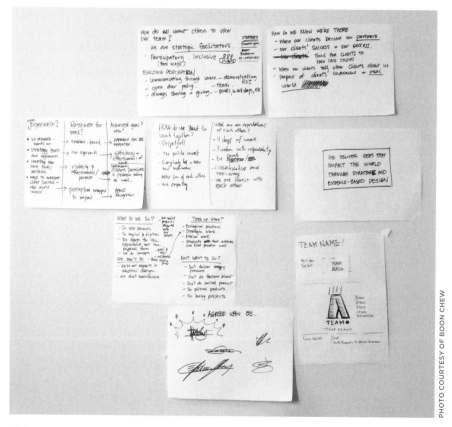

FIGURE 8.2
Outputs from a team charter exercise.

Sign, Show, and Share the Charter

After you've determined what's going in your charter, you've questioned every word so that your team is comfortable with the language, and as a whole it accurately reflects who your team is and how it fits in the company, then it's time to sign it, show it, and share it.

Every member on your team should sign the charter—these signatures reflect that the charter speaks for the whole team, not just the manager or a few select leads. Even if someone disagrees with a few of the attributes, they should feel heard, acknowledged, and likewise should understand why their disagreement ended the way it did. As such, you capture alignment, if not consensus, which as a manager is often far more elusive and useful.

The formal documentation of your team's charter should be shared with everyone on the team, the leadership of other teams, publicly within the organization wherever your team shares information, posted on the walls in the team's working areas, and anywhere else that it helps to gain visibility and awareness. Figure 8.3 shows a team, proud of their efforts—so take your own and share it! Not only does this increase the reach of your charter, but it also reflects and recognizes the distributed nature of your team and business.

FIGURE 8.3
The team and their team charter work.

Wrapping Up

The charter is a reflection of your team's desired culture; however, it isn't your culture. It's been said that if you don't define a culture, one will persist by default, and it's probably not the one you or your management wants.

The team charter goes a long way toward defining how you want to work and be seen—and what you want new members of the team to understand about your team's operational norms. For example, Audible.com wanted to specifically recognize that because some team members were remote, they all acted as if everyone was remote, even if they worked down the hall from each other. Other organizations crafted a motto to capture the elements of the charter in 3–5 sentences that everyone on the team could repeat and share if they were asked what team they were on or what they did for the company.

Like many design artifacts, such as customer journeys and personas, the process of capturing the charter is possibly more useful than the document itself. The charter as an artifact, be it a poster on the wall or a webpage or an infographic, gives you something to point to when you need to be reminded that there are commitments and agreements made by the team and everyone agrees to them.

Don't just leave the charter on the wall to collect dust. Revisit it when the world beneath you has changed—whether based on time (3–6 months), team size adjustments (either growing or shrinking), or remit (increasing or reducing responsibility). The charter reflects the culture that your team aspires to when you created it, so be sure to update it to reflect the next version of your culture as you meet and exceed your team's aspirations.

CHAPTER 9

Designing the One-on-Ones

Loosely defined, the one-on-ones (1:1s) are meetings that are utilized to learn how people are performing and what they're experiencing—both in their work and in their lives, and not necessarily to check the status of their work or a project. Work status is, of course, important, and the "person status" is equally important; when you know people better, you can adjust your approach to working with and supporting them.

It's important to remember that no person is an island on your team. That means that you need to have a way to keep up-to-date with what's happening with everyone, and also have a structure to make sure that reporting is happening continually. Left to our own devices, we'll all make assumptions about what's going on or not, and we all need to have someone who listens to us, guides us, and helps us solve challenges in our path—at least from time to time.

In a short period of time—usually 30 to 60 minutes weekly—you can have your finger on the pulse of your team for many nonimmediate issues. Those immediate issues are still going to crop up; however, understanding what's happening with the rest of your team when you're dealing with pressing situations can help prevent you from being the victim of surprise.

As leaders and managers, you don't really like surprises.

Designing the One-on-One Framework

Developing a framework for your 1:1 meetings establishes a foundation of structure and what to expect, both for you as the manager and for your team members who are participating in your meeting. It removes the guesswork of what to discuss and how to prepare, and generally leads to more productive, useful meetings.

Frameworks go beyond just agendas, and a 1:1 meeting is by definition, a meeting, so you know what that means: you'll need an agenda.

More importantly, however, you'll use the framework to drive the discussion on the following topics:

- What's important to your company?
- What's important to your team?
- What's important to the teammate with whom you're meeting?

How Richard Dalton Manages the One-on-Ones

by Richard Dalton, Head of Design at Verizon

I've always felt that 1:1 meetings with direct reports—which I try to do weekly for at least 30 minutes—are an opportunity to do a blend of three things:

1. Make ongoing personal connections with your colleagues.

2. Keep up-to-date with actual project work.

3. Give (and receive!) coaching and performance feedback and discuss longer-term career paths.

The great thing about regular 1:1s is that they force you to set aside time for these important conversations; however, they can be somewhat detached from the actual situation you want to discuss that may have happened a few days earlier. I always find it helps to keep notes of items to discuss, questions to ask, and coachable moments. You can do this electronically. I'm a big fan of using my email inbox as my "to-do" list, but more often than not, I'll simply use Post-its at my desk throughout the week.

One last important thing to remember: these times are 1:1s, not 1:0s or 0:1s. They are a two-way flow of information and feedback and not one-way!

- What unforeseen news or events should be discussed individually?

- What unresolved topics are still pending from the last time you met?

Like many successful frameworks, the utility lies in how you tailor it to your current situation to be the most beneficial to you and the teammate on the other end of the conversation. Let's start with the lynchpin of the meeting—the agenda itself.

Prioritizing the Agenda

First, it's critical to note that while 1:1 meetings are about helping you understand what is happening with your team and within your organization, they are also about making sure that you focus on the needs of your teammates. If you're meeting with people once a week, it's important to use that time wisely and do your best as a manager and a leader to understand the best way you can help people on your team be successful.

Sometimes, finding the balance between what is most important to the company and you as the manager and what is most important or best for the teammate can be a struggle. There are times when teammates have needs that outweigh the tactical updates that you seek to keep your team machine running, and that's when and where you need to make a judgment call. The type of manager or leader that you want to be will shine through in how you manage to prioritize what you determine is important at different times.

The best way to be prepared for adjusting what you need to discuss, relative to what your teammate wants to discuss, is to share an agenda in advance—preferably at least a day ahead; however, we've all been there when it's sent an hour before it's time to meet. (Or it might just have been "stuck in the Outbox—sorry!")

Seeing the agenda in advance also gives you enough time to schedule additional time if you estimate that your 30 or 60 minutes won't be enough. Here's a sample agenda (courtesy of Amy Jiménez Márquez) to get you started—and you'll definitely want to make this more specific to your needs, and the needs of your team.

Generic Non-prescriptive 1:1 Agenda

- Obstacles (currently in the way)

- Ongoing topics (project work, etc.)

- Special topics (organization or team topics, industry topics, nonindustry topics, etc.)

- Career development (What are you learning? What do you want to learn?)

- Productivity, happiness, work/life balance (How are you doing at work? How are you feeling? How much are you working?)

- Feedback (How can I help you? How can I improve? What would you like to know/what's on your mind that we haven't spoken about?)

This is a good start for a basic 1:1 agenda that you can modify to meet your needs. You'll want to brainstorm what makes the most amount of sense for you and your organization and adjust accordingly. You may also want to consider modifying your location—some people find that "getting out of the office" really helps to break down the formality that an office can impose.

Every manager in every organization will have a list of things that are definitely important to consider when they create their own prioritization for your 1:1 meetings. You should identify what the "must have" agenda items are for all of these, but there are bound to be some that may not be relevant to you and your teammates. Think about your organization size, team size, proximity to your team-mates, the way your team works, and the team's culture when you decide how you'll prioritize your own "must-haves."

Create a list of all the things that are important for you and your teammates to discuss. It may help to categorize them into "must have" and "nice to have" if prioritizing them from 1 to "n" isn't as useful to you.

After you've created that list, you've got the basis for what you need as an agenda for your 1:1 meetings. You've also got a set of expectations and a potential format that you can share with the other leaders on your team who need to conduct their meetings and share the notable outcomes with you.

Since effective 1:1s aren't just two people staring at each other waiting for one to say, "So what do you want to talk about?" then agreeing on an agenda in advance gives both parties time to mentally prepare to be present and actively participate.

Discussing Company News, Goals, and Goings-On

Your position as manager likely affords you unique access to company news and information, such as if its quarterly goals will be met or if a possible acquisition may impact a roadmap or release schedule. Your 1:1 meeting is a good opportunity to do two things:

- Share that information with your teammate

- Provide whatever context is necessary to make such an update useful for your teammate

In other words, if you mention that the sales team in Europe is outselling their projections and where they were a year ago, you may want to highlight how the designer's work contributed to that increase. Or you may need to remind the design team to revisit the demoware they are currently using to pitch the product, because the North American sales team will be expected to accelerate their targets.

Doing so may seem obvious, but it's also common to reflect on how the business is doing with little or no regard as to why that matters to a designer or what it means to them. Don't go there—keep them included.

This may not change much from week to week; however, consistently addressing how the team's work is contributing to the wider corporate goals is important. No one likes working on something without a sense of purpose or insight into the impact their work is having beyond their own team.

ADVICE FROM THE FIELD

How to Align Corporate and Personal Goals for Your Team

by Shay Howe, co-founder of Lead Honestly

Leaving nothing to chance, every six months I have each team member outline what they'd like to do more of, less of, and where they see themselves in six months and beyond. From there, I work with them to develop measurable and actionable personal goals that align with the broader team and organizational goals. Tying these goals together, even in the slightest manner, allows us to bond together, move faster, and accomplish more as a team.

There are times when you'll have to use your judgment of what to share and when, and, of course, to whom. Not everything you hear is for you to repeat right away—perhaps it's a missed sales target, an executive is being pushed out, or that looming acquisition may render features on the roadmap moot that the team still is expected to deliver.

Keep in mind how you learned of the news. If it was an official meeting, someone probably said whether or not that information should be shared. If it was a hallway conversation, it probably shouldn't be repeated at all. When in doubt, assume that big news stays quiet until you're told to share. If you're not sure, ask. Don't betray the trust of your management by being fast and loose with information—regardless of rumors or factual events.

What's Important to Your Team

Once you know what is important to your company and what is expected of you and your team, you should also have a sense of what is important to your team. Every team will have its own internal collection of needs and wants that are important to keep the team functioning at its best—perhaps it's something like increased knowledge and depth of skills or improved or enhanced communication and reporting, or any number of other expectations that you have hopefully set forth in your team charter (see Chapter 8, "Unifying the Team Culture with Charters").

Whatever those items are that you're tracking, it's important to make sure that they're part of your discussions so that you can keep tabs on progress and hopefully report those out as rolled-up metrics in your own 1:1 meetings or other reporting systems.

Talking to the individuals on your team about how they see the team performing is a useful way to sense a disturbance in the force—for example, if something may be beginning to fester or stew.

Try these questions to gauge how the individual perceives how their immediate team is performing:

- How do you think the team is working on this project compared to the last project you completed?

- Does the team find itself relying heavily on one or two people because the rest of the team isn't in a position to succeed?

- Do you think everyone on the team understands the primary goal of what they're working on and for whom they're working, including the business stakeholder and the end user?

- Is there anything that I, as the manager, need to be aware of that you haven't told me? In other words, please don't assume that I already know everything just because I'm the boss!

These questions should get your direct talking in such a way that any problems should be revealed, or show you where you need to step up and improve alignment, communication, or trust across your team and partners.

What's Important to Your Teammate

While using the 1:1 meeting to translate or relay corporate news and keep a pulse on the inner workings of the team, the primary focus is using the meeting to understand what's important to your teammate. This information includes understanding the teammate's morale and stress levels at work—and also as much as you need to know (and that they are willing to share) about their personal lives.

This is your opportunity to learn if there is anything in their work that is blocking them from being as productive or as successful as they can be—and how you can use your position to make their work seem as rewarding to them as possible. If you can help your teammates progress in their careers by creating opportunities for technical skill development, training and continuing education, on-the-job leadership efforts, and strengthening the purpose and engagement they feel at work, you will likely have happier, more fulfilled employees who bring their best selves to work every day. By doing so, you will also create a safe space to try, succeed, or fail—and learn—from something that they're passionate about and is related to their goals.

You'll also want to know if there is feedback for you that can help you improve how you and the company should work with your teammates. Every one of us has room for improvement, and the tone for your 1:1 should allow for this type of feedback in a safe way. It's also important to show your teammates that you genuinely are interested in finding the best way to make your interactions meaningful, useful, and beneficial to both of you.

When in doubt about providing or soliciting feedback, remember that we should all strive to provide and receive critique about processes and approaches to how we work. It's your responsibility to provide an environment where your teammates understand that critiquing an individual's behavior or work is a path toward continuous learning and improvement.

How to Have One-on-One Meetings

First, you need to schedule the meetings with your teammates, and that can be pretty challenging, particularly if you're not already doing them and you've got a fairly full schedule. The advice on how frequently you should hold your 1:1 meetings is all over the map. There are many determining factors for how frequently to schedule them, but the most influential factors will be the size of your team and the management structure in which you work.

Ideally, you should try to hold your 1:1 meetings as a recurring weekly meeting. We suggest a 30-minute time slot that you schedule from Tuesday through Thursday if you can. Mondays and Fridays seem to be popular for personal time off, travel time, and holidays, and some unfortunate timing can find you not checking in with your teammates for nearly a month if you're not careful. Some people will schedule all of their meetings on a single day to free up the rest of their week, and others will ask their teammates to schedule the time each week as calendar openings exist.

ADVICE FROM THE FIELD

Committing to One-on-Ones

by Abi Jones, UX Manager

It takes olive trees five years to fruit and another 60–75 years to reach consistent yields. While design teams mature faster than olive trees, it helps to view 1:1s as a long-term investment, not a quick fix.

When I started holding 1:1s, I made a commitment to six months of a weekly 30-minute meeting with each team member. That's 12 hours with each person. Within three months, we had a strong set of shared goals and improved our feedback cadence. Within six months, I wondered how I ever went without 1:1s in the first place. Now 1:1s are core to my management practice at Google.

If your first few 1:1s feel awkward or don't seem productive, *don't give up*. Instead, reflect on what's effective or ineffective about the 1:1 and make adjustments. The effort is worth the results that you'll see in your team.

Hopefully, you've included a standard agenda in your meeting request with your teammates. Once you have this in place, start having the meetings. Lead the first few meetings until things start to find their own rhythm and get comfortable, and then get out of the way and let your teammate run the meeting so that the list of important things can start coming from them a bit more. Essentially, get out of the way and let the 1:1 meetings become useful and productive to your teammates by letting them drive.

You can't always predict where people work; however, if you find that you and your teammates are in the same physical location, consider getting out of the office for your meetings, when appropriate. Take a walk out of the building, go grab a cup of coffee or tea, or just get away from your workspace so that your teammates can feel more at ease opening up to you. Wherever you decide to meet, make sure that you're *present*—put down the lid to your laptop, turn your phone upside down, don't look at your watch, and if you can't do any of these, for the sake of all things precious, don't type something to someone else.

Some meetings, however, will absolutely require a closed-door, private discussion. When that happens, ensure your colleague's privacy by doing your part to ensure that you're together and in an undisturbed environment.

It's your choice how, or if, you choose to document your 1:1 meetings. For some, this is important if there are several teammates to keep up with and keeping everything straight in your head can be challenging. That's okay! Do, however, keep in mind that some of your discussions are likely meant to be personal or private, and you'll want to respect the wishes of your teammate.

Ask Questions So That Team Members Problem-Solve

One of your core responsibilities as a manager is to coach team members, and the best coaches help others work through problems and identify solutions on their own. In this process, knowing what to ask is more important than knowing what to say.

During a 1:1 meeting, work with team members to probe a bit deeper, gather more context, and seek alternatives. Ask them to expand upon what they're thinking with questions such as the following:

- Can you tell me a bit more?
- What is your real challenge?
- What is your primary concern?
- What might you be missing?
- How might others see this situation?
- What do you see as your options?
- What are other possible options?
- What do you want to do?
- Where would you like help?

These questions should get the conversation flowing. As the discussion takes shape, the team member will get a better sense of how to proceed. Likewise, you will get a better understanding of how the team is performing and where to help.

When team members are able to answer their own questions, they execute at a higher level, have more confidence in their abilities, and you remove yourself as a blocker. All are great steps in helping grow and evolve the team!

—Shay Howe, Co-founder, Lead Honestly

Sometimes, your 1:1 meetings will fly by, and you'll be wondering if you've allocated enough time for them because there's still information left to share, and other times, you'll find yourself wondering what to do with the remaining time. Don't force yourself and your colleague to keep the full time if it's not necessary to you or them. That said, make a note when your meeting ends early so that you can see if there is a pattern of brevity, and you need to make an adjustment.

One last thing: don't save everything for 1:1 meetings. If something comes up, address it right away with your teammates so they will always have the most current information they need in order to succeed.

What If You Run Out of Things to Talk About?

Sometimes, especially if your design team is running like a well-oiled machine, 1:1 meetings can fall a little short and leave you and your teammate wondering what to do with the remaining 20 minutes of your time. Never fear! There are plenty of things to discuss and plenty of great questions that you can ask each other or topics that you can explore. In many cases, how your team answers these questions won't change much from week to week—after all, you're usually interested in when an answer changes from what someone said originally. So by all means, ask these questions once to create your baseline, and then after a period of time, revisit these questions to make sure that something isn't starting to go sideways.

If you're feeling that your 1:1 meetings are falling into a rut, or you're running low on topics to discuss, you can also use some of these questions to help reignite the conversation:

- What would you change in the projects you are working on?
- How would you change how you've worked on those projects?
- What is going really well on the projects?
- What isn't going well on the projects?
- What would you like to help solve for the company?
- How can I adjust the way we work together to make work easier on you?
- What kind of improvements would you like to see at the company?
- How can the company help you do your current role better?

- How can the company help me do my current role better?

- Tell me about your family or your hobbies, or the things that keep you energized when you're not at work.

- What would you like to learn more about to help you in your role?

- What would you like to learn more about to help you in your life?

- What would you like to teach others to help them in their roles here?

And if you've explored those, or would like to follow another route completely, we love this suggestion to discuss a current disaster, from Michael Lott's blog "Rands in Repose."[1]

NOTE MY CURRENT DISASTER

> Chances are, in my professional life, something is currently off the rails. It's selfish, but if you're leading with status, and I can't find an interesting discussion nugget, let's talk about my current disaster. *Do you know how many open reqs we have that we can't hire against? Who is the best hiring manager you know and what were their best moves?* The point of this discussion is not to solve my disaster, the point is that we're going to have a conversation where one of us is going to learn something more than just project status.

Additionally, Lead Honestly (https://leadhonestly.com) is a service that you can subscribe to that offers hundreds of questions for your 1:1 meetings, as well as ways to track your meetings, progress, and more.

If this finds you still struggling to fill the time, remember this: time is the biggest gift anyone can give another person. Go ahead and give your teammate some time back. They could probably use it, and so could you!

Don't Skip the Skip-Level

When your direct reports have their own teams, you need to make time to meet with the people whom they meet with. You need to "skip a level" (skip-level meeting) and meet with the direct reports of your direct reports.

---

1   http://randsinrepose.com/archives/the-update-the-vent-and-the-disaster/

Much like your 1:1 meetings with your directs, the participants in the skip 1:1 should also have ample opportunity to ask questions that perhaps their direct manager may not have insight into. These groups may be interested in what other teams are working on, what may be around the corner, or how the state of the larger company is. You may be asked what's keeping *you* up at night, much like how you're interested in what's causing your directs to lose sleep.

Camille Fournier shared a number of useful questions appropriate for skip 1:1's in her book *The Manager's Path: A Guide for Tech Leaders Navigating Growth and Change*[2] in groups such as lunches or other team events:

- What else, as your manager's manager, can I be doing to provide for you and your team?

- Is this team struggling to be effective with other teams?

- Are there other questions about the rest of the organization I can answer?

---

2 Camille Fournier, *The Manager's Path: A Guide for Tech Leaders Navigating Growth and Change* (Sebastopol, CA: O'Reilly Media, 2017), 128.

More importantly, Fournier writes, is that the group skip 1:1 meetings may make those participants more comfortable at approaching you for additional 1:1 conversations later, especially if something is troubling them.

If you're conducting your first skip 1:1 meeting with your team (because you read about how great an idea they are here), make sure that you write a note ahead of time to your directs and their directs—the attendees of the skip 1:1. You want everyone to be aware that the meeting is happening, and that it's not a top-secret fishing expedition trying to get some dirt on their boss without them in the room.

When you conduct your skip 1:1 meetings with individuals, you may have more leeway to ask a variety of questions that may have been difficult in the group setting. As with your 1:1s with your directs, you just need a few prompts to get the conversation moving, such as asking any of the following questions that perhaps you weren't asking your team:

- Do you have any feedback about your manager—things that are working well, things you need to learn more about, things you think could be improved?

- Are you getting useful or effective feedback from your manager?

- Do you have a good understanding of how your work is judged and measured?

- Do you have any questions about the business strategy behind what you're working on?

Reinforce that you are asking in the best interests of the individual and to also help you as the leader of the larger organization make more informed decisions. By better understanding your directs' lives at work—even if only in 30- to 60-minute increments—you're in a better position to change your own approach proactively to improve communication and expectations throughout your design organization.

Avoid Relying on Office Hours

There are cases when it may seem more efficient to establish office hours for your teammates to come and find you. Office hours can be an effective tool for supplementing 1:1 meetings, for sharing information, or for generally making yourself available, etc. A regular cadence of office hours may be perfect.

However, office hours may not help your introverts, your folks who are busy with other tasks and deadlines, or those occasional people who like to be a little invisible and unnoticed in the organization.

Be aware that relying on office hours switches the power dynamic between you and your directs because they are now supposed to find time to talk, instead of the other way around.

1:1S AS OPPORTUNITY

There was a time when I wasn't scheduling 1:1 meetings because I just assumed if someone on my team needed to talk to me that they'd schedule a meeting. It's an easy position to take—I moved the responsibility away from me as the manager and leader and onto the people who reported to me or my directs. I expected them to come to me with their problems or their challenges, instead of giving them a platform and an opportunity to open up—and that didn't happen.

As a result, I'd learn—oftentimes much later—about subtle dynamics between teams and individuals that didn't seem like a big problem but would fester over time. These behaviors then became compounded in size and impact because I had yet to intervene, which meant that I had more damage to repair once I was aware of what was going on.

Instead, I've learned to schedule—and keep—the 1:1 meetings. Provide the time and expectation that there is a forum in which to check in. You'll always do better with more information and more opportunities to help support your team. ■

What Happens in One-on-Ones

The subjects discussed in 1:1s are neither bound to secrecy like a priest's confessional or attorney-client privilege, nor likewise meant to be gossiped about to anyone who doesn't need to know what's going on with the individuals on your team.

One of the fastest, most sure-fire ways to erode—if not outright destroy—trust in a manager is if that manager cannot be trusted with confidential information. If, for whatever reason, you're not clear if you should share information, ask your teammate if you can discuss whatever you're talking about with someone else. Make it anonymous as to whom it came from, if necessary.

Consider these topics and evaluate the best course of action:

a. An employee doesn't agree with prioritizing one customer segment over another.

b. Your teammate says they are having issues with a product manager who is making belittling comments that may be misogynistic.

c. Your teammate confides that they have increased care for their elderly father and may need more flexibility in scheduling and what they are responsible for.

In many situations, the corresponding appropriate next steps would then be the following:

a. Do not escalate to management, but take time to better communicate why the company is making this decision. You may want to discuss with your manager that some of the team is unconvinced that the business strategy is sound.

b. Approach the product manager to better understand how they are communicating with your team and consider if the case warrants involving HR or the product manager's line manager.

c. Do not say anything to your team and colleagues at this point. If things get worse with your teammate's father, then you can mention that they'll be taking some time away from the office.

In short, many of the topics of 1:1s may seem mundane … until they're not. While you can rely on your own judgment, don't forget to ask your teammate what resolution they want to see happen to guide you in what steps to take next. Not every situation warrants involving HR, although some topics most certainly will. Nor will every situation require your boss to get involved—that could suggest you can't handle the tough conversations. Whatever you do, maintain the confidence of your teammate in those 1:1s unless your teammate explicitly asks you to discuss their situation with others.

Wrapping Up

It's all too easy to fall into the trap of hustling from meeting to meeting, presenting your team's work or ironing out what they'll work on next, and the next thing you know it's time to wrap up for the day. Days turn into weeks, and before you know it, you haven't learned that your own teammates are feeling lost, unclear, or skeptical of their mission. The consistent 1:1 meeting is your lever you can pull to keep focus, provide context, and uncover the cracks in the dam before they explode and flood the village.

Not every single 1:1 will yield compelling or incendiary insights. After you develop a habit of being fully engaged in a useful, honest space for communication with your team, you'll have a better understanding of their perception and reality for where they are as a member on your team and the larger organization.

One-on-one meetings are critical to both you and your teammates. The absence of regular check-ins can leave teammates feeling unaware of how they are progressing and, even worse, can leave them feeling alone, as if they're fending for themselves or even unmotivated. When people don't know how they are doing or if they're making progress, they can really only safely continue to do what they've been doing. Any issues that are left unchecked can percolate and build up to a boil over time if they're ignored.

The same goes for leaders that you manage. Leaders need leaders, too, and it's important to have opportunities to review what's happening in their worlds. A person may be more senior than you, based on a skill set and seniority; however, that doesn't exclude them from also needing check-ins.

Finally, 1:1 meetings aren't a replacement for in-the-moment feedback. When something's important, it shouldn't wait for a personal meeting. Address issues and support that your team needs on-the-fly, as well as in your scheduled meetings. The more feedback loops you can provide means that the dreaded task of annual performance reviews will be a lot less surprising as well, and that's something for which everyone should be grateful.

CHAPTER 10

Leading Continuous Critique

It's easy to visualize a small group of people sitting in a semi-circle around a wall of color-printed images of a product, a website, an advertising inventory item, or any other visual artifact. There's at least one person standing near the images, likely pointing or gesturing at some explicit aspect of it, with several others around them looking on with deep focus.

Sounds amazing! And it's entirely probable in an art school, or an organization where everyone is co-located, or where people aren't spread across multiple projects, and if calendars all line up perfectly to make this happen.

Enter reality, at least for a lot of organizations, and this type of scenario may only be a dream scenario. There are ways to weave critiques into the fabric of your team's DNA, without having to be in the same place and time (zone). Let's get past the excuses and into a culture of critique.

The Value of Critique

One of the best things ever stated about critique comes from Adam Connor, VP Design Transformation at Mad*Pow: "Critique is not a (just) design skill. It's a life skill. Any time we want to improve something we're doing, we can use it. We can step back, examine our goals and objectives, how what we've done does or does not work towards them, and adjust."

When you become strong in the critique of design work, you naturally start to apply the things that you've learned to other parts of your life, and only good comes from learning how to ask the questions to help others—and yourself—continually improve.

As an ongoing tool in your leadership belt, critique brings some additional value. Critique can also reduce the expectation that only one person can provide feedback to a work in progress to help one another improve, especially in teams with shared responsibilities. This is easy—because no one person is the sole proprietor of being able to provide valuable, actionable feedback, and no one person needs to feel overly responsible for providing critique.

Providing critique isn't a replacement for final approval of creative direction, nor is it a replacement for standard quality assurance measures. It is, however, a way to keep your team aware of the work of other members of the team, to improve general facilitation and critique skills across the team, and to identify opportunities for growth and new leadership across the team.

The (Self-Imposed) Challenges of Continuous Critique

Plenty of people will have reasons for discounting a way to have an ongoing cycle of critique in their organizations. That's okay! Change is hard, and so is giving up control of things that people think provide value or worth to the role that they perform.

Continuous critique can get shot down in cases where the following situations occur:

a. A design leader feels the need to be in control of or responsible for all aspects of design in their organization.

b. Someone in the organization feels that a distributed workforce can diminish the value of the critique, or someone in the organization feels that their feedback will be the most valuable and best delivered in person.

c. Someone thinks that the team is too big, too small, has too many disciplines, or some other reason that prevents critique from happening.

If people legitimately want to perform continuous critique within their organization, they will find a way to make it happen. Here are some quick counterpoints to previous nonstarter points:

a. Design leaders can still be the final gatekeeper for any design that leaves the organization. Critique is about getting valuable feedback from others to help a designer refine their thinking and help them move forward. Designers receiving critique get to decide how—and if—they choose to implement it. Unless, of course, it's from that design leader who needs to have the final say.

b. Is your organization only working with others who are in the same location? Are the clients local? Does everyone work in the office every day of the week? Does any work ever get done over the phone, in some form of chat, or in some other assisted way that doesn't require everyone to be in the same room at the same time? If you can answer yes to any of those questions, you can find a way to make continuous critique work.

c. This is more of the same—no team is too big, too small, or has too many different types of disciplines in it for someone to be able to provide valuable feedback. You're probably already reaching out to someone somewhere else to help inform your thinking, so it's time to stop making excuses and give it a try.

You can stop reading now if you think this just isn't for you—that's okay! Continuous critique is a choice you get to make, as is deciding whether or not you work for an organization that places value in critiquing work. We're pretty sure that adding critique to your practice will change the world, probably.

If you're interested in learning more, here's a way to kick-start continuous critique and put it into practice. Once you get up and running, you'll be able to modify this process to meet your needs, and it will only hurt a little bit.

Getting Started with Continuous Critique

The really great news is that you don't need a lot to start doing continuous critique across your team. The basics are the following:

- **An ability to share work while being able to discuss it.**

  - Screen-sharing technology is great for this—your organization likely has preferred options.

  - If screen-sharing technology isn't available and you're able to use email and telephones to share screens views and have discussions, this can work, too.

- **A team.** This seems like it works best with teams of six or more. We strongly recommend including diverse teams from product management, the development team, or others who may be stakeholders or partners at some point in the process.

  As an added bonus, you can also have the disciplines all spend time teaching each other how to provide valuable critique to each other (which works with any size team).

- **Work to share.**

This is a great time to mention that work that can be critiqued doesn't have to be something that has been designed with digital tools. You can—and should—test sketches, ideas, presentations, planning activities, important communications, or anything else that isn't "just" design.

And don't wait until your work is polished and pure—that's not what you're looking for with a critique. You're looking for actionable feedback from diverse teams that can get you to polished and pure, and with perspective.

Team Size

A team of six allows you to have two teams of three people. Each team consists of at least two people who are led by a "critique lead," which isn't an official position in your org chart, but it is a way for you to provide informal leadership opportunities to your team.

When you're establishing your critique teams, look for opportunities to connect people who don't normally get to interact or work together. If people are in different locations, or work on different projects (or both), give them time to get to know each other better and the work that they're doing. Doing critiques can be a great way to help your team get to know each other better than normal work might allow.

The Critique Process

by Elizabeth Goodman, Design Leader

The Benefits of Formalizing a Team Critique Process

A team that formalizes their critique process offers the opportunity for the members to continually learn from the insights of others across the team, while also providing additional benefits to their leader.

- **They are a safe ladder to leadership.**

  Running a critique group lets people flex their meeting facilitation skills. Serving as the critique group's lead helps people practice some core skills of management: developing projects, assigning work, checking on progress, and so on. It all scaffolds career growth—practicing skills, deciding whether progression along this path is interesting, and putting something on the résumé.

- **They can build community and morale—particularly on distributed teams.**

  When you have designers embedded on teams, they can feel isolated and alone. While giving or receiving feedback, members of critique groups are forming and strengthening relationships. Because there's no "official" manager there, critique sessions are also a safe place to vent, share anxieties, and feel heard. It also helps make sure that everyone stays in touch with design issues across a range of projects, so there's at least some institutional knowledge getting preserved.

- **They promote core skills.**

  For earlier career folks who aren't interested in leadership, meeting in groups helps them get comfortable presenting work and giving constructive feedback. This is particularly important for designers who are scared about showing in-progress or early-stage work. Even when members of critique groups shy away from showing their own early, messy work, they believe that it's helpful for them to see other people in the group model what it's like to share early, unformed ideas.

- **They lessen the burden on managers.**

  Knowing that less experienced designers are getting regular feedback from more experienced designers of all disciplines means less anxiety about quality control. From my perspective as a researcher/product designer, it also meant that I didn't have to worry so much about trying to give great feedback on content design! An actual senior content designer could handle that.

The Potential Costs and Burdens of a Formalized Critique Process

Every time you introduce a process or a policy, you're also running the risk of adding additional bureaucracy, time, and effort from the members of your team, and you need to be prepared to manage that, as well.

- **There is administrative overhead.**

  If no one is willing to serve as critique lead, that's going to fall on the manager.

- **They only work when you have enough people.**

  Let's say ... 10 people on the team? Otherwise, it's not clear to me whether the administrative overhead is worth it.

- **They require a critical mass of trusted leaders—enough so that each group has at least one person who can model constructive critique and give trustworthy feedback.**

  18F was perfect because the team was mostly composed of fairly experienced folks, so I could trust that critique group members were actually giving each other the sort of feedback I would want them to receive.

- **They take time.**

  I could see at about three years in and with staffing shortages, critique meetings started to get cancelled because people were just too busy. And then they start feeling like a "nice-to-have" rather than a commitment, and then (this didn't happen, but it could have started) they begin to wither away.

Continuous critique works best with teams of six or more. If you're in a team that's smaller than six, it's likely you're all going to know what other people are working on anyway, and you probably already have some established norms about how you review the work being done.

If you have a team of five people or less, you could consider attempting to add a critique to your 1:1 sessions, or you could make the critique a different standing meeting with a regular cadence that you decide upon with the team.

Team Roles and Responsibilities

Your critique teams will have a limited number of roles, which makes this pretty straightforward:

- **Continuous critique sponsor:** This is likely you, and the purpose of the role is to have regularly scheduled meetings with the critique leads to learn how the critique meetings are going, understand if there are opportunities to improve the way the meetings are held, learn if there are opportunities to grow the skills of teammates, and to update the critique manual (more on this later) as needed. Additionally, the critique sponsor will facilitate the decision-making when it's time to select new critique leads.

- **Critique leads:** These are, or should be, rotating positions. Critique leads will coordinate and organize the critique sessions, help plan the agendas for the critique sessions, and meet with the sponsor to provide insight into how the critique sessions are going overall, and to provide recommendations as necessary. Critique leads will also perform retrospectives to understand how the team perceives the usefulness of the critique sessions and to provide input for improvements.

- **Critique contributors:** These are the other people on your critique teams, and their role is to provide material for critique and to provide thoughtful, actionable feedback when critiquing the work of others.

You don't have to limit critique contributors to people on your design team. Product managers, developers, strategists, and any other roles you may have in your organization can all add value to critique sessions, as long as you provide them with a solid guide and the expectations of how they should provide actionable feedback.

Critique Manual/Guide

You should work with your critique leads to establish a critique manual/guide that provides a reference point for everyone on the team about how continuous critique works (focus especially on people who are newly hired or have transferred to your team). Everyone can provide input; however, it's best to limit the updates to the manual to your leads in order to ensure that changes are being made that are agreed upon by the critique leadership.

A critique manual should include the following information:

- **A brief overview of what continuous critique means to your team**

- **An overview of the roles and responsibilities, which include:**

  - Providing a thoughtful critique

  - Fostering a positive culture of critique

  - Determining how the critique sessions will be run

  - Deciding what meetings will look like for the team

- **Rules of critique:**

  - Look for positives and opportunities to improve

  - Focus on the design, not the designer

  - Don't assume or insert yourself into a project; ask questions to understand better

  - Lead with questions

  - Use a filter; these are your colleagues and everyone's time is valuable

  - Look for guidance that helps to improve the design and the designer where possible

- **Helpful tips/guidance:**
  - Things to avoid saying
  - Allow yourself to have time to understand the design challenge
  - Don't make assumptions
  - Avoid inserting personal "good ideas" into someone else's work
- **Timing guidelines for meetings:**
  - Meeting kickoff
  - Agenda sharing
  - Sharing background of the work to be critiqued and the focus of the critique
  - Summary of the critique received and potential next steps, if known
  - Planning next steps

Define Rules of Critique

Adam Connor and Aaron Irizarry have written a book, *Discussing Design: Improving Communication and Collaboration Through Critique,* that is worth your time to read—and quite likely worth investing in for everyone on your team and beyond. (If you're seeking a way to quickly get a team up to speed on critique, Nicole Maynard had her team read the book and discuss a chapter per week and found that it quickly added value.) Their book provides great insights into the value of critiques, as well as how to establish good rules for critiques in working sessions.

You can start with some very basic, simple rules:

- The person presenting the work to be critiqued defines the areas where they want feedback.
- Critiques should stay within the focus that the presenter has established.
- Critiques should be actionable; someone cannot say, "I don't like green" without providing an explanation that helps move the design forward.
- Critiques should be about the design/item and never about the individual presenting the work. Do *not* make the critique personal!

- The person presenting the work gets to make the decision about what feedback is incorporated—and how—and without repercussions from anyone. Implementing critique is also *not* personal!

- Consider thinking in positives and changes:

  - "I like this because …"

  - "Did you consider …?"

  - "If you changed this, what could happen?"

There is a lot of room to build upon these starter rules. These rules will be great for you to put into a critique guide that you share with your team and update regularly.

Choose a Critique Leader and Teams

While it's unlikely that you have room in your corporate org chart to add in a new "leadership" role for the critique leader, it is an opportunity to rotate responsibility across your team. Identify your critique leader through whatever method works best for you and your team—you can hold interviews, you can seek volunteers, or you can take on the role yourself (although it's better if it is led by someone else).

Once you have a critique leader identified, it's their responsibility to organize and coordinate the critique activities that happen across the team. They'll be responsible for helping to organize and structure the critique teams; they'll help identify the best cadence and operating rhythm for the critique; and they'll identify and collaborate with you when there are challenges that need to be addressed, skills that need to be strengthened, or any other issues that may arise.

Critique leaders can also help you identify various critique teams and the leader for each of those teams. Teams seem to work best when they are three to five teammates in size; however, your organization size may dictate something different, and you should adjust as necessary.

Establish Rhythm/Cadence

There are different ways that your critique teams can meet. Teams may choose from the following:

- **1:1 meetings:** Thirty-minute meetings (weekly, biweekly, etc.) between the critique lead and each member of the team in order to provide actionable feedback on the work in progress. It's important to note that this should be seen as a two-way street; critique leads should also be sharing work and receiving feedback from the teammates.

- **Group critique meetings:** Erica Deahl (www.ericadeahl.com) suggested that 1:1 critique sessions may work for some and may be improved upon by adding group critique sessions. You may want to try blending these approaches as well.

- **All design team critique meetings:** In addition to the group critique meetings and the 1:1 meetings, consider a regular meeting with everyone across all teams. Allow team members to sign up to receive critiques and let everyone participate across your entire design practice. This could also be expanded to include developers and other disciplines because it makes sense, and could also be done openly for others across the organization to attend and participate.

- **Retrospectives:** Identify a cadence for retros, as well, to ensure that people are helping you understand what isn't working and what can be improved upon.

And then, repeat this. Your mileage may vary as far as what works best, and you may find something entirely different is right for your team. Use this framework as a way to kick off a critique for your team and see where it leads.

Additionally, find a cadence to meet with the critique leads and learn how it's working. You should be participating in critiques as well, and it will be useful to work together to understand how to best shape the future of critique.

Keep It Fresh

Continuous critique is like just about any other system you may put into place: after some time, it may feel tired, out-of-date or out-of-touch, and people may no longer be engaged. Continually listen to the reports from the retros, and also look for opportunities to rotate the roles of the critique leaders—perhaps quarterly or semi-annually—to give others the opportunity to lead and bring other ideas to try.

Don't be afraid to experiment and fail—the only time you can *really* fail at a critique is if you're not actually doing it at all.

The Benefits of Critique

There are several benefits that may happen with the implementation of continuous critique, and these include the following:

- **Reduces your time as primary reviewer of all design.**

  The critique is happening all across your team, and you still get to be involved in the various group sessions.

- **Identifies leaders and leadership in the team.**

  Everyone gets an opportunity to participate, lead, and offer improvements.

- **Uncovers growth and training/learning needs and opportunities.**

  Discussions across multiple projects and products help identify areas of growth needed for the team.

- **Strengthens critique abilities across the team.**

  It's being put into practice regularly and becomes embedded in the design culture, which can improve how design is received by product teams and clients.

- **Increases distributed team communication, interaction, and engagement.**

  Team members who might not normally have reasons to interact get to spend time working together and learning about products or projects that they may not normally have exposure to.

- **Improves facilitation and presentation skills.**

  The more the team practices, the better it becomes at framing the scope of discussions and presenting work.

- **Improves design across the team.**

  A critique provides opportunities to hear and learn from different perspectives and take action that makes designs better. It can also improve design efficiencies when team members learn that problems they're working on may have already been solved in other parts of the organization.

- **Evangelizes design across the organization.**

  When critique is opened up to other disciplines to participate in, other people become more familiar with the work the design team is doing and vice versa.

There are a lot of benefits beyond improving the practice of critique across the organization. A relatively low investment (likely less than 5% of a team's overall utilization) can help a team learn more about its work and itself.

Every presentation is the sharing of information, and it's made even better when it's the telling of a story and not just a backward-facing report of history. Yes, the story can be the journey—the steps taken to achieve an outcome, the lessons learned along the way, the failures and successes that led to where you are today, and what you're presenting now.

Wrapping Up

Establishing a culture of frequent, inclusive critique is one of the most effective means of designing better products faster while also elevating your influence in the organization. Getting diverse teams involved sooner—not to see their sketches, per se, but to hear their feedback to the rest of the sketches on the wall—likely will reveal possible risk, lack of alignment, or conflicting priorities that can sink a project before a line of code is written or a prototype tested by a customer.

Suddenly, you're the flypaper that is attracting different teams to the project, ensuring greater buy-in, a shared sense of ownership, and fostering a healthy rapport across teams that very well could have seen each other as adversaries.

When you have the opportunity to coach teams, it's important to highlight the common business goals and challenges. This will help establish you and your team as leaders in the organization. Reinforce the value of critique as the language of continual improvement and innovation. While not everyone in your organization may have a design background or be a designer, they can all add value to the design process, regardless of their title.

Critique, as Adam Connor says, is a life skill. The more you invoke critique practices, the more you'll showcase that your team is grounded in making things better, regardless of where the good ideas come from. That's not a bad outcome for your team—and you.

CHAPTER 11

Presenting Work

M any actors in the theater will tell you that it takes a lot of practice to get to the point where they're comfortable in scenarios where something goes wrong, because as the saying goes, "The show must go on!" It might be difficult to believe that people who are performing on a stage will regularly practice and rehearse their craft so that they can appear to "wing it" with ease.

Athletes practice running their plays time and time again for the same reason. If something happens that drives a player off course, they can improvise, or they know *how* to improvise—because they know their teammates are following the script and that helps them understand their next best move.

The reality in both cases is that they've become really familiar with handling an environment where they know their actions and those around them very well. If and when something goes wrong for them, the back-up plan comes a little easier because they know where everyone else will be and what they will be doing.

Likewise, any presentation of work that you'll be doing is going to require preparation, as well. You may not need to invest the effort or energy as an improv team member; however, the more prepared, rehearsed, and familiar you are with your material, the easier it will be for you to adjust to scenarios where the agenda may be in your control, however, the other people in the room may not be.

Got it? Presentation requires preparation. Full stop.

Yes, there are those who make it look easy or even like they're winging it. That's because they've spent a lot of their careers and lives preparing for other presentations, and they have a wealth of experience and content that they're drawing from.

If you've not guessed it by now, we're going to cover a lot about the fundamentals of preparation for presentations in this chapter. And every presentation you give is preparation for future presentations down the road.

What's more, presenting work likely matters more as a design manager than when you were a design or project lead. Whereas before your presentations may have been focused on presenting client work for approval, or presenting prototypes to the development team, your presentations now may have far greater and lasting impact. Perhaps you're presenting to senior management about why you need increased head count. Maybe you're presenting to the executive team

Winging It

by Amy Jiménez Márquez, seasoned improv troupester (also works at Amazon; not as a troupester)

When you've practiced certain characters, themes, and types of story structures in front of people enough, you build a nice inventory of tools to pull from on a moment's notice. You're practicing so you can learn where your strengths and weaknesses are, and how to adjust to and for those moments, so your audience is never the wiser—even when things go off the rails.

And sometimes, off the rails can deliver serendipitous results!

about how investing in design has led to positive business value. Or maybe you have to present to your leadership that you recommend a reorganization of your design team from an agency model to a centralized partnership model. Regardless, the stakes are higher as a manager, so prepare yourself ahead of time not to let anything slip.

Presenting Work Matters

Every presentation is the sharing of information, and it's made even better when it's the telling of a story and not just a backward-facing report of history. Yes, the story can be the journey—the steps taken to achieve an outcome, the lessons learned along the way, and the failures and successes that led you to where you are today and what you're presenting now.

When you're sharing your design work in any form—napkin sketches, paper prototypes, low-fidelity wireframes, high-fidelity concepts, interactive prototypes, or the first final version of anything—you're selling. You're selling your knowledge of user needs, your expertise, and your trust that you made good decisions at the behest of the requesting authority, and you want them to believe in—and buy in—to what you've created.

You'll need to know why decisions were made along the way and how to map them to a desired and agreed-upon outcome. This isn't to infer that whatever you're presenting needs to be perfect; we already know that perfection in design is always just one more iteration away. It means that whatever you're presenting needs to be well prepared, and well prepared means that you need to have time to plan and practice what you're presenting. You'll need to know the desired outcome. Is it approval to move forward to the next phase? Is it additional funding? Is it an acknowledgment or a symbolic high-five from someone you report to? Whatever it is, you need to know that target and set the presentation to hit it.

By now, if you didn't know any better, you'd think you're not only rehearsing your presentation, but you're also basically establishing an agenda for a meeting.

Presenting Work Is a Meeting— Treat It Like One

As much as we'd like presenting work to be just about talking through design decisions, there's a lot more to it than that. Your preparation involves knowing all the things about the work you're presenting, of course, but it also involves everyone's favorite activity: herding cats!

Agendas

While you don't have to be the person who rides the hard line of "If the meeting invite doesn't have an agenda, I'm not going to attend it," it's still good to be informed about what's being asked of your time. If you want people to attend your meeting, leave them with no doubt, and do your best to prepare for a good meeting.

Good meetings start with good agendas. Good agendas include the following information:

- **A purpose:** Let everyone know why you're meeting, what the meeting is about, and why it is important that they are invited.

- **Topics to be covered:** Share details about what's being covered; fill in some backstory information, especially if the context isn't obvious or if everyone has not been aware of the same information prior to this meeting.

- **Outcomes/objectives:** Make sure to have a goal and expectation for the meeting, as well as explaining to attendees what actions are needed in order to continue making progress, if any.

- **Timing and high-level activities:** Let everyone know what's going to happen in the meeting and when. Set the expectation for how much is going to be covered and how much time is allotted so that attendees can understand expectations, and in some cases, when they may be able to join or leave the meeting.

- **Roles (who presents when, who is the scribe, etc.):** This will help people know what they're on the hook for. If someone is needed for an approval, it's best to let that person know they're needed in order for the meeting to be a success. If multiple people will be presenting, let everyone know in advance. (Even though, yes, they really should know already, and they really should be part of all that you are doing in preparation—in the real world, however, you can bet this won't always be the case.) If you're the presenter, you don't also have to be the facilitator. Facilitators have an important job to do, and they'll help ensure that you do your job as a presenter and that everyone else fulfills their obligation to the meeting as well. Facilitators will make sure to manage your agenda and the attendees in order to hit the objectives within the time allotted.

ADVICE FROM THE FIELD

Agendas as Crystal Balls

by Brad Nunnally, coauthor of Designing the Conversation: Techniques for Successful Facilitation *and* UX Research: Practical Techniques for Designing Better Products

Agendas not only help you prepare properly, but they can also help you predict how your meeting is going to go. If you've been working with the invitees long enough, it's likely that you know the various personalities and motives that are going to be in the room with you. With this insight, you can walk through your agenda and role-play how the conversations, collaboration, or decisions will go. This extra layer of preparation sets you up for success by helping you figure out how to handle known risk or conflicting motives.

This is a good start—for writing your agenda (see Figure 11.1). For the rest of the meeting preparation, keep in mind the difference between people who *need* to attend and those who *want* to attend.

Client: Missing Piece
Project: Website Relaunch
Date: May 30, 2020
Phase: Kickoff

Attendees

Missing Piece Stakeholders	[[Team Name]]
Cad Bane, Product Manager	Name, Role
Nute Gunray, Business Sponsor	Name, Role
Satine Kryze, Project Manager	Name, Role
Mina Bonteri, Technical Sponsor	

Agenda

Introduction	(5)
Empathy Map	(60)
Affinity Map	(60)
Site Map	(60)
Participatory Design	(60)

Workshop Objectives

- Discover user behaviors, needs, pain points, and goals
- Group project requirements based on type or theme
- Identify key content areas and pages that will contain them
- Map out key tasks to understand interaction points and areas of opportunity.

FIGURE 11.1
Sample meeting agenda.

Meeting Costs

While it's great to have people in the room who want to learn more about what's being presented, cost should be a factor that you keep in mind. There are many "meeting cost calculators" available to estimate how much you're spending for people in the room to be present.

NOTE MEETING ESTIMATOR

You can check out *Harvard Business Review*'s estimator here: **https://hbr.org/2016/01/estimate-the-cost-of-a-meeting-with-this-calculator**. You can also factor in billable rates versus annual salary to see what the costs to clients might be.

Another way to think of the cost of meetings is in time—for every eight hours spent in a meeting (eight people at one hour each), you're spending a full day's worth of time to accomplish a task. Is it worth it to invest a full day's worth of productivity into your meeting?

Meeting cost and meeting fatigue are real things—invest in your meetings wisely and do your best to avoid anything that's nonessential, including attending meetings you don't need to be at and inviting people who don't need to be in yours.

In addition, as the design manager in the room, monitor who is participating and to what degree. If you have a frequently reoccurring meeting and one person consistently doesn't contribute, or if they're only there to crack a few jokes or don't speak until the end of the meeting and just say "So what are the next steps?" then evaluate why that person is on the invite in the first place. They will likely be relieved they have one less thing to attend, and you'll reinforce accountability in who attends meetings and how they participate.

Setting Up

Welcome to the modern world! In addition to not yet having flying cars (and we have no misgivings that this text will find its way into a certain DeLorean of the future), we also don't have technology that functions perfectly every time, all the time. On a good day, it's more like 60% it works 100% of the time, so you'll want to do your part to make sure that the technology you're using is something that you're familiar with and is something you've tested.

Don't plan on walking into a meeting, or launching a meeting application from your cushy home office, and having everything work perfectly. We're still in the age of "Can you hear me?" and "Hi, who just joined?" and "Can everyone see my screen?" and ... look, just make sure the meeting isn't the first place you try to use screens, screen sharing, video chat, or anything else that is needed. At the risk of being counter to saving the environment, make sure that you have analog options available to you and supply in-room handouts if available, and share files prior to the meeting for your distributed attendees.

Don't Just Be on Time, Be Early

Consider this quote that we haven't been able to track to a single person and to countless memes online: "If you're early, you're on time. If you're on time, you're late." If you want to be a considerate presenter of work and scheduler of meetings, you could schedule meetings to end 5–10 minutes early so your attendees have enough time to gather their belongings, get a drink of water in the hallway, and stop by their locker to get their binder and books for their next class before Mr. Belding gives them a detention for being late to Miss Bliss's class!

When it's your meeting, it's your job to be there early and make sure that everything is ready to go, even if others may not be. Pre-block your calendar so that you're not in a back-to-back meeting schedule and you can arrive early to make sure that everything is set up in a way that makes you comfortable.

Expect that others will be late as well. The transition time from meeting to meeting can vary depending upon physical location, other meetings running long, and a number of other factors that can make things imperfect. Plan your meeting start time to allow for this, and don't be shy about buffering yourself—no one has ever complained about a meeting ending early!

Presentation Preparation

There are a lot of different approaches to preparation for a presentation, and most of them carry the same theme: *rehearsal allows you to give your best presentation.*

This should seem pretty straightforward, and yet ...

You could argue that, all along the way to the presentation, you're getting familiar with what you'll be presenting. You're learning all about the person you're presenting to, or the client(s), and that this is all the preparation you'll need. You could argue this, and you'd be wrong.

Each time you present your work affords you the opportunity to get feedback that provides you with opportunities to improve. Start small—don't wait to start walking through your material and how you plan to present until everything you have is 100% complete. Start rehearsing as soon as you're able—even if that means walking a trusted colleague through your outline to make sure that you're not forgetting anything. Then start building from there to include others, including others who will be in the presentation and may be close to the decision-makers, or the decision-makers themselves.

This may seem like a lot. To some degree, it is. However, if you work it into your work routine, it becomes a habit that is part of your DNA and is less of an event that you have to reset each time.

Here's an approach of preparing for a presentation:

- **Draft an outline.**

  Pull together your initial thoughts for how the presentation should go. Use this to make sure that you're thinking through all the parts and the order of what you'll present.

- **Share the outline.**

  Validate your outline with members of your team, or those familiar with what you'll be presenting, or even a sympathetic ear who will listen to how you set up the presentation and then attempt to track the flow of your outline.

- **Revise the outline.**

  After you've received feedback, make updates to your outline and start moving forward in creating your presentation.

- **Create the presentation while work is in-flight.**

  The important piece here is to get started with your presentation while you're still creating the work. Multitasking is tough, absolutely; however, with a clear outline, it will be straightforward for you to start generating content while you're working through the work you'll be presenting. Start taking notes for and marking placeholders in your presentation script.

- **Dry-run incomplete and unfinished materials informally internally.**

  Meet with your internal team—perhaps in 1:1s—and walk through your draft presentation, taking notes as you go.

- **Revise the presentation.**

  After you've collected your feedback, make updates to the draft presentation.

- **Dry-run the complete presentation internally.**

  Schedule time to practice your presentation in front of members of your team. Direct them to ask the hard questions, to grill you, to make you sweat, and to trip you up a bit, within reason. Every hard question you answer here will prepare you for the hard questions to come in your presentation.

- **Informally present to stakeholders.**

  If you can find time, present to other stakeholders who will be in the meeting and get their feedback. Insiders who can provide feedback that will help you be successful are always great to have on your side. As a bonus, they can always pre-share how the presentation will go and offer support during your formal presentation. These folks can be a determining factor to your outcomes; if they understand your intent, they can help position you and your presentation in the right frame.

- **Revise the presentation.**

  After receiving and distilling your feedback, make your final updates and make sure all of your preparations for the meeting are taken care of.

- **Send the presentation as a "read-ahead."**

  Whenever possible, send your presentation materials to attendees before the presentation. There are many different personalities that can come into play, including those who do not feel comfortable sharing feedback during the presentation. Some folks may not be comfortable because of the other personalities (or titles) in the room, some may tend to be more introverted, some may need additional time to process ahead of time, etc. When you can share your presentation materials ahead of time, you increase the chances of being more inclusive to everyone attending and in return you increase the opportunities to get feedback that you might not have been able to receive otherwise.

This may seem like a lot of steps to go through. It is—sort of. Instead of focusing on how much you iterate and rehearse, think about how you're becoming more ... agile. It will get easier over time as you start to make this part of your practice. You'll learn a shorthand for going through reviews and updates that won't be very time consuming, and you'll find yourself better prepared to present your work.

Along the way, you will have shown a lot of people your work. If you're able to, leave nothing to surprise anyone—constantly show your work and share ideas to help ensure that you're delivering the right thing and getting support from the decision-makers. Grand reveals, after all, are for amateurs.

It's also very important to remember: it's better to present incomplete work than it is to design until minutes before the meeting starts. You can always reschedule a meeting or explain incomplete work (and provide a plan for getting back on track); however, it can require a lot more effort to rebound from hurting your reputation by appearing unprepared.

Finally, regardless of your title, make sure that *you* present *your* work. If you've only been a resource for providing critique, state that, make introductions, and then get out of the way while the designer presents their work. In that scenario, your job is to be the Scottie Pippen to the Michael Jordan. You're the lead assistant, and you should take any necessary notes and action items, while happily stepping up to own mistakes for the team.

There's little excuse for not letting people present their own work, regardless of who the audience is. Part of your job is to lead by this example.

Presenting

After you've taken care of all the pleasantries, small talk, and introducing everyone in the meeting, you would think you'd be ready to start presenting your work. You'd think that, especially since it's taken so much time to get here; however, you'd be wrong.

Preparing for and Receiving Critique

Before you start presenting your work, you need to make sure that everyone in the meeting understands the type of actionable feedback that you're looking for. You'll want to establish what you are seeking critique about, and how you'd like to receive it.

When you define the scope for critique before you present your work, you establish the focus of every person in the meeting. In addition to providing the scope, you'll also want to define how you want the critique to be provided to you. You may decide that you want raw, unfiltered critique, or that you'd prefer to have critique that's framed in a way that establishes what is liked or perceived as good and working versus parts of the design that could be improved and how. You have options on how you choose to receive and document the feedback, and any out-of-scope comments and discussion can be directed to a parking lot or backlog, as you see fit.

Since you're likely delivering presentations *about* the design team in addition to the design team's *work*, the critique you seek will likely be different than what you were looking for as a practitioner. You may find yourself asking for critique on the clarity of your argument, how you positioned this work relative to how others either inside or outside the organization are attempting similar things, and if you accounted for enough of the dependencies that will be impacted by the decisions made based on your presentation.

Sample Rules of Critique and Helpful Tips

Rules of Critique

- **Find positives. And deltas.**

  Provide critique that informs the designer what they did well and what the areas are that could benefit from some kind of change.

- **Make it about the design.**

  It's *not* about the designer—even though it may seem like it is.

- **Don't assume. Don't be afraid to ask.**

  Make sure that you gain an understanding from the designer about why they took a certain approach or delivery method—this can help you understand how to provide better critique to them.

- **Lead with questions.**

  Ask the designer why they did something, how they put it together, and what their intention was in delivery. When you understand this, it's much easier to provide critique that will be beneficial to them.

- **Use a filter.**

  In essence, think before you speak. Be sensitive to the receiving party, as you would hope others would do to you when critiquing your work.

  You can learn more about how to address critique in Chapter 10, "Leading Continuous Critique."

Helpful Tips

- Avoid saying "You should have done it this way." "I would have ..."
- Take the time to understand the design problem.
- Don't make assumptions.
- Be mindful of what is helpful considering timelines. Be careful inserting your good idea at the last moment.

Presenting the Work

It's perhaps ironic that the shortest section of the chapter about presenting your work is about the actual *presenting* of your work. Except, by now, you've done a lot of preparation. You've prepared your outline and revised it, created your presentation and revised it (probably multiple times), and you've made sure that everyone understands why they are in the meeting, what they're going to see, what they're going to provide critique on, and how they're going to critique it.

And now, it's time. Remember that the work is the star of the show, and you're telling its story. Be aware of the time that you have available to you and make sure that you remember some basics about presenting.

- **Appearance:** Make sure that all the clothing items that should be tucked in are tucked in, and all the things that should be buttoned up are buttoned up, and definitely make sure all zippers are in the right places, too. Also, smile. You'll be surprised at the difference it makes to simply smile when you present. (Pro tip: Try smiling when you write emails, too, and notice the difference.)

- **Posture:** Stand up straight like your parents taught you and look at the people you are presenting to.

- **Attentive:** Be present in the meeting and engaged with the content you're presenting and the people you're presenting to. Most meetings cost more than a few hundred dollars from the moment they start, and you owe everyone your attention.

- **Enthusiasm:** Be enthusiastic—not only is it contagious, but people will sense your commitment to the work, and they'll appreciate the passion.

- **Speed:** Slow down when you speak. Time when presenting moves faster than normal time, and it's easy to begin to speak quicker when time runs short. It's better to run out of time and not present everything than to present all that you have and leave people wondering what they've been shown.

- **Podium usage:** You may not have a podium; however, if you're using one, be aware of how you lean on it, or how you use it while you're presenting. Also, pay attention to how much you're looking at your screen instead of the people you are presenting to—eye contact will be noticed, especially if it's not happening. If you're not using a podium and you're at a shared table, be aware of who is around you and what is displayed on your laptop's screen that is visible.

- **Microphone:** You may or may not have a microphone, depending upon where you're presenting; however, if you do use a microphone, be aware of where it's located and how it works. For example, podium or hand-held microphones don't need to be right up against your mouth and can often sound distorted if they are. Additionally, if you're too far away, the audience may not be able to hear you, so be mindful about where the microphone is compared to your mouth, especially when walking.

- **Sarcasm:** Don't do it. At all. This is difficult for all of us to do at different times, and do your best to leave it out of your presentation. The same goes for jokes that don't have any value or purpose, or anything that highlights negatives about others or the work of others.

NOTE CLIP-ON MIKES AND HEADSETS

Lavaliere or lapel/clip-on microphones allow you the freedom to move about easily; however, any turning while walking should be done with your shoulders to prevent your mouth from moving out of range from the microphone if your head turns and your torso remains in a different direction. If you get to use a headset microphone, things will be pretty smooth, although you may want to consider using a piece of clear tape to hold the microphone close to your face in order to pick up steady audio.

You should have a script worked out, or a series of speaker notes, bullet points, or whatever it is that you'll need to keep you on track. Make your way through your presentation flow and stay calm. You may lose your train of thought or break your flow—and that's okay! Take a moment and allow a pause in the room, acknowledge your mistake, and restart from where it makes sense. These types of things happen to the best presenters, but they know that the audience wants them to do well and will forgive them. There's a big difference between getting tripped up and being unprepared, and your attendees will be much more forgiving for the former than the latter.

Invariably, people will have their own ideas about what needs to be presented and when, or they'll have questions that they won't want to wait to ask. It's your choice in how you handle these scenarios. If you want people to hold their questions until the end, or you want to keep from getting into the weeds on certain topics, you can create and manage a parking lot so that you can come back to those questions later if there's time. And if there's not time, you can follow up after the meeting, if necessary.

There's a lot to remember when you're presenting, and the best way to keep yourself cruising on autopilot is to know your material. The best way to know your material is to be appropriately prepared and rehearsed. When you know your material, it will show, and the rest will come easier to you.

Those "Treasured Guests"[1] in Attendance

Sometimes, you're going to end up with some people in the presentation who have different motives than your own. There could be any number of reasons that don't really matter; all that matters is that they're going to be a negative force that you're going to have to contend with in order to be successful. As an added benefit, you'll make others in the room feel better, too, when you manage these disruptions.

---

1   Use your favorite search engine to learn more about this term (hint: adding "Disney" will help).

That said, respectful, nonconfrontational dissent or requests for clarification should not be considered personal attacks against you or your team. Looking defensive or taking conflict personally can undermine your maturity as a leader and can result in you being left out of meetings where leadership expects and needs to hear contrasting or dissenting perspectives before making a decision. As your career escalates to more strategic levels in the organization, you'll be participating in, and likely leading, conversations that don't have predictable outcomes and where the future is less clear, and where people will disagree—sometimes strongly. That's a good thing.

Bad behavior from others, on the other hand, in a meeting (or in general) when you're presenting your work is never really acceptable. It's also an occasional reality, and hopefully not a frequent one for you or your team. If you're in the facilitator or presenter role, it's your job to remain in control of the situation and steer it toward a resolution. Diplomacy is your friend, and you can remind everyone in the room of the purpose of the meeting as well as the timing. If you've defined a place for questions or comments, you can politely ask people to wait until you are at the point of the presentation where feedback is welcome. You can use your parking lot or backlog to manage these types of scenarios, as well.

No matter what, you and anyone in the room who is involved in presenting the work need to subscribe to the John Dalton school of dealing with people: "Be nice until it's time not to be nice."[2]

Essentially, this means that first you're going to need to engage any challenging person in the room with strategies that can mitigate or downplay confrontation, and then you have some options that may not be very comfortable:

Be nice:

- **Ask the person if they would be open to meeting with you after the meeting is over to discuss any issues.**

  This allows you to continue presenting work and hopefully sets the person up to feel heard as well. ("Let's discuss this offline" is a good approach to take here.)

---

2 From 1989's *Road House* starring Patrick Swayze as John Dalton, who everyone thought would have been taller, and was still the best bouncer, ever.

- **Ask the person to help you understand the underlying issues at hand so that you can help to resolve them.**

  This approach enables you to clear the air, and while it will potentially drive the meeting off course for a period of time (if not entirely), it can help remove stress from the room.

- **Ask whether discussing this topic here and now is critical.**

  This is similar to suggesting meeting later individually, but now you're framing any questions as an opportunity that may or may not advance the group toward making the necessary decisions for which the meeting was called in the first place. This person may be aware of a significant dependency or correlation to what you're advocating for that you didn't account for, and you may need to adjust course now rather than simply moving on.

Until it's time *not* to be nice:

- **Ask the person if there is something that needs to be discussed now in this meeting with everyone that was not discussed in the time between the meeting being scheduled and it happening.**

  This puts some responsibility on the individual causing the disruption and could be perceived as confrontational; this is kind of one of those last resort things to use.

- **Ask the room to take a quick break; then approach the individual and politely ask them to leave.**

  You may want to clear this maneuver with some supervisory/support staff beforehand. This allows you to remove the distraction altogether, unless the person is a key decision-maker for the work that is being presented, in which case, it's best to call in support. This is another last resort approach.

- **Ask the room to stop the meeting and reschedule.**

  This allows you to work with the individual to understand the challenges and to collaborate for a path to move forward. This is definitely a last approach and will require finesse and your best customer service chops.

Hopefully, most of your opportunities will be more energetic and exciting instead of anxious and antagonizing. First and foremost, getting through the presentation of your work is your goal and ensuring that everyone has an opportunity to be heard. Occasionally, you'll end up in situations that are difficult, where it feels like time stands still as everyone watches how you handle the situation.

When you treat the presentation of your work like a meeting, and you spend time planning your agenda and knowing who the right attendees are, this provides you with the opportunity to get out in front of any potentially challenging topics or personalities. You'll be able to seek support from others who were invited, learn how to handle specific topics or avoid them altogether, or even make adjustments as to whom is invited.

ADVICE FROM THE FIELD

Activating Your Data Shield

by Brad Nunnally, coauthor of Designing the Conversation *and* UX Research

One aspect of presenting is dealing with the inevitable situation when one of the invitees disagrees with you and turns a nice professional meeting into a war of opinions. Fear not, for you probably already have all you need to disarm the situation and redirect the meeting. The best way to deal with conflicting opinions is by ensuring that any material that is presented is backed up by some sort of data that informed the insight or decision that you are responsible for communicating.

When the work that's being presented is centered around data, it ensures that any conflict isn't a battle of wills between you and another person. Rather, the person raising their concerns, or voicing their opinion, is disagreeing with the data that is behind what you're presenting. Arguing with data, especially if it is data that was collected through known sources and valid research methods, is difficult and gives you the opportunity to defuse any conflict. This can come in the form of opening up the meeting to group discussion, scheduling a follow-up later to review the supporting data in more detail, or simply reinforcing the fact that the data represents what was found or observed.

By using data in this manner, it helps establish your credibility and professionalism as well with the other stakeholders. No one likes to have a squabble during a meeting, because it's embarrassing for everyone involved. It doesn't matter who was right or wrong, because all that people will remember is that folks got into a tiff and it derailed the meeting. Data is a core resource that leaders can use to properly manage a room and ensure that any work presentation stays on topic and reaches the expected outcome defined in the agenda.

Handling Q & A

You will get questions, and there's no way to avoid it. You're presenting work, and people will want to understand how decisions were made or the rationale for approaches taken, no matter how clearly you think you articulate them. Part of why you spend time rehearsing and revising is to help you prepare for the questions from people in the meeting. It shouldn't surprise you that you'll be surprised by some of the questions from the room, no matter how much you rehearse.

When taking questions from people in your presentation, consider the following:

- **Repeat the question.**

  Make sure that you understand what's being asked, in your own words, and that whoever may be scribing is also clear on what's being asked.

- **IDK is AOK.**

  Don't be afraid to say "I don't know" to a question asked of you. It's not possible, nor plausible, to think you can know everything asked of you. It is, however, an opportunity to check the question to make sure it's within your scope and to let people know that you will follow up after the meeting with a response.

- **Being wrong is okay.**

  There's a chance you'll get something wrong. That's okay, too. While you should do your best to acknowledge when you don't know, it's also okay if you miss an answer. Acknowledge the mistake, correct yourself if you're able to, or let people know that you'll follow up after the meeting with an accurate response.

- **Speak the truth.**

  Don't fabricate anything about the work that's been done, and don't work so hard to placate someone in the room that you end up overpromising what can be delivered. Nearly every bit of work is tied to a budget of either money or time, and don't overcommit against the reality of those budgets.

The Art of Meeting Ownership in Difficult Situations

by Gail Swanson, design leader

Everyone faces people behaving badly in work situations and sometimes they are the people you are presenting to—stakeholders, product owners, people in power. Interrupting, dismissing rationale, evading decisions, or derailing the presentation altogether are commonplace. Most of what you'll see when presenting work fits into predictable categories; thus, it's possible to train yourself to handle these challenges. When you have a plan for challenging reactions to your work, you're able to focus on the outcome and suppress the natural yet personal reaction that escalates these issues.

One of the best tools is your curiosity. During user research, we use a perspective of non-leading inquiry to understand people's reactions to an experience. The same perspective will help you ferret out the cause of someone's negative reaction or desire to push in a different direction. It also buys you time to think and adjust your plan. Listen and be open. There will be something in the most outlandish point of view, which will be useful if you can let go and be open enough.

If the stakeholder's reaction means that your presentation as planned won't be productive, don't give up. Spend the time gathering the information you need to iterate. Diffuse the room's anxiety by celebrating that you uncovered an approach to eliminate, and the work so far was the right stimulus to get going in the right direction. "Good news, we are being agile!" It sounds like fluff, but I've used that tactic with sincerity and it has brought focus back to the room.

A team with a bad communication culture can be the most challenging presentation environment. Overtalking, interrupting, and

- **Manage the question askers.**

    Sometimes, it happens that someone in the room wants to share a personal anecdote that isn't really a question, or someone asks a bundle of questions in a rapid-fire sentence. Slow your questioner down and manage the time in the meeting to ensure that people have time to contribute. Make room for everyone to get a chance to ask their questions and participate—for example, if people start to monopolize the time allotted. Don't be shy about cutting a question or response short to make sure that you're receiving the critique you need.

soapboxing are big barriers to sharing the information about the work that is needed to move it forward. I've found that practicing "go-to" phrases makes it easier to reset the behavior of a group, albeit temporarily. Build your own facilitation lexicon for bad behavior and practice saying them out loud.

For example:

- "I do want to hear more about that point, Joe, but we have limited time. Let's make sure we get multiple perspectives at this point. Sasha, you looked like you had some input ..."

- "That's an interesting proposal. Help me understand how that works, given the constraints we talked about."

- "That's an interesting point. Let's make sure we have it down so that we can keep moving."

- "Hold up a second, I want to hear the rest of what Jane was saying. She may answer the question you were about to ask."

Lastly, know when to discuss the difficult position they are putting you in and co-own the solution. If you've been caught in endless churn, or being asked to start over during a final review, don't pretend like you'll be able to do the impossible without personal cost. Get the impacts out on the table. Don't assume that they know that it impacts the cost or delivery date, or that they know the cascading effects of any shifts being made. Make sure that you are clear and they are clear. You may find that they are happy with the work, but felt they should keep pushing toward perfection as long as there is room in the budget.

- **Get out of the way—pass to experts.**

  Don't feel obligated to answer every question that comes your way. Ideally, you'll not be presenting alone, and you'll have other people in the meeting who have contributed to the work being presented along the way. Hopefully, they're wholly capable and should also be prepared to answer questions where they have expertise. Give others the opportunity to share their knowledge and be a good team player.

You'll never do enough preparation to answer every question that you'll be asked—and that's all right! Preparation sets you up to do your best, and knowing how to handle questions as they come at you will help you get through the presentation.

Leveling Up Your Team

Model how you present your work—be it recommended design solutions or your preferred org model—for your teammates who may not have as much experience. Take a step back and ask yourself if you really need to be presenting the work, or if there are others closer to the work who could benefit from the experience and exposure. It's great to feel like the boss in the front of the room holding court, but it feels even better to watch one of your teammates build confidence in themselves and portray them as leaders to other influential peers in the organization.

Prior to the presentation, make time in your calendar to review their agenda, materials, and what outcomes they want to achieve from the meeting. This simple review makes sure that your teammates are set up for success before it's showtime.

During the meeting, resist the urge to interrupt or interject unless absolutely necessary. You've agreed to let your teammate present, and you've worked with them in advance of the meeting to prepare. It's now up to that person to deliver the presentation, so let them do it.

After the event, provide critique immediately after their presentation. Any room for improvement and points to emphasize that are still fresh in your head enable your less-experienced presenter to absorb as much as possible instead of waiting hours or days. We recommend scheduling a 15-minute review after the meeting itself so that your teammate is expecting critique and doesn't feel caught off guard when you say you want to provide feedback.

Wrapping Up

Design managers will likely find themselves in more presentations than they want to be in *and* needing to present more work more often than earlier in their careers as practitioners. But it's a great problem to have. It means, of course, that in many cases your presence is needed before a decision is made. Let's face it: when we say design needs a seat at the table, what it usually really means is that design needs to be in more meetings—and sooner.

Meeting and presentation culture varies from company to company, and some can be vastly different than others. Netflix, for example, has (had) a standing policy that people can leave a meeting whenever they feel it necessary to be somewhere else. In other orgs, people getting up and leaving with 20 minutes left would appear disrespectful to the presenter and the rest of the team. Design leaders can set their own rules for their presentations—and they should establish what culture they want to have when it comes to reviewing design work. The rules that you establish are the rules that the rest of the team will follow, and it sets an expectation for the behavior and outcomes that are best suited for the work you and your team are doing.

Like many attributes of design and leadership, presentation preparation is a skill that can be strengthened with practice and repetition. Don't risk your reputation or allow your influence in the organization to wane because you were careless with how you and your team prepared for presenting work. When the spotlight is on you or your team to drive toward a business decision, rely on your methods of preparation and concrete expectations to show your leadership, stakeholders, and colleagues that you take the spotlight seriously.

CHAPTER 12

Saying No

It's almost impossible to start writing this chapter without breathing a heavy sigh.

Invariably, the friendly publisher or kind editor will ask, "Can you have that chapter finished by tomorrow?"

<sighs> "Yes."

Most people inherently want to help. Most people want to solve problems. Most people want to rise above a challenge, and as such, telling someone no can seem like we're letting someone down, or we're not trying hard enough—or even worse, we're failing.

That said, saying yes brings with it a set of challenges of its own. *Yes* generally leads to:

- Additional work for someone (hint: you)

- Negotiating with someone else to take on additional work (hint: people who report to you)

- The potential of failure that can leave others wondering why you ever said yes to begin with

No and yes bring with them baggage. The baggage varies depending on who is asking the question, what the effort requires to accomplish, what the outcome or reward may be, what the risk of your response may be to your reputation, or a variety of other factors.

Decision-making is hard. No seems to be much harder than yes for many people.

Why Say No?

If you say yes to everything now, you'll soon find there is very little you can say yes to later. Experienced leaders know that you have to say no to a lot of things to say yes to a few great things. That doesn't mean you need to turn people down; it just means that you need to help find ways to say no for you that doesn't land as a no to them.

Saying no will also help you do better at the things you're supposed to be doing with your day. *The Wall Street Journal* reported that companies' best performers didn't work harder than their peers. "Instead, top performers mastered selectivity. Whenever they could, they carefully selected which priorities, tasks, meetings, customers, ideas or steps to undertake and which to let go. They then applied intense, targeted effort on those few priorities in order to excel."[1] This focus—and ultimately, saying no to less important activities and being more selective with what you say yes to—will give you the breathing room to succeed.

It's really easy to want to curry favor from others. It's also easy to quickly get overloaded with so many "short" tasks that you no longer have any spare minutes left to do your own work, and that, too, is a reflection on you. Say no to make sure that you're taking care of your responsibilities to your team and yourself, and to make sure that you're not a doormat.

When you stay focused on the things that are most valuable for your team, your team can easily follow suit. Saying no allows you to also show people outside of your team what the right types of requests are that will help you say yes to them.

No is your friend, young Padwan. You learned how to say it very early in life, and it should not be more difficult as you get older. You'll need to be comfortable framing the way you say no, and making sure that you're choosing your opportunities for yes and no in such a way that they don't impact your ability to be successful.

You need tools and a framework to make these key decisions.

Power and Social Dynamics Shape Saying No

If you grew up in the 1980s, you probably remember the ineffective and inadequate advertising campaign *Just Say No* that was supposed to help fight the "War on Drugs." It was easy for the kids in the commercials to say no to a joint or a handful of nonspecific pills. But these ads were overly simplistic and didn't provide a way for kids to realistically deal with the underlying, systemic factors of the recreational drug epidemic they would actually face in their lives.

All too often, people are expected to participate in activity or event planning meetings, side projects that don't go anywhere or lead to anything, or take on additional work. If and when people say no, they fear retribution, or risk being seen as selfish or not a team

---

1   Morten T. Hansen, "How to Succeed in Business? Do Less," *The Wall Street Journal*, January 12, 2018, www.wsj.com/articles/how-to-succeed-in-business-do-less-1515770816

player. What's even more insulting is that people are expected to say yes *with a smile*.[2]

As you read this chapter, please realize that *your* mileage *will* vary. Perhaps by a lot. Know the context in which you work, the relationships you have with others in positions of power, and what you have at risk if you say no. If you're concerned that you may find yourself in harm's way, either overtly or tacitly, it may be a good time to take stock of what to do about it.

Finally, be aware of the gravity of your own words as a leader. If you mention something to someone that has any sort of potential action involved, even in a passing conversation in a hallway, it can be perceived as a directive. Make sure that you're giving people clarity around your own words and requests.

No Is Difficult—in Every Direction

When you take a look at your org chart, there are people above, below, and sideways from you who are going to ask you to do things that you may not always be able—or want—to do. Some of the questions you get may put extra effort on you with the promise of a favorable review or bonus. Some of the questions you get may completely throw you off guard in ways you never expected.

According to your org chart, there are really three main types of people who can put you into a yes/no scenario: direct reports, supervisors, and peers. Certainly, there are people from outside of your direct reporting structure who may bring to bear scenarios where you'll need to decide which path forward is best for you, your team, and the objectives you're already committed to accomplishing.

The people who report to you will bring you questions that, once answered, allow them to continue forward in their work. They are more direction-seeking than direction-giving; however, that doesn't mean that they're going to be easy for you to answer. In a lot of cases, you'll be able to defer to things like "company policy" or a "handbook" or something else that someone else decided long ago. These

---

2 Judith A. Hall, Amy G. Halberstadt, and Christopher E. O'Brian, "'Subordination' and Nonverbal Sensitivity: A Study and Synthesis of Findings Based on Trait Measures," *Sex Roles* 37 (1997): 295–317, https://link.springer.com/article/10.1023/A:1025608105284

questions are great in that, for the most part, the answers are already there for you to interpret and share. In some cases, you may decide to challenge the answers you find because times change and policies may not always keep up.

> **NOTE** DON'T HESITATE TO HESITATE
>
> If you get asked something seeking your approval—whether the person asking is a direct report, supervisor, or peer—and you feel your temper, blood pressure or anxiety spike, don't inadvertently rush to an answer. Even if you know the answer will be no, taking some time before you communicate your decision will help you appear easier to work with and more thoughtful and intentional in your decision-making.

Some requests may be pretty straightforward. Others may be a bit outlandish, and perhaps a few will leave you wondering if there are hidden cameras somewhere and you're getting punked because there's *no way* someone would actually ask that question to their boss. Some theoretical questions you could receive might be similar to the following:

- "I got invited to speak at this two-day conference in New Zealand, can the company pay my airfare and hotel for two weeks?"

- "Can I expense my trip to that Hobbit place, too?"

- "My band got asked to open for a Poison cover band on a state fair tour this summer—is it cool if I take vacation, then sick time, then rack up PTO-debt and then come back?"

These questions may require you to seek advice from others in your reporting structure or even Human Resources.

You may also see a different side of folks on your team when they're told *no* after they're used to hearing *yes*. They may try going answer-shopping and ask someone else. They may feel entitled to a yes. Others may take your no personally and feel like you're singling them out. Some may basically wait until you have to ask them for something so they can quickly say no to make the situation all square. You may even get dragged on Glassdoor, subtweeted on Twitter, or dunked on Reddit because you've said no, regardless of the clarity and logic you presented when you had to decline a request. Management is fun, remember?

It's important to remember that we're not discussing using *no* as a mechanism to quickly shut people down. The word "no" is very powerful, and what's said with and in support of it is as important as the word itself. Don't shortchange your team or yourself by forgetting the context for the request that is being asked. Invest time in providing thoughtful and compassionate responses when you're unable to deliver the yes that someone is looking for, especially when it impacts their happiness inside or outside of work.

In some cases, policy helps you answer the questions from direct reports. That's what policy is for. Sometimes, it's your job to seek clarifications or exceptions to policy for good, appropriate reasons, or to even suggest policy changes to meet the needs of the current work being delivered.

When it's not a point of policy, your role is to provide direction and support.

Sometimes policies are created because someone figured out a way around a system and pulled some less-than-admirable behaviors to get their way, and now everyone else has to pay the price. Sometimes it's not that bad, and it's still in the way, and you might not be able to get past that.

Telling the Boss No

"I can't wait to go to this meeting and tell my boss no!" says nary a happy employee. Hey, it's tough enough to tell the folks in your personal life no, let alone the person who is responsible for writing your review.

As if telling your boss no isn't tough enough, there are times when your boss's boss, or their boss, or however many steps are left in the ladder that is your org chart, will ask you to do something, and that could become "no multiplied by the number of boss levels above you" more difficult to deal with.

Most senior leaders really only seek a sincere and very real assessment of whether or not you can accomplish what they're asking for, within the time frame that they've requested it. In some cases, sure, there will be fire-drill scenarios, and you'll be scrambling to get something completed by a deadline.

In a perfect world, these types of scenarios wouldn't happen; however, someone always needs something at some time that isn't convenient to a bunch of people, and the opportunity to say no simply may not exist if you still want to remain gainfully employed. Sometimes, the gainful employment of others can depend upon you, and that doesn't help you much at all.

Exception to the No Rule?

There are countless reasons why fire-drill scenarios happen. If you've ever worked in a job that had deadlines, customers, partners, clients, bosses, or other people, you've probably found yourself facing more work than might be able to be accomplished in a standard workday.

If you've ever worked in an industry where there are "Technical, Code, Design Challenges" that require teams to form and deliver quickly against a set of requirements in a short period of time, well, you're probably familiar with it as well.

If you've ever participated in a hackathon of any kind, you have at least witnessed someone else cramming in as much work as possible into a very limited period of time.

The point here is simple: sometimes, we end up with more work to deliver than the amount of time at our disposal. That's rough, especially if it happens frequently. Hopefully, it does not.

In most cases, the best way to respond to bosses who are asking for something additional to the work you and your team are already doing is to ask them to help prioritize the tasks ahead of you *with* you.

This doesn't need to be a power struggle, at all. Explain how you see the consequences of accepting the new task(s)—especially how it could impact what you're already working on. You want to provide your supervisor with a transparent and objective view into what you and your team are focused on in order to help arrive at an informed decision.

Framework for Saying No

Good news! To some degree, you already have this. If you've followed along and created a team charter (see Chapter 8, "Unifying the Team Culture with Charters), you've already spent a lot of time framing what your team is and wants to be. You've also identified steps to help your team realize its goals, and any request that doesn't map to those steps and those goals should require a pretty clear and sound rationale in order to get you to deviate course.

Your team charter is your first step in saying no to others. There are also other questions to ask yourself, and to weigh, prior to making a decision:

- **Is there a policy you can point to that makes it easy to say no?**

  Or that requires you to say yes?

- **Is there a priority you can point to?**

  Who owns the priority and where do they exist in your reporting structure?

  Can you verify the request and the reprioritization?

  What can be sacrificed in order to meet this request and who can help make that decision?

- **Is there a deadline?**

  What is the reason for the deadline?

  Is there overtime or rewards/compensation for shifting to meet this deadline?

  Who owns reprioritization and communication of the impact of the deadline (see also prioritization)?

- **What are the risks/rewards and consequences?**

  Can you lose your job? Can you afford to lose your job?

  Even worse, could people on your team lose their jobs?

  Or much worse, could people across the entire organization lose their jobs?

  Can you get team- or self-recognition? Reward? Bonus? Extra time off?

  Can you get a promotion? A position change?

  Can you afford to take on additional effort for you or your team?

- **Will you gain or lose political favor?**

  Does saying no mean you won't get asked again?

  Will your team or you gain capital to make requests for your own benefit and betterment?

- **Do you really have the option to say no?**

  Are you being "voluntold?" Occasionally, supervisors like to frame things as a question ("Do you want to take this on?") in order to give the perception of choice; however, sometimes in these scenarios when you say no, there never was an actual choice presented to you. We've also learned that you really don't earn bonus points for calling out the disingenuous request, and unless this is part of your exit strategy, you should weigh your options wisely.

- **Do you want to do the thing?**

  Is it going to be fun?

  Is it going to remove all that is good from your soul?

  Will your team love/despise you if you say yes?

- **Is there a budget? Or a charge/billing/job code (depending upon your organization)?**

  Really. Is there a budget?

  Where do you record your time to show what you were doing and that you were doing it for someone?

  If you don't have a budget, how is this getting paid for and how does it affect your bottom line?

Can your team pay their mortgage or rent with someone else's appreciation and their auction proceeds from the office supply cabinet?

- **Are there second or third order of consequences or impact that need to be more thoroughly considered?**

One of the greatest gifts you can give your team is the permission not to feel compelled to respond to ad hoc, nonsanctioned-by-you requests for work. That doesn't imply permission to be rude; it's permission to invoke your name to help with the decision-making process. In many cases, suggesting that a requestor speak to the person's supervisor will be enough to diffuse the request and simultaneously save face for your teammate.

The good news is that this can even help diffuse requests from someone above you in the org chart. They may not be wholly aware of your team's obligations and priorities, and bypassing you to fulfill a need may seem like a harmless attempt. When teammates defer back to you, it allows you to act on their behalf as a servant leader and protect their time, commitments, and obligations.

Put the Framework to Work

Now that you've seen a few methods for saying no or asking for more information before you decide how you'll act, think through the following questions and consider which approach you may take when responding.

- Can I use sick time for this day I need off?
- Can I attend a conference?
- Can I get work to pay for my commuting costs?
- Can I expense my costs for working at home?
- Can I make this a business trip?
- Can I take a leave of absence?
- Can I use work tools for personal use?
- Can I switch projects?
- Can I work with other people?
- Can someone else perform <these tasks>/<my job> because <reasons>?

- Can I transfer to a different part of the organization?

- Can I go from a full-time job to part-time?

- Can I get converted from a contractor to a full-time employee?

- Can I get a promotion?

- Can I get a raise?

- Can you do this thing that was assigned to me, and I think you'd be better at?

- Can this team member start behaving as a better teammate?

- Can you help me get this presentation ready for our boss?

- Your team does design, right? Great, we need <this thing,> and it shouldn't take you long. Thanks!

- Can you make this slide deck for me/my team/my boss?

- I've got this side project I'm working on, and it'd be really great if you/your designers could look at it and spruce it up, okay?

- Your work looks so much better than mine. Can't you just help me out here?

- Can you add some UX to this for me?

- Can you give me something you've worked on so I can show what else we can do?

In each case above, relying on policy won't work every time. There's a gray area that the person asking the questions is hoping you'll be comfortable just agreeing to—usually only to their benefit, not yours.

Consequences of Saying No

In many cases, the perceived consequence of saying no can be more challenging than the actual impact to you and your workload.

There may be times when you're requested to do something, and if you say no, the request will continue down the chain to your direct reports. You'll have to look at yourself in the mirror and decide if you're willing to pass a difficult decision on to someone else—or an opportunity, and opportunities should always be easier to share across your organization than challenging scenarios. Remember that your decision—your yes or no—also influences how people perceive you.

The folks on the 18F Experience Design Team created a useful list for helping teammates (or you, or anyone, anywhere, ever) say "no" (or "not yes") to others.

Redirect to your supervisor.

"I've got to focus on this, and if you check with (supervisor's name) and if (they're) cool with it, I'm happy to help!"

Just say no.

"No, I can't do that."

Ask them to prioritize.

"Here's a list of things I'm working on: (Trello or ZenHub link). Can you help me prioritize your request?"

See if you're an optional attendee.

"Is this a critical meeting, or can I catch up on the notes afterward?"

Defer until later.

"I want to be in that meeting so I can be aware of the kinds of decisions we're making, but I won't be able to work on this until after I finish (my project work)."

"Do you need a decision on this now, or does it fit with the schedule to wait for me to finish (my project work) so that I can dig into this topic and give you better input?"

"I would genuinely like to contribute, but I need to focus on my billable project right now. Can we add this to the backlog?"

"I can't take that on right now, but let's schedule a meeting (next week) to pick this up when I have more bandwidth."

"Sure. How's (date months in the future) for a start date on that?"

Dig into the deadline.

"Can you tell me more about the urgency of this request? I'm juggling project work right now, but I have more time next week."

Offer a specific limited thing instead.

"I have to focus on my {project work}, so I can't join this, but I can find half an hour to chat over your ideas with you. Let's find a time next week."

Acknowledge the project's value.

And *then* defer.

"That sounds like a really amazing project! Sadly, right now I don't have the (time/focus/brain-space) to contribute."

"Thanks so much for thinking of me! I think this is important work, but I'm in a crunch time with my project, and don't have the time to make this work within this timeline. If I can help in a smaller way (like proofing or a short chat), I'd be happy to!"

Recommend someone else.

"You know who's great at this? (Name)."

Slow things down with strategic questions.

"Before we start working on that, can we talk about your larger goals for the project?"

Offer alternatives.

"I'm not going to do that right now, because I don't think that's the right thing to do. Here are some alternative suggestions: (link to guidance or include things to think about)."

Gather some data for yourself.

"I have 32 hours for this project, 4 hours of meetings, and 20 free minutes. I just can't do this right now."

Give yourself permission to focus.

For yourself: "Choosing one thing to do for the next half hour doesn't mean I won't ever do the other things—the stakes aren't very high if I do the wrong thing for half an hour."

Courtesy of 18F's Handbook (https://handbook.18f.gov/how-to-say-no/)

There will be individuals—those "treasured guests"—who sometimes might be easier to just deal with than to constantly have them undermining your efforts or those of your team. It may be worthwhile to seek out opportunities to head them off at the pass by taking on tasks that they might not be fond of, or that they frequently ask for, in order to build a better rapport or working relationship. It may be easier to sign up for some of those efforts on your own terms rather than to have to litigate them later in a court of public (work) opinion.

There may also be scenarios where you've just said some form of no, a few too many times, and it's having a negative impact on the way you—and your team—are being viewed. That's rough, and while there is no shortage of designers in the industry who have stood up for the "right reasons" to do the work, there also happens to be no shortage of designers who might have been labeled "difficult" for the wrong reasons. (Those numbers are probably pretty close, not that we're counting.) That means that, unfortunately, you may have to decide between taking a hit on the image of you and your team or taking on a task you might normally deflect or defer in some way.

When you say yes to something difficult or challenging, so others don't have to be put into a position to say no, that's called *leadership*. Sometimes, the consequence of leadership is ensuring that others aren't faced with dilemmas you're willing to shoulder. When you say no to something difficult and you stop the request from moving any further while you seek clarification and understanding of the "why" behind it, that's leadership, too. Yes or no, let the buck stop with you, until it makes sense not to.

When Not to Say No

There are times when saying no may not be the best option. We've all been asked to do things we don't want to do or don't like to do, and sometimes, that's the way your work goes. You, too, will have the pleasure of asking people to do things that they don't like to do or don't want to do, and it probably won't be fun.

You made it to a leadership position, and while this may come across slightly as a cop-out, you should have a good sense for what some of the things are that you can say no to. When it's mission-critical, and you're being asked to do your part and pitch in, it may not be the time to say no (and this can help build trust and relationships that you may need throughout your work). When it's not a work-essential project, you're already overloaded, or you can't see a way to be successful, push back on the request and identify the challenges in place.

Got that? When you get a request, determine where on the scale from "Lose my job" to "Everyone else is pitching in and it makes sense" to "You're killing me, Smalls, I'm so underwater here!" you find yourself and your team.

Also, the people who are requesting the time of you and your team have an obligation of explaining to you the reasons you should be saying yes. Don't let others off the hook before you jump into answer mode.

Additionally, and not without importance, there may be other people in your life who depend upon you. You may be the sole provider in your household, you may be responsible for debt, you may have any number of reasons for which losing your job is something you cannot afford to do—especially when it's not on your terms. This doesn't mean you shouldn't have your own strong set of ethics; however, it does mean that saying no can be exceptionally challenging and have an awful lot of stress associated with it.

You have to make your own decisions about where your boundaries are for the types of work and the amounts of work that you are willing to take on.

What About Yes?

Look, we've been treating saying yes like it's not a great thing for almost an entire chapter now. That's really not the case! *Yes* is not the Lex Luthor in this Superman story by any stretch—however, feeling unable or uncomfortable to an approach to a no could be your kryptonite if you're not careful.

Yes is perfectly acceptable, and something you'll probably say much more often than no. That said, yes is really, really easy to say, frequently, even when you probably shouldn't. It's difficult to see ourselves as not being helpful, or as letting others down—because we're human, so we want to be liked, help others succeed, and be a team player!

Here are some perfectly valid reasons for when you may very well want to say yes:

- The request is for a senior leader with whom you haven't worked with yet and you want to grow the relationship.

- When the project is considered to be a stretch assignment—just out of your daily routine and job description so that you can learn and be recognized from the experience.

- When you can delegate some of your existing responsibilities to your team instead of doing everything yourself.

- When the project is aligned with your career or annual goals or values.

We're not suggesting that you should always say no or never say yes. We want to help you and those who report to you have options at your disposal to use in order to feel comfortable and empowered *not* to say yes. Sometimes, Admiral Ackbar, saying yes is most definitely a trap.

Saying No to Gender-Coded Requests

You may find yourself inadvertently asking people on your team—or being asked by others—to perform tasks that are heavily gender-coded. These situations almost always involve male managers in positions of power asking women to perform routine or administrative work that they would prefer simply not to do themselves.

Women are all too frequently asked to take notes in meetings, to get coffee for the rest of the team, or to do other errands. Refusing these requests can be tricky—especially if there's a pattern of people complying with the requests in the past.

In the 2014 edition of her book *Nice Girls Don't Get the Corner Office*, executive coach Lois P. Frankel suggests that women should decline these requests by referencing the fact that they have already completed other menial chores, and someone else can help out. In other situations, Frankel writes that women can avoid saying no outright by saying that the work they've been hired to do has to take priority, and if there's time, they'll try to complete the task. (This approach only works if you don't rush through your day job to pick up the balloons.[3])

---

3   Monica Torres, "How Women Should Say No to Thankless Office Tasks," Huffpost, July 23, 2019, www.huffpost.com/entry/women-serve-coffee-at-work-how-to-say-no_l_5d35c9bfe4b004b6adb352a5

So dudes: if the office table is a mess with post-birthday cake plates and beverages, don't ask or suggest that the women clean up while you go back to your email. Additionally, don't ignore the obvious signs that this is happening and continue to let it happen. Publicly distribute the tasks to everyone equally, at a minimum, and adjust when the efforts are off-balance. Likewise, don't expect your junior colleagues to perform workplace labor that you as the manager may feel is beneath you—lead by example and show that you're a member of the team.

Wrapping Up

As leaders, we're pretty much as afraid of people saying no to us as we are of saying it to others. There's no magic here: we want others to say yes to the things we ask them to do—and really good leaders will also tell you when you can say no, what your options are, and what their motivations are for asking you to take on more responsibility.

The best advice is to tell people all the things you'd want to know about a request, be as transparent as you can be, and be as flexible as possible. Then have the backs of the people you are directing. Be the umbrella for the crap that may head their way as they move forward at your behest.

Don't hesitate to draw lines between your work life and your personal life; you deserve to have both of those things, and you have a right to keep them separate. You'll likely not look back later in life and think, "I'm sure glad I worked extra that one week and didn't go … <do whatever is important to you in life>." Don't get so caught up in someone else's priorities that you forget your own.

Oh, and don't ask someone to do something you'd either not do yourself, or haven't done at some point in your career already. Don't get so caught up in your own priorities that you ask someone else to compromise their own.

Developing Designers

There is no shortage of activities that quickly fill the weekly calendar of most high-performing, effective design managers. Making sure that the team delivers awesome work that adds value on time. Maintaining a pipeline for hiring. Interviewing designers. Talking with your directs in one-on-one meetings. Forecasting. Shaping research. Scoping roadmaps. And probably lots of PowerPoints and spreadsheets.

But it's easy to find yourself with a full calendar and making your leadership happy, yet inadvertently neglecting one of the most important roles you can have as a manager: leading the development of your people's skills and helping them grow in their careers. In a study by global staffing firm Randstad, 73% of employers said fostering employee development was a priority, but only 49% of employees said leadership were actually adhering to this practice.[1]

In many cases, developing your people isn't just an altruistic mission that will make you feel like a good boss. It's good business for you and your employer to help your employees learn new or deeper approaches to skills they are interested in and give them an opportunity to apply those improved skills to their real world.

It makes sense: people generally want to feel like they are getting closer to mastering something, or trying something new, and if not, they'll leave to find those experiences elsewhere. In fact, a 2017 Gallup poll[2] found that 45% of Millennials and 31% of Gen Xers— basically the most populous generations in the workforce now— say a job that accelerates career development is very important.

But saying career development is important and actually developing careers can be difficult for some managers. How do you create time to focus on development? How do you know if it's working? What if these teammates take the skills you've helped build and leave to work across the street?

The good news is that, in most cases, career development isn't a zero-sum game where adding or building skills in one person is taking them away from someone else. Likewise, career development, when done well, is an emergent practice, where creating opportunity

1   "Developing Employee Career Paths and Ladders," Society for Human Resource Management, www.shrm.org/resourcesandtools/tools-and-samples/toolkits/pages/developingemployeecareerpathsandladders.aspx

2   *State of the American Workplace* (Gallup, 2018), www.gallup.com/workplace/238085/state-american-workplace-report-2017.aspx

for advancing in one skill or field yields advancement in others and among more people. In short, fostering an environment where career development is a priority becomes less about a finite activity and more about ingraining professional development in the culture itself. And, as the design leader, you may have to mandate that your team takes advantage of career development initiatives, whether that relates to attending conferences or contributing to projects. Because it's also easy for teams to lose a sense of their own development when they're in the consistent, repeatable cadence of delivering work.

We've seen that the demand for design work is increasing with no sign of slowing down.[3] Before you can scale the design practice to do more work across other parts of the organization or lines of business, you first need to identify how to develop the team you have today to meet not only the needs of the business, but also the needs of your teammates and colleagues.

Skill and Interest Mapping

Prior to any comprehensive development program (which doesn't necessarily have to be formal to be effective), it helps to start with an understanding of where each person is in their career at the moment and where they want to be in the future. It's highly likely that you've had these discussions during your one-on-one meetings with your directs, but if you're considering a more proactive, designed development program, you may want to revisit that conversation. Some people may have different responses when they know there may be some action behind their responses instead of what may have been said under different circumstances.

The initial assessment doesn't have to be comprehensive or digital. In fact, analog skill assessments can alleviate some of the unintentional pressure some of your teammates may feel if their manager asked them to complete some comprehensive skill matrix as if their job depended on it.

Jason Mesut, a UK-based design leader, has written extensively on a variety of the dimensions, arrangements, and visualizations to map

---

3   Babar Suleman, "UX Design Careers in 2018 and Beyond: The Future of the UX Designer," Boxes and Arrows, November 13, 2018, http://boxesandarrows.com /ux-design-careers-in-2018-and-beyond-the-future-of-the-ux-designer/

designers' skills, qualities, competence, and interests.[4] He even uses color-coded Skittles (see Figure 13.1) in professional development workshops to indicate what skills people currently have and how well they think they do these skills relative to a variety of design-specific and career frameworks. (They also provide a much-needed sugar rush after an intense day of self-reflection.)

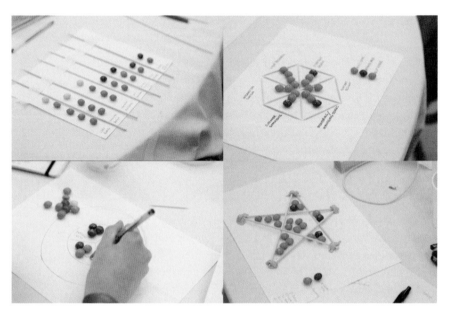

FIGURE 13.1
Jason Mesut uses a variety of methods, arrangements, and approaches to map where designers want to improve their skills or spend their time.

NOTE SHAPING DESIGNERS AND DESIGN TEAMS

Find the complete collection of Jason Mesut's Shaping Design series on Medium at **https://medium.com/shapingdesign**.

To conduct a similar skill assessment, create a radial diagram (see Figure 13.2) where each axis is a particular skill or activity, such as prototyping, visual design, or design systems. Leave a few blanks so that the participant can write their own, such as designing motion graphics, illustration, or well, just about anything else.

---

4   Jason Mesut, "Skittle Mapping," Medium, December 20, 2018, https://medium.com /shapingdesign/skittle-mapping-e0ec4d639ab7

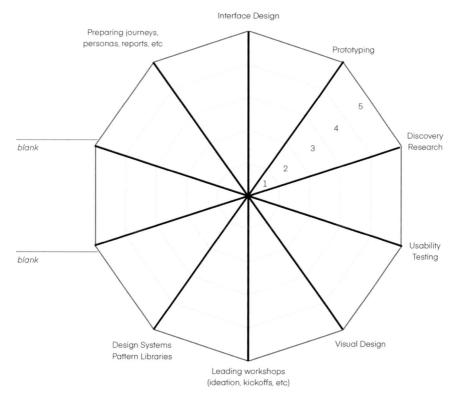

FIGURE 13.2

Use a radial diagram to represent how interested designers are in a variety of activities. We recommend allowing the participant to add two of their own interests.

Ask each participant to identify how often they do each of these skills or activities on a scale of 1–5. The perimeter of the radial diagram should reflect what each designer spends most of their time on, and closer to the center of the diagram should be things the designer rarely, if ever, does.

Next, repeat the activity but now mark how interested the person is in each of these skills, attributes, or activities.

These diagrams now reveal any gaps between what your teammates are doing that *doesn't* interest them, what they're *not* doing that *does* interest them, and what they *do enjoy* day in and day out.

It's important to do this task individually so that each designer feels comfortable accurately describing themselves. But just because it's an individual task doesn't mean the collective group responses aren't valuable. On the contrary, you now can identify patterns across your team that you may be able to address. For instance, if four or five designers on a team of ten said they want more opportunity to participate in more research, you can investigate where those feelings came from and take action. That may mean working with the research lead to try to develop those designers, or you may need to improve how research is positioned and offered to either clients or stakeholders.

Ultimately, you need a clear understanding of your team's interests—both collectively and at the individual level. You also should know how those needs align with what the organizational needs from your design team are. For example, if your firm doesn't have a glaring demand for visual design skills, don't set the expectation that everyone on your team must strive to reach a level 5 or mastery in visual design. It's just not necessary for them or you.

Use the following bullets as a lens in which you should balance individual, team, and organizational needs when planning your development program:

- **Individual interests:** Where an individual wants to grow and improve

  "I want to get better at managing up."

- **Team/group interests:** Where the entire team or group of individuals want to develop

  "We all need to improve our approach to discovery research."

- **Just-in-time development:** Where you may be weakest and who is interested in getting better to meet a near-term need

  "We need someone with front-end development skills, who understands CSS and wants to improve their comfort with public speaking to try leading next month's Design System workshop."

- **Long-term practice development:** Where your team can begin addressing needs for skills or specialization you expect to materialize later

  "We have strong visual designers who are interested in developing into data visualization specialists."

Starting with where the individuals on your team want to improve is a more positive and honest experience than asking "Hey, Steve, what are you terrible at?" and fixating on weaknesses or negative traits. Likewise, seeing the gap between how frequently a person is doing something relative to their interest secures a useful foundation where your team can learn and grow. However, you now need to structure your design team to accommodate that growth.

Career Ladders and Paths

Tiered career ladders, often composed of bands of different levels of rank and seniority, are nothing new to organizations. Originally designed in the early 20th century, these paths outlined how doting, grateful employees could climb from rung to rung for decades until their retirement.

Today, these ladders and paths still exist throughout organizations of all sizes and industries, but it's now clear that many of these ladders haven't been designed for designers and other important roles of the 21st century workforce.

If you've ever had the official job title of Product Development Associate Level 2, or Graphic Arts Developer, or Computer Developer Class B, despite your business card or your email signature more accurately labeling your role as UX Designer, Visual Designer, or Interaction Designer, you've probably felt like the organization didn't know what to do with you—at least for the long term.

As a result, many design leaders have taken it upon themselves to establish more specific career ladders for their design and product teams, both for managerial roles and independent contributors.

These design-centric career ladders provide practitioners and managers alike with a shared understanding of what is expected in each role and how to advance from one stage to another. (It's important to note that not all career paths go straight up. Some people want and should have the opportunity to take on different roles across an organization or to move in and out of management.)

These ladders can provide some autonomy and ownership of the designer's time in the organization, as well as clarity and structure with how their current role fits into the broader company. Furthermore, these career ladders also help the organization understand and compensate design roles more fairly with the broader market, hopefully making it easier for you to hire great people (and keep the already-great ones you have on board).

However, left unchecked, it's easy for career ladders to create unrealistic expectations or a punch list–like mentality to your team's work, where if you can just do four things, you can collect your merit badge promotion and advance to the next rank.

Creating your own design team career ladder can also be problematic if you don't tie parallels to other nondesign parts of the organization. If you are going out on your own, be sure that senior designers map in pay and performance to senior engineers, senior product managers, and senior business analysts. This improves compatibility with the rest of the company—for example, you'll see greater respect for your titles if *senior* in the design team means *senior* everywhere else.

Ladders, Not Checklists

Avoiding the checklist mentality is important for two reasons. First, designers will likely be averse to doing any work that's not in their particular career ladder because they won't think they're getting credit for their labor to advance. Second, you'll reduce the expectation that immediately doing one thing means it's time for an advancement. Instead, write your ladders to emphasize a pattern of exhibiting broader behaviors instead of tasks.

For instance, independent contributors should execute work autonomously despite ambiguity. Design managers should be expected to make sound decisions for the business and the broader design team. Neither of these are behaviors are easily just done once, and you can reinforce that your team will be expected to show they can perform these behaviors over several months, if not years.

Design Your Ladders: Pro Tips

If you see the need or benefit of crafting your own career ladders for your organization, there are some useful approaches that will get you started on the right foot.

- **Identify** what ladders already exist in your org (where'd they come from?) and how are they used elsewhere in the org. Determine if creating new design career ladders could also help your product management team.

- **Estimate** the scope of the undertaking to see your ladders become a reality, given the constraints and culture of the larger organization.

- If you have multiple design teams within your company, be sure to get the other design leaders to **buy into** a career ladder effort. Creating ladders for only one business unit among several teams will create a fragmented experience, even worse as you won't be aligned with your own design teams, let alone other teams in the organization.

- **Articulate and capture** where existing ladders fall short and why.

- **Review** recent job descriptions for skills, responsibilities, and expectations of roles and titles.

- **Plan to draft ladders for practitioner and manager tracks.** Manager tracks may be more similar to other pre-existing career ladders elsewhere in the company.

- **Socialize** your drafts with your team so they are aware and feel involved. Let them ask questions about where they stand and why.

- **Articulate** what people need to do, show, or accomplish to advance up or across the ladder.

- **Highlight** observable differences between roles and levels. If two traits sound ambiguously similar to you, it's likely your team won't understand the difference either.

- **Don't paint yourself into a corner** with the attributes or categories—keep them broad enough to allow for flexibility across specialties, roles, and seniority. For instance, resist the urge to say a senior designer must be able to prototype via a specific software tool, because your team may not be using that tool in the future, or such a tool may not be appropriate for your colleagues designing mobile apps on your team.

Career ladders—particularly those crafted just for designers—can vary as much as the organizations themselves in detail, scope, and format. Most, however, follow one of the following formats:

- One screen capturing every position, as seen in Basecamp's handbook available on Github here: https://github.com/basecamp/handbook/blob /master/titles-for-designers.md (See Figure 13.3, left.)

- A grid, matrix, or spreadsheet that displays criteria down the left and titles across sheets displaying how each progression is different than the last, such as Zendesk's approach in Figure 13.3, center.

    These approaches all have a few things in common that your ladders, at minimum, would likely benefit from, including the following:

    - The specific job title and where it fits among other titles

    - Functional and technical knowledge

    - Other teams with which they frequently work

    - The level of complexity and scope that each position is responsible for in a project, product, business unit, or other classification or structure

- Single-page descriptions of *each* step in the career ladder, with references and links to other positions in the ladder. Gov.UK follows this approach in Figure 13.3, right and is available at www.gov.uk/government /collections/digital-data-and-technology-profession-capability -framework.

Other ladders may also mention any management or leadership responsibilities, achievements, successes, or thought leadership expectations. Some ladders also call attention to what roles will not do, or who these roles will not work with, to create more clarity from position to position. For instance,

- **Frame** how to advance within the context of your corporate values and the design team charter's values.

- **Create** some tie into other senior titles that senior designers can grow into if they choose to evolve away from design, such as leading broader product development, customer experience, design operations, or across multiple business units. This starts with knowing what other career options are available through other ladders and paths in the organization.

the ladder may indicate that the Senior Product Design Manager may not facilitate mid-sprint demos to give Associate Product Designers the opportunity to grow their presentation skills.

If you need inspiration, check out progression.fyi and find what may work for your team.

FIGURE 13.3

These examples show the variety of methods you can use to structure your design practice's career paths. From left to right: Basecamp, Zendesk, Gov.UK.

- Likewise, don't just make your career ladders reflect an up-or-out approach to moving throughout the organization. **Show** where there are other opportunities to move horizontally to other teams. For instance, map how a research role can also move into marketing, or a prototyping role can move into the development organization.

- **Publish, maintain, and edit** your career paths: don't throw them in a drawer or stuff them onto an intranet site never to be seen again. Remind your colleagues that the ladders are available at all times and keep an edit log so people can see them as active documents.

- Similar to above, don't just throw your work onto a shared drive never to be seen again until you have a new head count or someone is eligible for a promotion. **Implement** and work with HR to enact your new ladders with the team you have today. If your company only converts or promotes groups in batches or windows, plan your implementation months in advance with HR.

- You may leave out something, or not fully understand the implications of a ladder attribute, so don't hesitate to **iterate** and change. As mentioned above, maintain a change log of what you edit, who made the change, and why it was necessary.

- **Revisit and recalibrate** at least two times a year to make sure that the career ladders represent current and future needs and continue to be aligned with the broader organization.

Then with a career ladder in hand, it's time to start framing how you'll actually rethink developing your team.

Designing a Development Playbook

It's pretty easy to say that managers should talk to the individuals on their teams to develop their interests and skills. But sometimes developing employees can seem amorphous, and specific development programs can be ephemeral.

But there is good news. Researchers have explored how people learn, how they're motivated, and how they acquire new skills and deepen their expertise in familiar fields for decades, and continue to be studied today. The tricky part, of course, is mapping that body of knowledge into an actionable, sustainable plan that integrates into your larger business objectives, team priorities, and the day-in, day-out routine of work.

A development playbook helps build a foundation to identify situations and approaches to develop your team, without being overprescriptive. Such a playbook coincides nicely with your career ladders and your individual skill and interest assessments as well, since those documents shape what your team wants to do and where they'll be striving to advance and grow in the company. This development playbook ultimately helps you define how you'll set your team up to succeed.

Expand the Scope of Responsibility

Creating more space for the individuals on your team to take on more ownership is fundamental to broadening or deepening skills, either as an independent contributor who wants to improve her craft or a manager leading people. Responsibility isn't just doing *more of the same*, though.

For example, to expand the scope of a visual designer's responsibility, don't just expect them to increase their output from five screens to ten screens. Completing more tasks won't grow their skills, other than perhaps looking for shortcuts while they update their résumé.

To help expand the scope of their role, work from a baseline of what a person has been responsible for and identify where you can expand some of that work. Revisit the career ladders you established to see if you've already outlined what next level of participation or engagement is necessary to officially advance, too.

Expansion of scope may mean your colleague will now be responsible for any of the following:

- Communicating decisions and questions to stakeholders
- Prioritizing how the work will be accomplished
- Spinning up the team of available people
- Improving how data influences decision-making
- Setting the cadence of check-ins with you as the manager
- Trying new research methods

When expanding scope, be sure to emphasize any constraints or limitations to the designer who will be venturing into unfamiliar territory. Communicate where there may be stress points in their process or workflow where you may need to be involved again to make sure things are progressing as they should. Likewise, provide feedback as quickly as possible if you see your colleagues start to bite off more than they can chew or make a questionable decision that may have adverse or unplanned consequences.

It will always be a judgment call when you have to involve yourself—do it too soon, and you'll seem like you're hovering and eliminating any chance of growth. Reassert yourself too late, and you risk something going sideways, if not south.

Instead, keep the outcome in mind. Ask yourself how much damage can really be done if someone tries something that hasn't been done before and fails, or doesn't complete something exactly like you would have done it.

Enable Autonomy

Creating an environment where your team feels empowered and engaged greatly improves their productivity and sense of purpose at work.[5] But some managers struggle with finding a balance between autonomy and ambiguity—after all, some say, how can you as the manager know what's going on if you tell your team to just come back to you when the project is complete?

But it's exactly that space where individuals can push their comfort zone to experience firsthand what works well and what may need adjustments if attempted again later. Often, the best approach to supporting autonomy—especially in less experienced individuals— is to emphasize outcomes and accountability to those outcomes.

This puts you as the senior manager in a position to care less about *how* the work is done, and more about making sure the work meets its goals and *is* done well.

Also, be clear about how frequently you expect check-ins, and be careful not to just ask for a status report during these check-ins. You risk neutralizing the potential for growth if you set the expectations that your colleagues should now just tell you everything they've been doing. Instead, ask questions about how they're perceiving their role, if there is anything they'd already do differently, and what they've learned since you last met. Ask when they've had to decide how to do something, and ask them about their thought process that led them to that decision.

That said, it's natural—and your responsibility to your team, the person you're developing, and your company—not to be totally checked out in the spirit of instilling autonomy. To effectively create an environment to improve autonomy, the answer isn't in reducing ambiguity through more check-ins, but instead *ensuring alignment* across individuals, teams, and management.

---

5   Jalal Hanaysha, "Examining the Effects of Employee Empowerment, Teamwork, and Employee Training on Organizational Commitment ," *Procedia - Social and Behavioral Sciences* 229 (August 19, 2016): 298–306. https://doi.org/10.1016/j.sbspro.2016.07.140

Alignment sets your team up for knowing where they're going without necessarily involving you in how they get there. Furthermore, the communication, conflict, and resolution for establishing that alignment across teams is an immensely valuable experience for your teammates who are trying to grow.

Emphasizing what has or hasn't worked in the past is another method of making sure that the folks on your team are improving autonomous decision-making while also making sure they're operating in a safe space with reduced risk. Laying out a series of options that have been tried before gives your colleague a starting point from which to try things or the opportunity to explore something entirely new. Either way, you are building an expectation that this person has the autonomy to make their own decisions, without being totally left out in the cold to survive on their own.

Show Their Work Matters

Creating an environment where people know their work matters may initially seem like a no-brainer or so obvious that it's not worth discussing here. But it's unfortunately all too easy to become so absorbed in your own day-to-day work that you, as the manager, neglect telling the team why their work is important.

Creating meaning and purpose in your team's work can be easy in some industries. In others, establishing this strong tie may prove more challenging. But to anyone who has ever spent time refining a prototype, mock-up, or customer journey that seemed like it never made an impact—if it was seen at all—can become demoralizing.

Instead, strengthen the connection between an individual's contributions and why those are important to them as designers and the company. In some cases, this can be as simple as reinforcing the broader ecosystem in which the designer's work will be used. Designers generally don't want to think they're only coming to work to move around boxes and arrows on a screen without knowing how the system will actually be used. Even just keeping designers involved in customer research improves their empathy with who is ultimately using the systems they build.

In addition, go beyond just providing greater context into how the team's work will be used and get involved yourself in more of your team's work. This is what Wharton School of Business faculty and author Adam Grant calls "closing the power distance."[6] Grant isn't suggesting that you meddle in your team's work or suddenly turn yourself into a hovering art director. Instead, he suggests that sitting in a few meetings can go a long way in reinforcing that this work is worthy of your time.

You'll need to communicate that you're making time for this meeting because things are going well, and not the opposite direction. Be engaged, supportive, and ask questions to reinforce to the team and its individuals that they have the autonomy to do the work as they see fit. Try to feel comfortable enough to let your team know what you don't understand in these meetings as well, so they see you respecting their expertise and how they go about their work.

Be sure to actively participate—so no phones, emails, or laptops—in design studio, mid- or end-of-sprint demos, research interviews, or prioritization exercises. In short, show respect. Ask questions—even if you think you know the answers. Let them answer when you ask before speaking again. Include the team members who don't always ask *you* what you think.

You can also inherently stress that your team's work is important to the company by involving the team or individuals in decisions that will impact them one way or another. As the leader, you'll likely need to exercise judgment to gauge when to involve others and to what level of detail you share. There's no shortage of topics that would likely be off limits until you're explicitly told what and when to share: mergers or acquisitions, reorganization efforts resulting in layoffs, and personal matters of individuals on your team. All of these topics should be explicitly shared only if and when you've been advised to do so.

But that said, you could certainly involve your team and stress the importance of their work if you were trying to improve a specific design practice or competency in the team and you're pursuing funding for more head count. Likewise, asking your team if they thought the current design team organization model was enabling them to do great work or getting in the way would also stress that you value the team's input. Even though you likely won't be able to do everything you discuss with your team, they'll still feel like their work is more important than if you didn't talk to them at all.

---

6   Adam Grant, *Power Moves: Lessons from Davos* (Newark: Audible Original, 2019).

Delegating Work

One of the most effective ways to develop your team and prioritize your time is to delegate work to the teammates you lead and manage. But sometimes it's much easier said than done, especially among recently promoted design managers who are leading teams for the first time in their careers.

Delegating work doesn't mean throwing the busy work to your team to offload it from your schedule. In fact, the more important the work is that you delegate, the greater chance your team recognizes you're taking an active role in improving their skills and their standing in the company. And in many cases, effective delegating will likely foster more opportunities for autonomous development, creating a virtuous cycle for you and your team. The more work you delegate, the more autonomous they become, and then you have higher profile, more strategic, or more challenging work to delegate all over again.

To practice your own ability to delegate meaningful work to your team, keep these tips in mind to ensure that all parties—you, your teammate to whom you're delegating the work, and your company— are satisfied and successful:

- **Focus on outcomes, not the process.**

  We covered focusing on outcomes instead of the process of how those outcomes are achieved in establishing autonomy in your teams, but it's worth repeating when delegating work as well. The focus of delegating work is making sure that your people can accomplish the task, however they see fit.

- **Set boundaries for failure.**

  You risk increasing the stress and anxiety levels of your colleague to whom you're delegating work if you don't address what happens if they stumble. Try to recommend moments or milestones they should reach. If they encounter some trouble achieving those expectations, they'll have a better understanding of when to pull their lifeline for help.

- **Provide context.**

  When delegating work, provide as much context and background information as necessary, including political implications of the project, personalities of other people they may not have worked with in the past, what led to the design team getting involved, and the business goals and intended impact of the engagement. This context is significant in not only ensuring the team's success, but also in drawing the bigger picture of why their involvement matters.

- **Show how it's been done before.**

  Chances are whatever you're delegating has been done before in some capacity. Share what worked and what didn't with your colleague so they aren't starting from scratch and repeating similar mistakes. Point to supporting research, such as personas, journeys, or prior prototypes and let them determine how to figure out if they're still relevant. Highlight parallels between projects they've already led and let them see if they can apply lessons or approaches to this new assignment.

- **Establish a cadence for feedback.**

  Create a set schedule (ahead of time for less experienced teammates, early in the engagement for more experienced colleagues) for when you can get status updates, ask questions, and see any work underway to avoid looking like you're micromanaging or don't trust the team or the leader you're trying to develop. Make sure that your colleague is comfortable with how often you'll check in. If you schedule updates too frequently, you risk looking like you're overbearing. If you schedule updates too far apart, it may look like the project isn't important enough for your time. Find that balance and adjust accordingly throughout the project.

- **Ensure psychological safety.**

  Try to remember that delegating work is meant to grow your colleagues' skills and their approaches to work in new or different capacities, relative to their normal duties. Therefore, you probably have a higher risk of something going sideways that you can use as teaching moments throughout the engagement. Before assigning anything, make sure that your colleagues are interested in the work and motivated to accomplish the job to the best of their ability. Stress that you're there to help guide when necessary or called upon, and that any stumbles are okay and manageable. If you need to provide corrective coaching, like most difficult discussions where there may be conflict, do it privately, and celebrate their leadership and accomplishments publicly to the whole team.

Be Clear with Limitations, Scope, and Authority

Establishing boundaries, expectations, and the scope of your team-mate's authority improves the chances of success for everyone when delegating work. When delegated work goes wrong, you can likely point to a lack of clarity in and alignment about what was expected of the person to whom the work was delegated in the first place. Articulating the boundaries between different levels of delegation ensures that there's little risk of mistaking what's expected of both you as the manager and your teammate.

Figure 13.4 visualizes where you need to commit the most time. The less experienced person to whom you're delegating work to will need more of your time to help support their efforts. The more experienced the teammate, the less you need to be involved when delegating work. Level 1 can be broken down into more distinct stages to be more granular if such additional structure is necessary. When in doubt, overexplain your expectations, particularly with teammates to whom you've never delegated work.

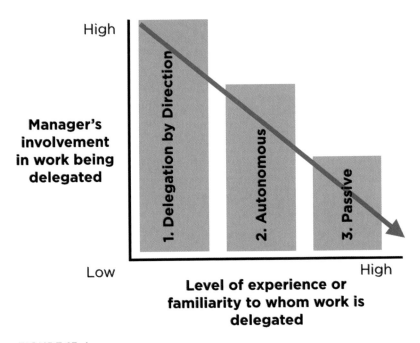

FIGURE 13.4

When delegating work, expect your level of involvement to decrease when tasking work to more senior or experienced colleagues.

Level 1: Delegate by Direction

The earliest level of delegation, delegating by direction, is usually appropriate for junior or early-career team members. At this level, you as the manager assign your colleague to research and assess an opportunity, issue, or problem. In this case, you would likely instruct the colleague where to look, what to look for, and how you want the results to be presented. Check-ins may be frequent and tactical to monitor progress. This is delegation only in the sense that this person is doing the task instead of someone else.

Stage 2 of level 1 loosens the expectations you provide to your teammate. You'll likely describe the end result you're expecting, but leave your colleague to decide how and what to research. They can provide alternatives, options, and approaches for solving the problem, but you'll ultimately decide how to continue. You may agree to check in with each other at each quarter or even at the halfway point of the effort.

Stage 3 of level 1 is where you've still delegated the work to your teammate, but you no longer need to structure the engagement. Your teammate may determine how to provide their conclusions or recommendations, but still is seeking your sign-off on which option to pursue before continuing. You may establish that your colleague determines when you both need to meet again once they have begun the project, rather than up front.

Level 2: Autonomous Delegation

This level is when you establish the challenge or opportunity you perceive and then ask your colleague to see it through and report back what they found, or how they addressed it, or if there was anything there in the first place. Your colleague makes the decision to pursue the opportunity, structures how action should be taken, executes the plan, and shares their findings after the fact. Scheduled check-ins will be focused on coaching the person's decision-making and prioritization and not about the status of the project.

Level 3: Passive Delegation

The highest level of delegation is when your teammate is able to identify opportunities, efforts, or projects that they feel deserve their attention and exploration. They bring back the results of their work and collaborate with you as to how to proceed. You as the manager may need to involve yourself to manage their availability, or the time of others, but your teammate isn't necessarily asking permission or reporting back with status updates. This level is framed as *passive* because you are trusting your colleague to prioritize their time to a project or opportunity that is out of their daily routine, and any interactions with your colleague are focused on either coaching or having you learn more about what your colleague is uncovering.

Delegation Pro-Tips

Delegating work is likely the fastest track of developing employees as they get real practice building skills they don't normally get to exercise during their daily routine of work. But it can go sideways fast if you and your colleagues to whom you delegate work aren't clear on outcomes, expectations, or other details. Keep some of these *dos* and *don'ts* in mind when delegating work to colleagues the next time you have a project on your desk that could grow the skills of someone on your team.

- **Don't swoop in if you think something is going astray.**

  Inserting yourself into how your colleague is approaching the problem undermines their tactics to address the project. Unless you see something dangerously going wrong, wait until your next check-in to talk about their decision-making that led them to what you see as wrong.

- **Don't describe how you'd do the work.**

  It can be easy to say, "Well, this is how I'd do it ..." when describing a new project you want to delegate. But doing so immediately robs your colleague of the valuable opportunity to learn what works and what doesn't for their own comfort and ability.

- **Do delegate real projects with real impact.**

  Your team will notice if the only projects you delegate are the ones that won't further your career. Chances are so will your boss. Instead, position your colleagues to lead the projects that can grow their own careers and set the future of your design and product team up for success.

- **Keep your own records of what you delegate and the results.**

  Keep a simple spreadsheet or running document of what projects you have delegated, to whom you delegated the work, and your impression of the results. It can be too easy to inadvertently keep delegating one kind of project to one person, so maintain a list to reduce the likelihood of unintentional bias and spread the wealth.

- **Do give positive reinforcement.**

  At the core of delegation is that the work isn't supposed to be something your colleague would normally do under typical circumstances. Make sure that you recognize their effort, even if it doesn't make a huge impact on the team or business, to show them that their interest in trying to grow and develop something is recognized.

- **Foster a delegation mindset across your team.**

  If you manage other managers, set the expectation that you want them to be delegating work to their directs as well. Create and sustain a culture of delegating work to continuously improve skillsets and keep your team interested and invested in the company's work.

Setting Goals

Establishing goals to meet either annual corporate human resources requirements or your own team's standard for measuring improvement over time can be challenging. After all, you may feel like you're forcing yourself to cram design goal pegs into corporate HR system holes, or you may feel like you're trying to predict the future. In other cases, you realize that product development is a team sport, and it's not always easy to just set goals on meeting deadlines or figuring out if something shipped or not.

While some goals may be tied to corporate performance that may be out of your ability to alter, there are some useful, if not creative, ways to set your team up to monitor how they've developed from one point in time to another.

First, try to establish goals that are aligned to corporate priorities and what your teammate is also interested in accomplishing. Goals that don't serve the business aren't likely to be approved in whatever checks and balances there may be in human resources, and likewise, goals that the designer doesn't feel vested in will create detachment and disinterest. For instance, don't create a goal for the designer to design a vision of the corporate website if there is no actual project to implement a new company web presence, and don't ask a user researcher to learn JavaScript just to satisfy a goal.

Also, make sure that the goals you set are quantifiable. Resist the urge to set goals with criteria such as "Designer ships clean, effective, and usable design solutions." Management or HR will see right through these goals as unsophisticated attempts to just give your teammates the highest grades possible because they work for you.

Be sure to review goals with your teammates periodically—no one wants to be surprised that they may miss a goal or that they're inadvertently underperforming. Clearly communicating progress toward goals—even if it's bad news—will always be received and respected more than the person who waits until the last minute to tell someone they didn't meet their goals.

Instead, try riffing off of these examples in Table 13.1 to see if they work for you and your team.

TABLE 13.1   EXAMPLE GOALS FOR DIFFERENT ROLES

Role	Goal	Reason
UX Designer	Prepare and present a design strategy deck establishing your approach to testing, validating, and implementing a solution for the summer and fall release.	You're expecting a designer to articulate the problem and approach to solve a valid business problem that not only helps frame their understanding of the context, but also improves their speaking and presentation skills.
UX Researcher	Summarize principles of customer research to three teams in the company who don't currently interview customers. Stretch goal: conduct one campaign of discovery interviews with one of these teams.	This goal evangelizes good customer research and creates an additional benefit if the publicity campaign results in additional research. The researcher working toward this goal expands their network and influence in the company, as well as presents to audiences who may not be entirely supportive.
UX Manager	Create development plans and delegate at least three projects to every direct report.	To maintain and support a culture of developing your team, incentivize your own managers to develop their directs as well.

Regardless of what goals you select, there are a handful of tips to keep in mind when crafting goals for your team:

- Rely on your career ladders to act as a roadmap for where your team is ultimately progressing.

- Be careful not to conflate tasks with goals. Designing a website home page is a task; leading a multidisciplinary team for a three-month, high-profile engagement and presenting its successes to management is a goal.

- Keep goals consistent within roles and titles of your team.

- Communicate if, and to what degree, how goal performance impacts compensation.

- Monitor how other peers of the design team are measured in their goals, such as product management, marketing, and front-end development teams.

Performance Reviews

In many ways, performance reviews are like a useful customer journey or an effective persona—the value may initially seem like it's the deliverable itself, when under closer analysis, the real benefit is in the exercises completed to create the document.

Performance reviews are most valuable when they're not a surprise to anyone, because you've been developing your team members year-round. The review becomes a formality.

However, in some organizations, the performance review can still be a high-stress event where the outcomes are unknown, there is little or no relationship between the reviewer and the reviewee, and the person who is getting reviewed doesn't feel like they've grown at all or even knows a path forward to grow.

To conduct an effective performance review, your work starts long before the meeting is on the calendar. You'll want notes, records, and artifacts that will help you recall how your colleague performed relative to their own goals and the company's expectations. This isn't to create a Big Brother state of monitoring everything that your team does. Instead, you'll be able to avoid recency bias when discussing projects across a 12-month span. It's way too easy to focus on what your colleague did two weeks ago relative to the significant project they led 10 months ago.

To reduce anxiety in your team, be up front with the format of the performance review—describe to everyone how long it is, what you'll discuss, and what you hope you'll both leave with at the end.

Finally, if the corporate or HR approach to performance reviews is overly cold, detached, or doesn't reflect how the design team's culture operates, don't dismiss the idea of crafting your own approach to a more humane, respectful performance review process.

Continuous Feedback

Many organizations that are concerned that the annual performance review is rife with problems are shifting to have their employees provide continuous feedback throughout the year. In many cases, these companies will enlist an online tool to dispatch surveys of three to five questions with cheery questions and responses to choose from about your colleagues and management. These tools can be great to say that you're now operating in an environment that supports continuous feedback, but like many things, it's what you do with the data that really counts. You also don't necessarily need yet another software platform to create this environment either.

Much like critiquing design work, the best feedback is specific, actionable, timely, and attainable. (*Oh, is that all?*) Let's examine each in the context of providing feedback relative to the career development of your colleagues instead of the artifacts they design.

- **Specific:** Make your feedback as specific as possible, particularly relative to the employee's development goals and the career ladder. Cite the behavior you observed, and how they should either continue doing that same behavior or recommend an adjustment to continue toward their goals. Few things are worse than hearing hand-wavy vague descriptions of behavior that are ambiguous and can't be attributed to a point in time.

- **Actionable:** There should be a way that your teammate can listen to your perspective and put it into practice. Providing actionable feedback can be as simple as recommending a blog post or a book that seems relevant to observed behavior. In other cases, you may want to provide an action plan of smaller tasks, intentions, and outcomes to change or improve a skill. Regardless, resist just settling for "you should try harder" or "that wasn't what we were expecting," which doesn't do anyone any good.

- **Timely:** Continuous feedback implies that you're not waiting for dates on a calendar to indicate when you'll give feedback—it can and should be expected at any time. As such, try to provide feedback as close as possible to when an event was observed. Naturally, if tensions rise or you sense defensiveness in either you or your colleague, don't hesitate to call a time-out and continue the conversation later.

- **Attainable:** Any feedback you recommend should be feasible for your teammate to accomplish, particularly when you're trying to target your feedback toward goals tracked over weeks and months. Strike a balance between things your colleague can do in the short run that build up to bigger accomplishments over time.

Finally, continuous feedback shouldn't be mistaken for a reactionary model for managers to talk to their teams. Yes, we've discussed observing behavior to trigger a conversation, but that doesn't imply you as the manager can't proactively address a colleague. Imagine reading something on your commute that would benefit someone on your team—you'd probably send it to them without hesitation. Similarly, if you have the opportunity to volunteer an insight that will help with your colleague's development—even if it may mean asking what initially feels like an uncomfortable question—you'll be improving your relationship with your teammates while continuing to foster an environment of continuous development in your team.

Coaching, Mentoring, and Sponsoring People

Coaching, mentoring, and sponsoring designers can be especially rewarding to you and valuable for the people you help. To many people looking back on their careers, the most influential and most impactful people aren't their managers, but their mentors or allies who coached them through difficult decisions. Let's explore the basics of each role and where these roles can apply to your work.

Coach

There are two varieties of coaches—the manager who coaches more established or senior colleagues who may not need the tactical oversight they did early in their careers, and secondly, the people who are trained and certified as coaches.

When coaching people on your own team, you strike a balance between helping your teammate adjust their behavior to meet their own goals and their responsibilities to your mutual employer. In many cases, whatever advice you give will be delivered through the lens of acting in the interests of the company.

Much of your job likely already involves some coaching, both in your one-on-ones with your team, when you're providing feedback, and when you're doing your best to resolve a conflict or set a good example for your team with your own behavior. Often, when you're asking open-ended questions and listening more than you are giving answers or your point of view, you're coaching. While coaching, you're a conduit for helping people realize what next steps to take, how to get there, and how to know if they've been successful.

Coaches who don't actively manage the person they're coaching may have a different mandate. In many cases, these coaches have undergone rigorous (not to mention expensive) training and a certification program to be officially recognized as a coach. While some coaches may work with their clients through your employer, other coaches may have nothing to do with your day job. As such, it's unlikely these coaches will share your background, know your domain or industry, or understand the personalities or politics of your organization. That's almost always a good thing.

These coaches will often work within an established period of time to define your goals and the outcomes you want to see. They'll give you explicit exercises or tools to meet those goals. Coaches aren't hired to be your friend or your champion—they're there to make you better than you are today.

> **TIP** COACHING TIPS
>
> **When *coaching*, you might say:**
>
> "Let's develop a three-month plan to improve how you're prioritizing projects."
>
> "What led you to choose that path? Would you do it differently knowing what you know now?"
>
> "What do you think success will look like in six months? How will you know you've achieved it?"

Mentor

Mentors are different than coaches in a lot of ways—they probably have extensive experience navigating the waters you're swimming in. They probably have some industry or professional experience similar to you. And they probably aren't your boss, nor should you expect to mentor the people who report directly to you. In many cases, the further mentors or mentees are from your daily work, the more effective they can be.

Mentors listen to your challenges, offer advice, and will talk through available options to a given situation. For example, if you're mentoring someone, they may ask you about negotiating salary, or if they should consider undertaking a new challenge at work with high risk but a big upside.

Mentoring is usually pretty passive, which distinguishes it from sponsorship. As a mentor, you're usually providing advice; likewise, when talking to your own mentor, you're likely expecting their perspective, anecdotes, and stories.

When considering if you could use the advice of another mentor, take stock of who you already consider to be your mentors. It may be a good time to consider diversifying the experience, background, or industry of those you consider to be your mentors so that you can have a wider network of people to draw from.

> **TIP** MENTORING TIPS
>
> **When *mentoring*, you might say:**
>
> "I want to share how I encountered a similar situation."
>
> "When I was in your position, I was too risk-averse. This is how I started to change that behavior."
>
> "When I had a difficult boss, this is how I approached it every day."

Sponsor

Sponsors take a more active role than mentors in developing the person they're working with. Instead of giving advice from their own experience, or asking how they can help, sponsors effectively make things happen to improve the visibility or responsibility of the person they are sponsoring.

The Center for Talent Innovation's Julia Taylor Kennedy and Pooja Jain-Link summed up sponsorship as follows:

> A sponsor has three primary responsibilities: to believe in and go out on a limb for their protégé; to use their organizational capital, both publicly and behind closed doors, to push for their protégé's promotion; and to provide their protégé with "air cover" for risk-taking.[7]

In short, it's more action and less talk.

Sponsorship is critical for developing colleagues—particularly women and people of color—who need improved access, promotion, and visibility. Without sponsorship, it's too easy for people to go unnoticed; as a sponsor, you take it on yourself to see that doesn't happen. Sponsorship also mitigates the risk that what worked for you may have the opposite result for others. It's easy for a mentor whose success was enabled by privilege to say "When I wanted something, I spoke up and worked hard and made sure I got it." It's far different for someone who isn't in a position to speak up, or whose cultural upbringing downplays speaking up, to succeed without someone else moving a chess piece here and there to help that person succeed.

Sponsorship, it can be said, is dropping down another, sturdier ladder that helped you get to the top, instead of just pulling up the ladder you used to get to the top.

TIP SPONSOR TIPS

When *sponsoring*, you might say:

"I suggested you present the team's work at the annual Sales Kickoff."

"I reached out to the conference organizer to ask you about speaking at their event."

"I nominated you to participate in the company's Leadership Development program."

---

7   Julia Taylor Kennedy and Pooja Jain-Link, "Sponsors Need to Stop Acting Like Mentors," *Harvard Business Review*, February 26, 2019, https://hbr.org/2019/02/sponsors-need-to-stop-acting-like-mentors

Developing New Managers

Managing new managers can be one of the most rewarding endeavors of your time with the team. You have the front row seat to see someone grow from individually contributing successfully to trying something new and uncomfortable, and later witnessing them grow the careers of others.

To ensure that the new manager and their team of directs are successful and fruitful in the new working relationship, set clear expectations of what is expected of the new manager, and be on the lookout for a few warning signs that you may need to intervene for the benefit of the new manager and their team.

Much of this work begins before the new manager is managing anyone. First, stress that management is going to be a different job, using different skills that the manager-to-be hasn't used as frequently or as importantly as they will be expected to do now.

Talk to the team that they will be managing as well. Let everyone know you'll want to do a skip interview after 30 and 90 days to just get a better understanding of the relationship, so the team doesn't think their manager is doing anything wrong when you start putting time on their calendars.

Also, reinforce to your new manager that if they don't think managing is a fit that it's okay—in fact, preferred—that they return to their role as a contributor, rather than trying to manage people when it's just not working.

Expect yourself to be more proactive when coaching your new manager, even if it just means offering books or blogs to read, and in the spirit of continuous feedback discussed earlier in this chapter, recognize and act on coachable moments when you see the opportunity—don't wait for your one-on-ones.

Occasionally, there are some warning signs that the new manager may be struggling. If you see or hear about these situations occurring, intervene quickly and decisively for the good of the manager and the team.

- **Struggling to separate the prior role and new role:** Watch for signs that the new manager is still in a delivery mindset, or focuses too much time on the assets that the team is producing and not the team itself.

- **Micromanagement:** You may not see this directly, but your skip-level meetings should reveal if the new manager is constantly checking in, requesting status updates, or monitoring when their new team is arriving at work, how long their lunches last, and when they leave for the day.

- **Little or no delegation:** Since delegation is often difficult, even for experienced managers, look for signs that the new manager is taking on too much for himself or herself. Prepare yourself to coach your new manager on how to identify opportunities for delegation within the team based on the criteria discussed earlier in this chapter.

- **Increased hours:** This can be a by-product of many aspects mentioned here—still trying to deliver work, micromanaging team members, and doing work themselves because nothing has been delegated to others. If you observe a significant and consistent change in when your new manager arrives at or leaves work, begins sending emails at all hours of the day (and night), and exhibits more time at their desk, be sure to explore why, even if your next one-on-one isn't scheduled for another week.

- **Fixing the work of their team:** Effective managers have learned to suppress any feelings, no matter how common, that they can just do it all themselves, and it will be done sooner and better. But new managers haven't developed that skill yet, and they may intervene with their team's work instead of working with their colleagues to give them a chance to improve it themselves. While the manager fixing their team's work feels like they're doing what's best for the company and the team, this manager risks losing the trust of the team they are trying to earn by diving into their work and assisting.

Helping new managers develop their interpersonal skills, communication techniques, prioritization abilities, and trusting their teams are invaluable to their careers and your organization. Make the extra time now to improve everyone's chances for success over time, in order to find yourself creating another virtuous cycle of growth in your design organization.

Developing Yourself

It's so easy to focus on developing your team and their time at your design team that you can inadvertently let your own development wane. To make sure that you continue looking out for "number 1," take a few moments to take stock of where you are right now and what successes you need to experience to consider yourself fulfilled.

If your design team career ladder has means of crossing into other cross-department leadership roles, work with your own manager to identify how you can continue working toward those outcomes, if that's what you want. If such a career ladder doesn't exist, you'll likely have to look to your bosses and their peers to see if and where you could fit in should you plan to stay in your organization for the long haul.

Even when things are going well at your job and you think you could stick around for years, keep your résumé up-to-date with personal and team wins to monitor what jobs you're attracting (even if you're not officially on the lookout for a new job). If you keep getting calls about jobs that aren't interesting to you or were appropriate five or ten years ago, consider if the recruiters are terrible at sourcing, or consider if you need to rethink the material in your résumé to better represent who you are today and what work you'll be doing in the future.

Interview with companies that seem to be doing interesting things with interesting people. Not only is interviewing a skill that can atrophy without practice, but you'll also clarify what you actually want next in your career by talking to others, gauging the landscape of what is available, and also identifying what you clearly don't want to be doing.

Take stock if you're growing professionally at your job, leading design in your organization. It's valuable to question whether you're developing into a senior leader, or if you're just doing the same things, at the same levels, with the same caliber of people, year in and year out. If not much has changed, chances are neither have you.

If you're not seeing exactly what you hoped for when conducting this brief personal audit, talk to your own manager to see what options the company has available for you. Perhaps the organization has professional coaching opportunities available to its staff, or it may agree to fund a career coach whom you can work with.

Here are some questions to ask yourself:

- Do I still believe in the vision of this company?

- Is what I'm doing today any different than what I was doing a year ago? Is this what I want to be doing?

- What have I learned in the last 12 months? Is that in line with my own career goals and aspirations?

- Am I getting enough feedback to know where I could be growing?

Be careful to avoid basing your own career path, or what you should be doing, or what titles you should have, based on others, regardless if they're people you know or just people on Twitter (or people who write books, *trust us*). What works somewhere in someone else's situation probably doesn't wholly apply to where you are in your career, and it's just not worth the mental energy keeping up with the Joneses, regardless if those Joneses are VPs of Design, Heads of Design, or calling themselves Chief Design Officers on LinkedIn.

Finally, resist letting developing your own career path consume you, but don't take it for granted that the company will always look out for you. It's totally understandable that you don't know exactly what you want next, but you can write down questions to ask yourself to determine if you're getting any closer to seeing if you're heading in the right direction.

Wrapping Up

If design is the rendering of intent, as some say, then the designer's career development is the rendering of design leadership. Whether you're leading a scrappy few people in a startup or you're navigating a large matrixed enterprise, identifying how to grow your team's skills and interests plays a huge part in your own success as a leader.

Learning the constraints and opportunities within your organization is one of the first steps toward knowing what you can build from, or where you'll need to start from scratch, and it can seem daunting at times.

But doing nothing because your team is too busy, or you have too many projects underway right now, or your team is happy where they are, is a myopic perspective that will quickly fester into resentment, contempt, and ultimately a toxic environment where the team feels detached from you, as the leader, and the company.

Instead, turn developing your team into an opportunity to differentiate from other teams and companies. Invest the time to know when the individuals on your team are ready to manage others and help them along their journey. Proactively provide feedback under safe circumstances to show that you're thinking of your team long before performance reviews begin.

It's yet another tall order for the design manager, and it can be all too easy to neglect yourself when making sure that your design team is developing according to the plan. You should coach, mentor, and sponsor the people around you, and in the process, grow your own abilities, too.

Scaling Design

Actively scaling the design practice to meet the changing needs of the larger organization can be the inflection point where you start evolving from a competent design manager to a strategic business leader.

It means tailoring your approaches, people, and delivery in a repeatable, governed framework that can be applied consistently as the needs of the organization grow. Often, this means identifying which design methods work as a team of five and determining how those need to change to produce similar results as a team of 15, 50, or 150.

As the design manager, you'll be the expert on how to make those adjustments, identify how those adjustments are working, and make sure that you have the right people in place at those new levels of size and responsibility.

Consider any of these situations, all of which will test the scalability of a design organization:

- Your company undergoes a corporate reorganization, and you're now expected to manage another design team in the organization that previously didn't report to you—and the products that team designs.

- Your team gets the budget to hire 15 more designers in the next six months in order to address growth.

- Your team's budget is cut by 50%, but you're still expected to service the same portfolio of products.

- Your development organization agrees to use your CSS across the company's portfolio.

- You join an organization that already has other self-reliant design teams working on different projects with design leadership that doesn't report to you, and with development teams that use different technologies than your team's development partners.

- Your team is expected to design and research for an additional business unit without adding resources.

While no one likes to hear "just do more with less," doing more with more can be equally challenging, or doing more differently can also bring new challenges with which you may not be familiar. How resilient your team is will determine how well you can adapt to the demands of the future.

Resilient, robust teams are prepared to handle these challenges through a range of approaches and techniques that can prepare you for the unknown—both the good and the bad, for scaling up, down, or across the organization, and the type of work you do for the company.

The best way to prepare for the future of your team is to be honest with yourself when assessing the team that you have today. The issues threatening your ability to scale likely are not found in whether you have good designers on the team or not, or even the tools you have at your disposal. It's more about how the team functions. Note that we've covered a lot of techniques in this book that will improve your ability to scale, such as improving hiring beginning in Chapter 3, "Designing Your Hiring Process," onboarding those new hires in Chapter 7, "Offers, Negotiations, and Onboarding," and presenting work in Chapter 11, "Presenting Work." The methods discussed in those chapters will be worth revisiting when seen in the context of how to better prepare your team for adapting to the new demands of scaling up.

Threats to Scaling Design

Most threats to your team's ability to scale are often similar to those that many people face in other organizations, regardless of market cap, team size, age of the company, or industry. In many cases and with few exceptions, the challenges to successfully scaling have very little to do with the practice of design. Instead, the political and cultural climate of the organization in which design is expected to do more often creates the roadblocks and the headaches.

Let's look at some of the symptoms facing design teams trying to scale, and how and why attempting to scale in that environment will be particularly challenging.

Threat 1: Tunnel Vision

- **Symptoms:** The design team is closed off from the rest of the organization. Designers usually don't know what happens to their work after it's completed or why they are working on their assignments

- **Threats to scaling:** It's difficult—if not impossible—to grow in an organization if you only focus on one thing. Tunnel vision limits how your work or your methods could be used elsewhere in the organization. What's worse, without a clear understanding of the impact of their work on the business or their users, designers don't feel vested in their work or valued for their contributions.

Threat 2: Overly Specialized Approaches and Techniques

- **Symptoms:** These design teams do one thing and do it well, often in a familiar, expected way by management and the rest of the organization. Teams may closely follow a discover—> design—>develop—>deploy process flow that produces useful, effective wireframes or high-fidelity comps. But on new projects with new teams, designers are unclear or uncomfortable about how to begin if they have to start somewhere else in that process or aren't seeing the process completed. Or perhaps the designers don't have sufficient feedback loops built into each stage of the process. Then if another team or project needs new work, there may not be enough opportunities to make sure that the design work is aligned with the goals of the organization and customer.

- **Threats to scaling:** The best teams have diverse skill sets that can adapt to the changing needs of the organization. If your team needs to shift its methods, delivery, and output to meet the expectations of another department, client, or project, how you deal with that change will determine your success. For example, if none of your team is comfortable prototyping because you've never had to do it with your current projects, you risk letting your organization down if you're unprepared to prototype new projects.

Threat 3: Ineffective or Overmatched Tools

- **Symptoms:** Similar to the threats of overspecialization, the tools your team uses may only be appropriate for how you work today and aren't easily shared with other teams, or applicable to another project. These pain points usually rear their head when teams want to reuse past work, artifacts aren't where they should be, or you have to copy and paste one design solution to another, rendering both implementations susceptible to being out-of-date. As a design manager, you're likely aware that your team is trying to create repeatable tasks, or asking for new tools, but you recognize that these decisions shouldn't be made just as they arise and make the situation worse. You realize you should be talking to other teams, but are not sure where to start or how to articulate the problem or suggest alternatives.

- **Threats to scaling:** Your tools, much like your team's work, need to be shareable, accessible, and editable without courting disaster. If other teams can't use your work, build on your prior efforts, or pick up where you left off, you reduce the likelihood those teams will try to work with you in the future. This situation often happens when teams discuss the benefits of design systems to better reconcile what tools are best for the jobs of the design teams today and improve resiliency for the future. We'll explore this more later in this chapter in "Scaling via Design Systems."

Threat 4: Organizational Misunderstanding of Design

- **Symptoms:** Unlike the prior issues, such as process or tools, an organization's misunderstanding of design initially seems like the one challenge that has the least to do with you and your team. You might believe that if you put your head down and produce work, you won't get caught up in politics. But the symptoms are there: executives who think design is decoration; engineers who think design holds them up; and marketers who want style over substance. Even fellow designers may think they have their remit to make or do one thing and nothing else. Resources are scarce, information security is overly restrictive, and little early access to customers are all signs the organization doesn't understand the value of design.

- **Threats to scaling:** An organization that doesn't understand design won't be prepared to address the steps to make scaling possible. If design is viewed as decoration, then head count won't be strategically allocated; rather, as a design manager, you'll get contractors at the last second. Management won't review processes to adapt to more work completed by more teams. You may find yourself with more work, but you're not scaling, you're just busier.

Threat 5: A *LOT* of Design and a Lot of Designers

- **Symptoms:** If you've worked in a large company that employs several design teams, many of these symptoms may sound familiar: one technology team practices waterfall software development, while another team practices agile. The back-office design team isn't allowed to talk to customers. The designers over there call a six-person, one-hour design studio to solve the simplest design problem. Some teams only meet at sprint demos. Some code. Others email annotated PDFs. A few teams still use Axure. And then there's always one team that tries every single new tool they can get their hands on.

- **Threats to scaling:** Just having a lot of designers or design teams doesn't necessarily solve more problems. In fact, having more designers usually compounds the difficulties in collaborating with partner teams, such as efficiently communicating what everyone is working on so that people can share or reuse each other's work. Replicating what works well in one team to other teams can seem impossible when so many teams do things their own way. Inevitably, teams can't do their best work if everyone is working so differently that lessons learned by some teams can't be applied to others. If practicing design feels like an organizational free-for-all with 50 designers, it's hard to imagine that it can be successful with 100 designers.

In short, scaling design is a complex, multifaceted challenge that could strain everything from the processes within your design team to the way you work with other teams and even to the cultural or organizational composition with which you've become familiar. What's more, scaling teams isn't just additive—it practically causes a reinvention of how you work. Such a change can't be undone just by removing the people or projects.

Navigating how to work with more designers, more products, more developers, and more customers may not always be straightforward, and you may not even know if your decisions and choices are working for months, if not longer. Let's explore how to make such a navigation more likely to succeed by breaking scaling down into three manageable chunks—operations, culture, and the design organization itself.

Scaling Operations

Over the last few years, many people have discussed the role that operations play in enabling teams to deliver work consistently over time and across projects. The myriad approaches, methods, and systems that provide design teams with a framework for how they work—both among their design teams and with their partner teams—are commonly referred to as *design operations,* or *DesignOps*. As a nascent subfield, definitions of DesignOps vary depending on who is doing the talking and who is listening.

But the intention of DesignOps is clear: to create reliable, repeatable processes that support design work across teams, projects, and technologies, throughout various periods and milestones of time and throughout the product development lifecycle.

The primary benefit of DesignOps is to help put more routine tasks on autopilot, or to make activities that occur frequently more routine (so they can be put on autopilot). Fully exploring DesignOps requires a book of its own (they're already out in the world), but let's look at a few common elements of DesignOps and how they enable operational scale (see Table 14.1).

TABLE 14.1 DESIGNOPS IN PRACTICE

Effort	Description	How It Enables Scaling
Design Research	Processes, directions, and guides to help make design research more consistent and therefore more efficient. It often includes details about how teams can request new research, participant recruiting, how to write scripts, and where reports, recordings, and more are found.	By making a checklist of steps and repeatable processes throughout design research, teams increase their likelihood of conducting successful research, without needing one person to make sure that everyone follows procedure. Ideally, research operations deploy a framework so that more people can do more research, more frequently.
Project Kickoff	A list of who should be involved, what questions should be answered, what existing materials are available, and any activities or events conducted at the start of a project.	Starting projects off with a consistent foundation that addresses fundamental questions, including clarity around roles and timelines, and gets projects and teams off on the right foot.
Sprint Cadence	A schedule of when ceremonies, meetings, approvals, and demos are held.	Similar cadences across teams and projects increase the likelihood of reusable artifacts, predictable methods, and easier ability for people from other teams and projects to contribute sooner.
Project Delivery/Handoff	A list of dates, what files will be made available, how these files are named, where they'll be posted, and how teams will be notified.	Similar to kickoffs and sprint cadences, standardizing how work is delivered reduces unknowns, questions, and risk.
Onboarding New Hires	The steps, introductions, and other details necessary for new team members to be effective.	Starting all new team members, regardless of project or business unit, from the same place every time reduces the risk of something important falling through the cracks.

TABLE 14.1 DESIGNOPS IN PRACTICE (continued)

Effort	Description	How It Enables Scaling
Discipline and Corrective Coaching	Progressively elevating steps to apply and enforce when team members don't meet expected standards of work or behavior.	These uncomfortable moments are more easily resolved when designers and the teams know what to expect and how everyone will work toward a resolution. Actions seem less personal if everything is communicated beforehand.
Job Tracks/Career Progression	A document detailing the primary responsibilities of specific job titles and how individuals can advance throughout the team.	As design scales to new business units or teams grow in head count, having a shared path to promotion is important so that everyone is aligned around titles and how to progress in their career.
Status Checks	A script or workflow used to assess where and to what extent a project is completed.	Asking and expecting the same information across projects, products, and lines of business ensures alignment and reduces surprises.

Some design managers may resist buying into DesignOps for a variety of reasons. Perhaps they aren't convinced there are repeatable processes across different business units, product portfolios, and development teams. They might think that knowing what work is getting done and by whom is their job, and they fear that relaxing their grip on project status will be seen as a weakness.

Or maybe they're concerned that process begets assembly-line dogmatic conformity that squelches creativity. But having the *right* processes in place means that you don't have to reinvent how to do things you've already done, and it lets you, as the design manager, focus more on what's important to your team, your organization, and your career.

If the best design work comes when constraints are clear and up front, then the best design management has processes in place so you don't have to rethink how to get design work done and delivered.

Deviate when necessary, but let the rote decision-making be addressed by repeatable, agreed-upon procedures up front.

Reflect, Observe, and Adapt

It's also wise to reflect regularly on what is working and what needs to adapt to new conditions. If you don't have formal design operations in place, conduct a current state analysis of how much time you spend making sure that projects and work meet these criteria:

- Projects are designed with a clear, aligned vision throughout the team.

- Work is completed on time.

- Deliverables are provided to stakeholders or partners the same way every time.

- Projects are accurately scoped and staffed.

- Work is archived and easily accessed in the future.

If the answer is the majority of your day, or if these all cause stress in every single project, it is probably time to formalize more design operations across your design team and larger product development organization.

Try to gather feedback from a diverse population of who interacts with your operations guidelines—ask designers, developers, your stakeholders, to find out where you or your team have made life harder on itself. It's critical to listen with an open mind—don't be defensive and do encourage honesty. After all, you can't improve if you don't know what to improve.

Detail a clear understanding of that baseline or current state before you enact new governance or process so that you can clearly show how far you've come with the process in place. You can do this through hard metrics and data, or even through anecdotal stories from your teams and your partners.

You need enough time for these DesignOps processes to be in place to measure the impact of your approach. A good rule of thumb is to reflect on your efforts every six months unless something occurs that triggers new measurements. For instance, if a new team joins your design organization, get a new baseline of how they ship work or kick off projects so that you can monitor their improvements via your DesignOps efforts.

Be sure to make your findings easily shareable and findable. Full disclosure of what's working and what needs to be changed lets others know you're on the right track or willing to adapt as necessary.

Promote Your Operational Team Wins and Your Pivots

Because much of DesignOps is focused on *how* design work gets done, it's all too easy to overlook the changes that make work easier to implement, test, and deploy. Don't let that go unnoticed—either by your own design team and your peers, management, or partners. Similarly, be sure that everyone knows when you adjusted course because the process you were trying to establish wasn't hitting your targets. You'll have more credibility when you mention what's *not* working than if you just shout from the rooftops about what *is* working.

Your own design team needs to hear about the successes because so much of DesignOps will directly affect your team first and foremost. By sharing the positives of changing course, you'll continue to get more buy-in faster than if you just mandated new ways of doing things.

Likewise, your partners and peers should hear that your DesignOps successes are paying dividends as well so they continue to support your efforts the next time you approach them with new ideas. They'll feel better about supporting your new ways of doing things if they have a track record of you clearly describing results.

Be willing to adjust how you communicate your DesignOps success based on your audience. When meeting with your product development leadership, you may rely on anecdotes by your development team, describing improved collaboration with designers. But you may only share hard-and-fast metrics when describing the improvements found in your six-month reflection to your executive management.

As we discussed in Chapter 8, "Unifying the Team Culture with Charters" about creating a team charter, sharing your DesignOps successes should be frequent and across a variety of channels. Don't just post metrics buried in a deck onto the intranet, and likewise don't just drop an @here message in Slack with an anecdote that will be forgotten as soon as the next funny Giphy is dropped in the channel 30 seconds later. Use your multiple channels—the intranet, town halls, weekly status update emails to management, your design team blog, etc.—to reinforce and reiterate that your direction is creating positive changes.

Q: *Tell our readers who you are and what you do.*

A: I'm a Senior Director of Design Operations. Our mission in design operations is to be great creative business leaders and business operators for design. We attempt to do that through providing systems infrastructure and programs around design org management, production operations, continuous growth, and business operations that help to create creative flow and fluidity for the design org and for the larger organization.

Q: *What types of roles and structure do you advocate for and see as successful both in your own DesignOps team and in other organizations?*

A: I've talked to a lot of design leaders looking to add DesignOps to their organizations and the reality is that people are looking for very similar people, experience, and qualities. You have Producer roles: people who are good at being on a project or cross-functional team, building great design plans, being a great cross-functional communicator, and supporting quality design work.

You have Design Program Managers, people who care most about the architecture, systems, and infrastructure; they understand the big picture, come with a rich history of production or project management, and know how to get things done.

Then you have a Director or Head of DesignOps, someone who knows how to build a world-class operations team. They build career paths for ops and cross-functional alignment with other operations groups to serve the greater business purpose. They define the strategy of DesignOps and its role in the design org.

Then you have a Chief of Staff role, the role that is the right hand to the leader of design. This role plays a critical role in aligning the design org and supporting strategic initiatives and orchestration of the design org in support of the leader of design.

For a DesignOps team of one, a single person may have to play all of these roles. For a more mature DesignOps team, you have more specialization, separation, and clarity between roles. As I mature in my tenure in DesignOps, I am often playing more of a Chief of Staff and Head of DesignOps role.

—Jacqui Frey, DesignOps leader

Hiring DesignOps Management and Specialists

As one of the primary tenets of DesignOps is to make design more effective and valuable, you risk making yourself less effective as a leader if you try to solely manage design operations yourself. Many well-known firms, such as 18F, Dropbox, Capital One, Pinterest, and Google, have documented how and why they employ teams of teams to monitor design operations and program management. They understand that design leaders need operational support in order to be the best leaders they can be.

If you already have design operations as a formal team, that's great. But if you don't, you may be in for a challenge to secure resources to hire a DesignOps leader, or at a minimum, a specialist who monitors how DesignOps is executed across your teams and projects.

There are essentially three methods to establish DesignOps leadership:

- Create brand new head count
- Ask a motivated designer already on the team to change their current role to focus on DesignOps
- Identify someone in your product development ecosystem (product management, development, business analysis, project management) who is interested in leading DesignOps and could maneuver to take on new responsibility

Not surprisingly, each organization has its own attitudes and philosophies and budgets that determine when head count is granted and for what roles. But hiring for DesignOps specialists has its own unique benefits and challenges when pitching the idea to your executive leadership.

For instance, you'll be finding yourself lobbying for new head count for people who won't, at first glance, create new design work. You'll have to fight the perception that there won't be more comps or prototypes or research if you hire this person instead of another visual designer, interaction designer, or researcher. Instead, you'll likely need to create a sense of urgency that you can't scale further if you don't introduce more operations-focused professionals on your team.

At risk of stating the obvious, make such a position more than a design role that a design manager wants to have filled. Work with your dev organization to point out where DesignOps can smooth the delivery of design work to dev, and that throughput could be faster, and the output could be more accurate. Get product management on board that there will be more uniformity in writing stories, acceptance criteria, and how meetings will be run from team to team.

Be careful, though, not to inadvertently conflate DesignOps with project management, or else you'll just be told to work more closely with Todd or Erin in PM to make sure they can do all the DesignOps stuff.

In other instances where you may try to tap the shoulder of someone already on the payroll, be it yours or someone on your extended team, be sure to articulate what DesignOps means to you and the company, and what they'll be leaving behind. Reinforce who their new stakeholders will be, and how you'll measure their success relative to how they're incentivized today.

Silencing the Skeptics: Make DesignOps Visible

Above all, though, reiterate to whomever may join you, that managing DesignOps will result in more updates, more conversations, and more transparency into what work is getting done, and less risk of duplicate or misaligned efforts. In many organizations, you may face early skepticism that you're hiring people to make work smoother, but aren't shipping more designs or closing out more tickets. These skeptics may think you outsourced some of the primary tenets of your managerial job to someone else.

You want to have answers on hand for when those skeptics ask what your new DesignOps person actually does. Getting defensive usually doesn't help these situations. We don't recommend replying with "Well, what have *you* done for me lately!" Instead, use it as a reminder that you may need to increase how regularly you communicate your team's successes and milestones to your wider team of partners and stakeholders.

Perhaps as a manager, your project plans or status updates were just a few lines in a weekly email. But now your operations leads use a visual map of where projects are and how they're staffed. Make sure those artifacts are front and center when you're communicating what is getting done, and post those updates across a variety of channels, such as SharePoint or a Confluence site, through team emails, Slack, and even printed on a whiteboard.

You may find that showing where your team was before you began deploying DesignOps specialists compared to where you are now will show the positive changes in and across your teams. You could look for a variety of metrics to help paint this picture of positive change.

For instance, consider any of these factors as possible snapshots of how your design operations have improved your team as it grows:

- Improved time to post job descriptions, hire, and onboard new team members

- Reduced number of delays when delivering work

- Better quality of life for design leads and design management who no longer are also responsible for operations

- Improved consistency and reuse of design assets across teams (many design systems can surface this data)

- How fast new teams or projects can be spun up as the work increases since new processes are now in place

Remember, the goal of successful design operations is pretty simple in theory: to provide the foundational processes and approaches that can be consistently applied over time to make sure that the design team can do their best work and the rest of the organization can best utilize the work of the design team.

Scaling Culture: Managing Designers and Expectations

We mentioned earlier that scaling design up and across an organization isn't simply additive. Hiring 20 new designers to a team that was formerly 20 doesn't simply double the team's output and the team's lunch order. The fundamental identity can change, and when an identity changes, culture isn't far behind.

Perhaps your team started out small and scrappy—a bastion of creativity and expression in a larger company devoid of character or anything, well, interesting. But when your team has grown to a greater size than the accounting department, or is more widely recognized than marketing and communications, you're not scrappy—you're the institution.

There's nothing wrong with that—many design managers wear a Black Flag shirt under their business casual oxford button-down. But keep a few things in mind as you see your team's culture ebb and change as your team and influence grow in any of these circumstances.

If a design team that previously didn't report to you is now part of your larger organization, don't do anything drastic to force assimilation into your team. Instead, ask the team to complete their own design team charter (as discussed in Chapter 8) within a few weeks of the reorganization. Show them how your team's charter and their charters are similar and where they are different. Since the charter probes on values, behaviors, and beliefs, you have the opportunity to better understand who your team *was* before they became a part of your team *now*.

Then tie these different charters into the common, shared vision of the entire organization. Show the leaders of these individual teams that despite any differences in the charters themselves, you're still marching toward executing a shared vision. Surfacing the ties between the (formerly) separate teams and the larger corporate mission should start to show these design teams that they're more alike than different.

Likewise, share unifying approaches to work sooner than later. If you have a defined experience or design framework documented, you and a few of your directs or leaders from your design team could socialize how this framework is applied to projects in practice. Similar to the charter comparison exercise, use the framework as an artifact to drive further collaboration and discussion with your new colleagues.

For instance, take the experience framework and explore it like a customer journey with this new team. Again, look for divergences in practice, such as when the design team is initially involved, to when everyone expects or conducts research, and when any prototypes are finalized. By taking the time to explore these approaches to design work across different, existing teams, you'll create a rapport and credibility with these new teams that you're now responsible for, and also show that you're genuinely interested in how they currently work. You'll likely find they have been doing things you could adapt into your process, and likewise identify things that you'll want these teams to adopt, based on your team's approaches to designing at your organization.

That said, be sure to extend some token of your own team's identity to the new team to show that they're a part of your organization, even if they maintain their own identity. Don't create an *us* and *them* environment where there are no shared traits beyond getting paid by the same company. Invite the new team to design reviews, conference recaps, kickoffs and any other events that don't require heavy subject matter expertise to follow along or participate. If the CEO or another executive is dropping by your office, be sure to extend an invite to that team to be there, too.

Also, temper your expectations that everyone wants to work on a large design team. It's perfectly reasonable that a designer might feel most effective and fulfilled in a smaller team and will look for another position outside the company. That's okay and to be expected.

What you can do, however, is find out what traits that designer appreciates and values from working in a smaller team that she now feels she can't experience on the larger team. Do your best to support those attributes, but it is unrealistic to assume that you can maintain a similar environment under drastically different circumstances.

It's also reasonable to expect that some designers would have done things differently when the team was smaller or before it moved under your watch. Turn these into learning opportunities when you talk to your larger team about why such practices were especially effective or special. What they say may reveal more fundamental or important practices you can draw from and add to your own toolkit and also show the rest of the team that you're not set to only do things the way you always did them with smaller teams.

Make your vision of the team and how your work influences the larger organization everyone's vision. You can do that by including these teams in your vision-setting activities, even if they may not contribute to the actual project. By including them now, you'll be sure they feel included later when there are fewer boundaries across your design teams, and a shared sense of culture will tie your disparate teams together far more tightly than simply sharing email addresses.

Scaling the Practice

The larger the organization, the greater the likelihood that there will be multiple design and product teams who conduct business differently—sometimes starkly—than your own team and the projects you work on. In some situations, this is tolerable. Teams continue to do things the way they've always done them, and the work gets done, and people get paid.

But cracks in the dam can start to appear when that status quo begins to shift into a new state, and expectations, needs, and practices change, and you risk those cracks leading to a flood of inefficiency, misaligned expectations, and a general unease that no one is happy or performing at their best.

In some cases, you may not even have a mandate to standardize how design gets done across your organization. In others, you may be on the hook to fix it by year-end.

Let's look at a number of ways that standardizing how design functions work in your company can lead to improved chances of success as your practice scales. In the best case, you'll work with your design operations manager or team to help see these through.

Create a Design or Experience Framework

Similar to the design team's charter we discussed in Chapter 8, a design or experience framework captures the spirit and principles of how design work gets done, shows what is valued as good design work, and outlines the process you regularly apply to deliver the work. As design grows in scope and responsibility across an organization, it's critical for both designers and nondesigners to be able to say "This—this right here, is how we design here."

Such a document isn't just a pattern library of components, or a style guide of colors, or a comprehensive design system.

> **NOTE LABELS MATTER**
>
> Choose a label that will get the most traction in your organization. If your company identifies design as a process to solve business problems through a variety of methods and approaches with and by different teams, you can probably call such a framework a *design framework*.
>
> However, if your organization thinks of design as something that the visual designers do at the end of a project, calling your declaration of operations an *experience framework* may get more adoption. Both are used interchangeably here.

A design or experience framework should articulate the steps and the decision path you and your larger product team pursue from start to finish, and how you define and use terms like *good design* and *usable*. Furthermore, an effective framework sets constraints and limits as to what is acceptable and not acceptable in your design organization. In some cases, you may not need to mandate change in one team's process if the journey and destination still are within the boundaries of what you declare in the framework.

The UK-based food delivery company, Deliveroo, created posters illustrated by Sam Ailey promoting their experience principles (see Figure 14.1). Rather than risk overly flowery language that might seem impractical or difficult to apply, each principle features three or four examples of how to practice the principle in everyday situations, such as finding user needs to address, or checking if something already exists before building something new.

Similarly, Gov.UK designed posters (see Figure 14.2) to capture their own approaches to how they design in a way that not only captures the reader's attention but is also easy to understand.

FIGURE 14.1

Deliveroo's experience principles clearly communicate how the design team practices its craft.

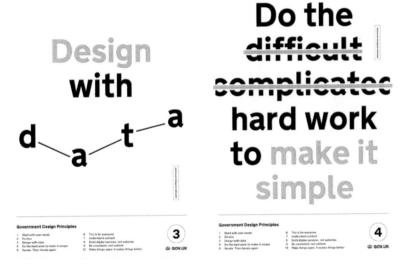

FIGURE 14.2

Gov.UK's design principles are clear, concise, and can be easily understood by anyone in the organization.

Don't let such an important artifact be written by you alone and stored on a shelf. Instead, start with identifying the structure of what should be in the framework, then task your teams, including those on other design teams in your organization, to generate their perspective on what should be included. A wider-team involvement ensures greater buy-in and support both now and in the future when a decision to possibly deviate from the framework is at hand.

In some corporate cultures, the Deliveroo or Gov.UK posters may be less effective in sharing how the team works together and what makes them who they are. In those instances, workflow or process diagrams may be more well-received when showing how the team works with others, and when they should be involved. For example, Jeff Gothelf's Scrum and UX process diagram[1] (see Figure 14.3) may help convince skeptical engineers when to involve the design team because they can clearly see what to expect from them when they're involved.

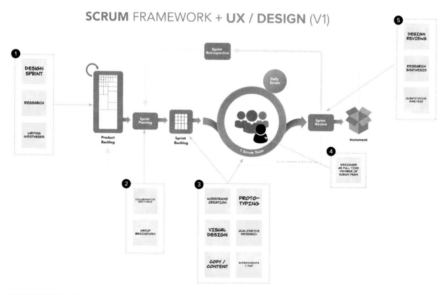

FIGURE 14.3
Jeff Gothelf's Scrum and UX framework would be especially useful in cultures where engineering teams lead decision-making.

1   Jeff Gothelf, "Here Is How UX Design Integrates with Agile and Scrum," October 11, 2018, https://jeffgothelf.com/blog/here-is-how-ux-design -integrates-with-agile-and-scrum/

Much like your team charters, socialize the design framework as part of your story in the larger organization. Print and display it prominently where people congregate. Include it in decks to show how decisions are made and why. Share it when interviewing designers and reference it when you're considering promoting designers and furthering their careers.

> **NOTE** MORE RESOURCES AND EXAMPLES FOR
> DESIGN PRINCIPLES
>
> Browse over 200 design principles: **https://principles.design/**
>
> Gov.UK Design Principles: **www.gov.uk/guidance/government
> -design-principles**
>
> Jeremy Keith's archive of design principles: **https://principles
> .adactio.com/**

By having a foundation that documents and shares how design is done as one team *and* multiple teams in the organization, you give yourself and these teams, who previously weren't under your leadership, a roadmap of how to act as one unified force and how you know it's actually working.

Scaling via Design Systems

Much has been written about design systems over the past few years as a way to improve consistency and delivery within and across product and development organizations. As a design manager tasked with scaling the design practice further throughout your company, design systems could be the key that unlocks opportunities to work more closely with development and product teams, not to mention the additional products themselves.

Design systems—loosely defined here as *reusable pieces of code and components complete with documentation*—will provide a number of tangible benefits to scale design across your organization, both tactically and strategically. Not every benefit is as influential for different groups of people or teams in your organization, so be sure to tailor how you approach promoting an existing design system or starting from scratch.

For instance, design systems are often useful for providing a single source of truth about what components should look like and how they behave, whether your team is designing websites, mobile apps, or any other digital system. As a design manager trying to scale the practice across the company, a design system gives you something to point to and say "Executive management wants these components to look the same way in our organization, and they should all look like how they're defined here." Even if your team isn't responsible for designing web applications built by another team, the design system can still support those products.

That brings us to another useful attribute of design systems for a design manager scaling how design works at her company—the collaboration and exposure necessary from other teams to create or improve a fully functioning design system.

No design system can be effective if built in a vacuum or silo and dumped on another team to build into their products. Instead, the conversations, meetings, and milestones achieved together—be it development teams, other product teams, and even marketing and communications—should all be included when developing a useful, living design system that supports multiple products across a company.

Rather than fully exploring how to build the most effective design systems, let's focus our attention on what your role as the design leader should be when either planning for a new design system across products or taking a style guide or pattern library to that next level.

Getting Buy-In

You'll want to be the person spearheading the conversations driving a design system across products. Don't think of a design system as a tool for design to own the look and feel across everything—you risk looking like you are land-grabbing and possibly overreaching. Instead, talk to development teams to hear how shared style sheets fall short, how code could be reused more effectively, and how other design teams could focus on hard problems instead of searching for specific colors or fonts to use in new design work.

Securing Time and Resources

Following buy-in, you'll need to get teams to dedicate people to start doing the work. Be careful going rogue and relying on a skunk-works model to start the design system without approval. Many managers don't like surprises—especially ones that take time away from projects they thought were getting someone's full attention. Instead, create a plan that shows how much time will be needed to deliver a simple component of a design system—even just a button. Quickly share the usefulness of that component to get momentum for securing a fully staffed team later.

Identifying Which Projects Will Use the Design System

As the design leader and proponent of the design system, identify which products in your organization's product portfolio are useful candidates to pilot the system. Use these meetings with senior leaders to show that you can prioritize what's most important to the company, while also minimizing risk and cost by not lobbying for a one-size-fits-all mandate. Emphasize that waiting for a brand new project starting from scratch may be idealistic, and incorporating the design system into a product currently in the market is a more realistic approach to see real value from the effort.

Evangelizing

Don't let the design system just be a technical solution to a technical problem. Be the champion of a system that crosses lines of business, provides artifacts that multiple teams can use and benefit from, and that creates a consistent face of the digital product portfolio that will be easier to maintain and support.

Better yet, elevate the folks on your design team and the development organization who made the design system possible. Evangelize anecdotes and stories about how design, dev, and even QA are working more succinctly together, and improvements can happen faster than ever before.

Showing That It's Making a Difference

Much like evangelization, promote positive impact that can be traced back to the design system. Even if in the early stages the results are just developers feeling like they have more autonomy or that designers feel that they can focus their talents on addressing their biggest challenges, share these results with the senior leaders who signed off on providing resources in the first place. You'll show that their support is paying dividends, and they'll want to continue that support in the future.

Standardize, but Don't Fetishize Uniformity or Conformity

Scaling design in your company isn't about achieving maximum efficiency, commodifying creativity, or turning design into an assembly-line-like factory that eliminates risk and gets the most productive hours out of a designer. In fact, nothing could be further from the truth. Good design will never be an outcome—or output—in a command-and-control environment.

Instead, scaling design is, much like when we discuss design operations, reducing or eliminating the things that make work unproductive so that designers have more time and spirit to innovate and solve the hard problems we all face today.

It's unproductive to have to look up what color a primary submit button should use. It's inefficient to have to prototype the same navigation bar for another project. It's draining to only show your work at the end of a project and then have it shredded by a boss because you didn't get effective feedback sooner, especially if another team in the office does get feedback earlier.

The constraints you establish shouldn't reduce creativity—rather, scaling design the right way should unleash more creativity than ever before because the nitpicking decision-making is a thing of the past. Don't drive yourself crazy trying to turn designers into automatons who will do everything the same way. Instead, rely on your experience framework, your design system, and your team charters to show your process, the tools you and your team used, and the values your team shares to grow the design practice across the company.

> **NOTE** USEFUL READING TO LEARN MORE ABOUT DESIGN SYSTEMS
>
> Here's a decent start to better understand how design systems may enable smoother scaling for your design team.
>
> *Expressive Design Systems* by Yesenia Perez-Cruz, available at **https://abookapart.com/products/expressive-design-systems**
>
> *Design Systems Handbook*, by Marco Suarez, Jina Anne, Katie Sylor-Miller, Diana Mounter, and Roy Stanfield: **www.designbetter .co/design-systems-handbook**
>
> "Design Systems" by Nathan Curtis: **https://medium.com /eightshapes-llc/design-systems/home**

Choosing Your Battles

The first step in identifying how to scale the design practice across active design and product teams is to identify where you can make a change. You may recognize that changing the organization's software development methodology from waterfall to agile could result in a more iterative, incremental product development process. But is that really your hill to die on?

Instead, start small with things you can control and measure the difference between the old fractured way and your way. But don't just throw a dart while you're blindfolded at a list of things you could change—at a minimum, identify one small fix that could lead to bigger changes later. Figure 14.4 illustrates a continuum of easy-to-challenging changes to drive in your organization. Starting your efforts on the left side of the spectrum may improve your chances of addressing gnarly problems with scaling later. You can also expand on what you can do by estimating what efforts will generate the most impact relative to the effort you and your team will have to exert (see Figure 14.5).

For example, if designers on these separate teams admit that they don't always know the bigger picture of what they're working on, adjust how you approach kickoffs with more vision-alignment exercises.

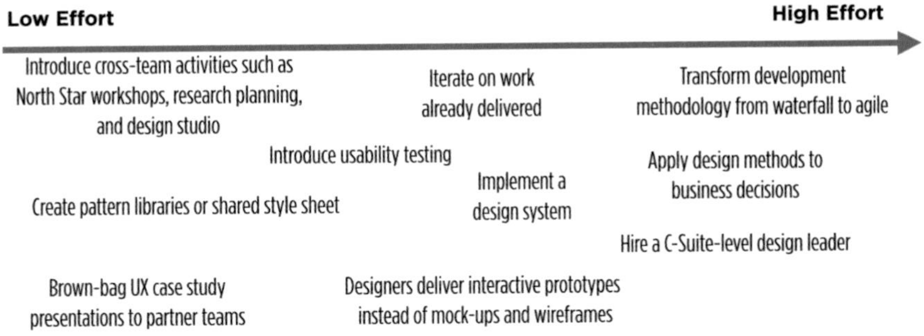

Low Effort → **High Effort**

Introduce cross-team activities such as North Star workshops, research planning, and design studio

Iterate on work already delivered

Transform development methodology from waterfall to agile

Introduce usability testing

Implement a design system

Apply design methods to business decisions

Create pattern libraries or shared style sheet

Hire a C-Suite-level design leader

Brown-bag UX case study presentations to partner teams

Designers deliver interactive prototypes instead of mock-ups and wireframes

FIGURE 14.4

Decide what organizational or procedural challenges you want to tackle and rank them from easy to challenging.

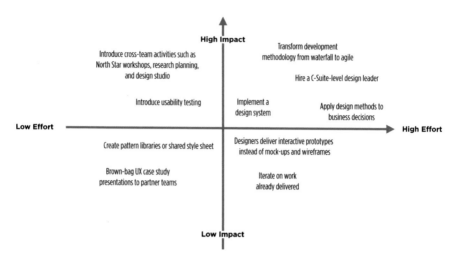

High Impact

Introduce cross-team activities such as North Star workshops, research planning, and design studio

Transform development methodology from waterfall to agile

Hire a C-Suite-level design leader

Introduce usability testing

Implement a design system

Apply design methods to business decisions

Low Effort

High Effort

Create pattern libraries or shared style sheet

Designers deliver interactive prototypes instead of mock-ups and wireframes

Brown-bag UX case study presentations to partner teams

Iterate on work already delivered

Low Impact

FIGURE 14.5

Evaluating the impact relative to the effort you and your team will need to exert to create change can help you prioritize where to start.

Not all change efforts are created equal. If you're in an organization resistant to change, lower design maturity, or unfamiliarity with design, we suggest starting on the left side of the continuum.

If designers feel that they only get feedback at the very end of the process, and then it's just a punch list of what to change, dig into when teams present work and the general format of sharing work for sign-offs. These adjustments may be far more achievable in the short term and can get these designers on your side sooner rather than trying to overhaul entire departments that many would see as an overreach of your remit as a design manager scaling the design practice.

Show It Can Be Done

Instead of trying to change the entire product development organization at once, find one practice, approach, or team you can work closely with and shift their behavior to your desired end state.

Publicly share this one example of how standardizing design methods and practices created a better result for the teams, especially when you approach the next team with whom you'll be working.

For instance, in 2018 a 100-year-old telecommunications company wanted to improve its approach to innovation by applying design thinking across the enterprise. In a company with over 300 designers across various projects and business units, some people may have tried asking those designers to each educate their respective teams on how to use design thinking.

Instead, they asked one design leader to work with one team and assess what was possible, given the scope of the program at the time, to deliver a plan that could then be extended to other teams.

By starting with one team he knew well instead of broadly across multiple teams, the design leader was able to show success, build rapport with executive management that his task was achievable, and create momentum that what he was trying to accomplish would benefit the larger organization.

As a result, the executive team had more confidence in their design leader, expanded the scope of the program, and increased the resources available. The design leader, in turn, had a more willing, engaged audience when he started working with the rest of the organization.

This approach also works well with cross-functional teams within your product development organization.

"Working on many different product teams over the years, I've found that the best way to build trust and respect for product design is to start small, show success, and then take those learnings to another project or team. It's important to influence the product strategy and process over time, not make broad, sweeping changes to an existing company-wide approach," said Kim Lenox, VP of Product Design at Zendesk in San Francisco.

"A key technique I've used at many companies is to share the success with your cross-functional partners by scheduling a lunch-and-learn presentation or co-creating a case study together. When design, product, engineering and program management are standing together speaking about their approach, their mistakes, and their learnings, the other teams will be much more likely to try out the new approach," she continued. "Start with one team, find your design allies, and build from there. Eventually, the whole organization will embrace the new approach as their own and often iterate to make it even better."

Start small to show that scaling to a larger practice is possible and your strategy is working.

Get Top-Down Support

At some point, you'll need senior management to set the expectation that design should be a priority in your organization. In many cases, you don't need executive sponsorship to kick off standardizing how design works to scale its efforts. After all, who actually wants inefficient, duplicative teams doing similar work whether they're in accounting, marketing, or design? Eventually, however, you'll likely encounter some resistance to change that will threaten your efforts. That's when you need executive support.

When the finance and HR software company Workday had lost 25% of its design team to attrition, yet had plans to grow by 30%, senior management knew it had to make changes—both in the team it had and in the team it wanted. The executive leadership understood that improving effective design could deliver value to a software company, but in order to deliver that vision, the company would need more designers, as well as a way to improve the maturity of the design practice itself.

The company asked design leader and then-newly hired Global Head of User Experience Todd Zaki Warfel to develop a plan to shore up the designers already on the payroll and to develop a strategy to support the planned surge in new hires. Like many large organizations, Workday had several design teams throughout the company, some of which came from acquisitions and others from departments that hired their own teams, some of which had been in the company for years. As such, Todd knew he had to offset any concerns that this scaling effort was a power-grabbing consolidation.

Using his first month on the job as a listening tour, Todd then built a plan of timelines and outcomes over six, twelve, and eighteen months that executive leadership would support. Prior to attempting to implement the scaling strategy, he then sought out the leaders of those design teams that weren't under the same reporting structure. He showed them the organizational structure he was proposing for each of the six-month segments, and reiterated that he wasn't just looking to increase his own head count.

"One manager had been overseeing a design team for three years," Todd said. "And I recall him saying 'You want my designers to report in to you?' I responded with I didn't care if they reported in to my team in practice—but I wanted those designers to know they can participate in what the larger design team will be doing."

Todd made sure that his scaling plans took into account the skepticism that he might encounter when seeking support from management. "By removing every *no* from the table, I knew what I needed to do to get [leadership's] support," he said.

The Senior Vice President then knew that Todd's plan for scaling the practice had the support of the managers who would also have to buy into the scaling strategy. He approved the plan and awarded the funding, ultimately leading to the hiring of over 60 designers—bringing the total head count at the time to 100 designers—in only four months.

Show Grassroots Value

The natural foil to getting top-down support from executive leadership is getting the buy-in from the designers on the ground who will be asked to change how they work.

In many cases, this may not be as difficult as it seems. In 2015, a financial services company with a design team of about ten people absorbed another six-person design team via acquisition.

The acquired team was relieved to learn that their new colleagues had successfully cultivated an expectation of customer research to validate, generate, or refute ideas. This was quite a change from their prior approach to design. Their former product development process had little to no exposure to customers. While they knew they should be sharing their design work with customers, the broader corporate culture didn't prioritize research. As such, when they joined the acquiring, larger team, they welcomed the day-to-day change of how they actually worked.

That's not to say it's always that easy.

Let's revisit the above example where one team is establishing a consistent design process. Imagine the acquired team wasn't as eager to share their work with customers early and often. Perhaps they believed the work had to be perfect. Or their approach prior to acquisition had required approval by layers of team leads and managers before it was perceived as solid enough to be released to production. It's easy to imagine how the differences in approach could lead to frustration among designers on both the acquiring and acquired teams.

It's true that some managers may try telling the new team to fall in line. But that approach isn't leadership, that's just barking mandate. Instead, start with a clear outcome. In order to grow a design practice that scales across the company, design teams need to operate with a customer-centric approach to design, with frequent external feedback throughout the product development process.

Now ask your own design team to talk through how customer feedback made their design work more useful, effective, and valuable. But don't stop there.

Make time to show the newly acquired team (or team from another department or business unit) how to do it themselves—in this case, show the team how to write an interview script, to declare what they want to learn and what they'll do with that information, and help them with the interview, either as a note-taker or the primary interviewer. Then help the team translate the observations into insights and show them how to adjust the design accordingly. Show how consistent practices help enable scaling by having someone from their team shadow or attend a few research sessions, and ask someone on your team to do the same with them. You'll be reinforcing that establishing similar operating models in one company can usually make it easier to get design work done.

Bringing them along as colleagues who could be coached instead of a top-down mandate from the boss can get the team on board for more significant changes later.

But as your leadership grows and the expectations of your teams increase, you may realize you've outgrown how you are organized within the company.

Scaling the Organization Model

As your larger organization expects more out of design and your team, you may find that the organizational model that worked when your team had five people doesn't address the same needs when you manage five teams of 10 designers across three lines of business. Often, these growing pains assert themselves when senior program sponsors are unclear how to fund designers, or who designers should report to as they join a dedicated project for a long-term commitment. In other cases, designers working in different lines of business are aware of the great work you and your team are doing, yet they feel like they're on a deserted island with no one who understands their profession or how to advance in their career.

Kristin Skinner and Peter Merholz addressed many of the benefits and risks associated with the most common design organization models in their 2016 book *Org Design for Design Orgs*.[2] Instead of revisiting much of what they wrote, let's examine what design leaders should be aware of if they find themselves changing from one model to another to address scaling in the company:

- **From centralized org to decentralized design teams:**

  Opportunity: You may have the chance to lead multiple design teams across the company and be expected to make strategic business decisions on what to prioritize, how to resource, and how to grow the careers of the leaders of those new decentralized teams.

  Risk: You'll be even further removed from any design work, and you may find yourself going from being *the* boss to being *a* boss with many peers in the organization. That's certainly not a problem, but it may impact your own goals and how you see your career trajectory at the company.

- **From decentralized design team to agency model:**

  Opportunity: You and your design team, and the new teams joining your internal agency, will likely have more unique projects to work on that you didn't have access to previously.

  Risk: Agency models continue to struggle with designers and researchers being involved from the beginning of a project to post-launch; you and your team may now be seen as a cost center just looking to be capitalized on a balance sheet. There will likely be fewer traditional leadership and management roles, but you should see a greater need for lead roles.

- **From decentralized teams to one centralized org:**

  Opportunity: You'll likely have more responsibility to establish design quality and how design work gets done as more teams who were independent now report to you.

---

2   Peter Merholz and Kristin Skinner, *Org Design for Design Orgs* (Sebastopol, CA O'Reilly Media, 2016).

Risk: Some of the lines of business that had their own design team may not see the value in changing models, and designers who were leads or managers may not have those same roles in the now-larger team.

- **From agency model to hybrid/decentralized teams:**

  Opportunity: You should find the design team is engaged earlier and throughout the product development process. More leadership roles should open up for designers.

  Risk: The team that was used to paying for only what it needed via the agency model will now likely have more design overhead to support. Be sure to emphasize how bringing design into the full product development process will be more valuable to the organization. Also, beware that designers will likely lose access to the breadth of projects they had been enjoying in the agency model. Prepare how to accommodate rotations across teams, if possible.

As many of these summaries above are broad generalizations, look for cues within your organization to determine if you need a change of organizational model. For instance, look for other teams, such as the software development organization, that have reorganized recently to better scale throughout and up the company, or if they're feeling similar challenges as you and your team. If so, you may find better luck being part of a broader organizational realignment than trying to reposition the structure of your own team alone.

Communicate how and why these reorganizations are necessary before, during, and after any organizational structure change. Reinforce the benefits that the team and the company will realize. Furthermore, emphasize the ways that your team will work differently in the new model versus the prior model, so everyone understands any new expectations or responsibilities.

Scaling Leadership

At this point, you may feel overwhelmed and think that scaling the design practice is a heck of a lot for one person to undertake. In fact, it should feel like way too much, because it *is* way too much for one person.

As your organization wants more out of design, you have the fantastic opportunity to grow new leaders who can shape the impact of design in not only your vision for the company, but their own as well.

Don't make the all-too-common mistake to only consider the best practicing designers for leadership roles or the same usual designers who have already led projects in the past. Rather, look to the people who have been with you on this scaling journey, whether it's the people speaking up in favor of collaborating with development teams to implement the design system, or those who are working with the other existing design teams to draft their team charter.

Be on the lookout for those designers who are building bridges, opening new venues for communication and collaboration with different teams, and becoming recognizable across the organization and invest in them—not just the folks who are happiest designing amazing experiences.

In addition, pay special attention to women and people of color in your organization who may not have as many role models at the leadership level within the organization. Identify, train, mentor, and sponsor them to prepare them for senior roles in your larger, more influential design organization (and hopefully for their growth, even outside your team).

In many cases, simply providing access to your meetings with a pre- and post-meeting conversation about what happened and how you acted is a great start to growing these new, more diverse leaders in the company. As those new leadership roles emerge, the stale, pale, and male candidates will no longer be perceived as the only option, and younger and earlier-career designers will have more people in positions of influence like them to show that success is achievable and possible.

Wrapping Up

Scaling design further throughout the organization is ultimately much more than a tool challenge, a process challenge, or a production and output challenge. Rather, scaling design is ensuring that the right people are empowered to shift behaviors and expectations in ways in which the organization may not be initially familiar or comfortable. That's a people challenge.

As the design leader, you're in a position to set yourself and your team up to be successful with more at stake and with more visibility than ever was possible before when you were serving only a slice of the company.

Let's revisit a few recurring themes you'll want to keep top of mind as you undergo this journey, with not only your team and your partners in the company, but yourself as well.

- **Do maintain a systems-thinking view of your position.**

  Keep the big picture of company goals at the forefront and look for how your design team influences the likelihood of exceeding those goals. Beware of zooming too far into the design work at the expense of understanding how the teams, projects, and products all fit together and influence one another. Furthermore, be transparent, up front, and collaborative with how you work with other teams so they can see your value firsthand. Keep feedback loops frequent with these diverse teams of stakeholders to make sure that bad ideas are caught early by scaling communication at a similar pace as you scale delivery.

- **Don't overspecialize roles at the expense of skills.**

  You risk making your design organization fragile and subject to disruption if you build your team around too many specialists who can only do a few things really well. Instead, build teams around skills, such as leading effective interviews, versus roles, such as design research. As your organization takes on more of these specific roles, challenge the experts on your team to help the generalists know more about their domain.

- **Do prepare for the politics.**

  Increasing your design organization's reach, expectations, and responsibilities will be an inherently political undertaking as you navigate existing systems and cultures—some of which will be, more than likely, resistant to change. Try to keep the vision of the larger company front and center in your work, and look for the common ground between those who are threatened or skeptical of your new remit. Search for ways you can make those who doubt you look successful as a result of your efforts, and keep your allies on your side by reinforcing how their support has made these collaborations possible.

Designing Influence

Depending on what you read and whom you talk to, design may very well be the driving force behind the success of modern, digital companies such as Netflix, Uber, Airbnb, and Google. And then you may find yourself seemingly living on a totally different planet, where you get asked if the "UX slash UI is done." Or you're in a conference room reading spreadsheets row by row of locked-down features you're expected to design over the next six months. Or perhaps the engineering manager has emailed you four times already this week asking how many wireframes can be delivered to keep the dev team busy.

It's true that companies of all sizes and industries are successfully unlocking the potential of design. It's also true that many organizations want to embrace design and reap its benefits, even as they struggle with understanding the value of design in the first place.

"Design is notoriously difficult to define, tough to measure, hard to isolate as a function, and tricky to manage, making it challenging for many nondesigners to comprehend," wrote innovation strategist Jeneanne Rae in "What Is the Real Value of Design?"[1]

In many cases this *lack* of understanding design value looks something like this:

- Design involvement isn't connected to business results.

- Design is only seen as a step in a process.

- Design is only seen as a team.

What's more, Leah Buley led a Forrester survey that asked large organizations what barriers prevented user experience from having a larger impact. Twenty-five percent of respondents said that partial implementation limited the impact of UX in their organization—likely attributed to an inability to adequately scale. But right behind at 24% was a lack of understanding of user experience approach, methods, and value.[2] In other words, one out of four design leaders works in an organization where the biggest challenge is getting the company to understand what it is they do.

---

1   Jeneanne Ray, "What Is the Real Value of Design?" *DMI Review* (Winter 2013), www.dmi.org/page/13244RAE30

2   Leah Buley, "How to Modernize User Experience" (Forrester, March 23, 2015), www.forrester.com/report/How+To+Modernize+User+Experience/-/E-RES119568

This lack of understanding design isn't harmless or to be taken lightly. It likely limits your ability to create sustainable change that can make a difference to the company, your team's success, and your own career.

As a design leader, you are the one person who is best suited to help educate your colleagues and executives on the impact that design can have on your business. In some cases, you may have to get the executive team on board. In other instances, the executives have bought in and are ready to see results. In those situations, the middle management are the people you'll have to convince that there's a better way to do things.

And even though it's easy to throw your hands up and vow to just pack up and go work for people who actually do get it, many of us aren't in such a position that we can work for whomever and wherever we want.

Instead, we can educate our colleagues and raise design's influence among our partners, stakeholders, and peers. By doing so, we'll increase our chances to get involved sooner in higher priority projects. We'll explore more challenging problems, and our teams will feel more empowered and connected to their work.

To create this change, let's explore the following:

- Improving how we communicate with executives
- Examining the broader industry via maturity models and other research
- Building a case with data
- Applying the fundamentals of change management to design
- Tweaking regular design exercises and activities to activate culture change

If you're not exhausted at the sheer thought of it, or it's easier to educate your peers about the value of design than update your résumé, let's get started.

Influencing Up

"You are not the user" is a pithy reminder that designers need to know who their audience is to deliver a well-designed experience. In other words, designers can't rely on their own worldview to accurately determine what to design and how it should be designed for someone else with a different background, skills, values, and more. Likewise, helping executives understand the value of design will require you to tailor your messaging differently than when talking to another designer. In this case, you'll likely adjust how you're framing success and why you're taking on the challenges your team is addressing with the appropriate level of detail.

Many design leaders make the mistake of talking to the executive team like they would talk to their immediate manager. They'll want to show work, roadmaps, or staffing models for how the work is getting done. The problem with this approach is twofold: one, the executive naturally assumes this work is already getting done because there are teams and management in place to do all of this, so talking about it may be interesting, but not necessarily compelling. Two: talking about *outputs* of design work is time you're not talking to executives about the *outcomes* of all this design work.

Instead, try to frame your conversations in one of three ways—by capturing the broader business impact of your design work, tying your design work to improving the top or bottom line, or showing how research is shaping decision-making.

Positioning your work as influencing the broader ramifications for the business may be easier than it initially sounds. The research firm Altimeter Group surveyed organizations asking what the key drivers of their investments in digital transformation were.[3] The top three results were as follows:

- 51% cited growth in new markets

- 46% selected evolving customer behaviors

- 42% said increased competition

As a result, you can craft a narrative that the design team's work addresses all of these primary motives of the company's executive team. If the design team isn't influencing this work, they should be empowered to do so because it's right up their collective product development alley.

For example, high-performing design teams should be researching, prototyping, and testing new products that address the needs and opportunities of those new markets. A comprehensive research practice should be expected to talk to customers throughout the entire product development lifecycle, because it enables you to see how customer behaviors evolve over time. This approach also gives you insights into how the competition is trying to position itself against your own company.

Likewise, knowing how your design work contributes to increasing revenue and profit (known as *the top line*) or reduce expenses (*the bottom line*) is useful when discussing your team's work with the executive team. Even knowing which customer journeys are the most valuable to the business and how your team has adapted if those priorities have changed can elevate your conversations with your company's leadership.

Finally, many senior leaders would love to talk to customers as much as some designers do. Take advantage of that by finding ways to include them, even if it's just a recap of what you assumed versus what you ultimately learned. We'll discuss how to make design research a more inclusive activity later in this chapter.

---

3 Brian Solis, *The 2018-2019 State of Digital Transformation* (Altimeter, January 3, 2019), www.prophet.com/2019/01/state-of-digital-transformation-2018/

Stay Humble and Empathetic

It can be way too easy to project an aloof attitude when trying to educate senior stakeholders or executives as to why they should care about design. After all, it could be reasoned that these are the same people who have impeded progress, if not outright made a series of decisions that made your work a lot harder than the designers you follow on Twitter or whom you see speak at conferences. But remind yourself that even getting the opportunity to talk about your design successes is a victory for you and your team.

Resist the urge to correct an executive who says "user testing" instead of "usability testing" or admonish someone who says you should run *focus groups* more often. Instead, see those statements as opportunities that leadership is willing and interested in expanding the opportunity for design in your organization. Listen to what they're saying and unpack what they actually mean. Hopefully, if an executive says *focus group*, they want user feedback, regardless of how you get that feedback. It's often too easy to poke fun at people who don't get what we do, but never let such contempt surface, or you won't be invited back.

Instead, be sure to come prepared with your own questions that could give you more insight into how to prepare yourself and your team for the future. Effective questions to consider asking an executive in a design meeting might include the following:

- Who else in the company might benefit from knowing more about our customers?

- Can you think of anyone else who could use this research?

- Who else would benefit from having a similar meeting to this one we just had?

Ultimately, the senior leadership team wants many of the same things you do, too. Focus your discussions, presentations, and relationships on showing how your outcomes are the foundation of those successes, and you'll continue to grow your political capital with leadership.

We'll talk about how to tweak many of your existing design methods and approaches to include executives later in this chapter in "Tactics and Exercises," too.

Align Corporate Goals to Design Outcomes

It's important to steer your design successes in the same direction as the company in order to show that your contributions are improving what the organization cares about.

The best part? If you work for a public company, your organization describes what they're up to four times a year and provides an annual summary of their accomplishments, and that's just the bare minimum. In almost all cases, these organizations will also address the current business climate to provide context to their performance (or lack thereof).

The documents may describe positive themes, such as commitments to innovation, improving customer experience, or they'll announce a new mobile product later in the year. In other cases, these press releases may refer to the headwinds the company is facing. These challenges could include anything from an unclear regulatory future, shifting consumer tastes in Europe, or even buggy or delayed software. (In fact, many cite lousy weather in winter and great weather in spring for hurting business—nothing is immune from being blamed for poor sales.)

In any of these positive or negative examples, you can tie how your design efforts either have contributed or should contribute to the company goal. See Table 15.1 for possible connections between your design team's work and the events or conditions mentioned in earnings announcements. Note how the design outcomes tell a far more compelling story than the outputs alone.

TABLE 15.1 TRANSLATE CORPORATE GOALS TO DESIGN OUTCOMES

Corporate Goal	Design Outputs	Design Outcomes
Committing to innovation	Research summaries, prototypes	We researched, designed, and prototyped a brand new product to enter an adjacent market.
Improving customer experience	Research summaries, customer journeys	We've interviewed 30 more customers than last quarter to better understand their most important journeys with us.
Introducing new mobile product this year	Responsive prototype	We need to prioritize our resources so that we have our best people working on this new project.
Facing regulatory challenges	Customer journeys	The design team can journey map the regulatory process so that we don't get surprised later.
Changing consumer tastes in Europe	Research summaries	We should prioritize a discovery research campaign to better understand these changing attitudes to our product.
Buggy or delayed software	Prototypes	We need to rethink how and when design and development work together.

Even design managers who lead teams at agencies, nonprofits, or private businesses should be able to identify what's important to the larger organization by studying how they market themselves to the outside world.

It's much easier for an executive to understand how your work is addressing stated company goals than letting your accomplishments stand on their own, devoid of any larger business context into the impact your choices made that are critical to the company's success.

Show Connections in the Media

To help senior leaders and the executive team learn more about the business value of design, find and share articles from sources that are already familiar to them. In other words, instead of forwarding the latest Medium article by the conference speaker you saw last year, send stories, reports, and other materials from names they trust. These probably include such stalwarts as the following:

- *The Wall Street Journal*
- *BusinessWeek*
- Forrester
- Gartner
- *Harvard Business Review*

But don't stop at sending a link or a PDF. Be sure to clarify how what you're sending is relevant to what you're dealing with or working on. Keep your summary brief—after all, you want your recipient to read the actual article or report—but establish a strong tie between what you're sending and why. *TL;DR:* Include a TL;DR.

Pay close attention to your tone and word choice as well. You don't want to risk sounding condescending or even patronizing in your commentary when sharing examples from the media. Remember, you're trying to create an empathetic connection where executives are seeing the world more clearly through your eyes—don't just use that time to admonish them for not knowing about these topics as well as you do.

Reinforce these trends or news in other meetings and presentations to continue sharing a consistent message across multiple audiences.

> **NOTE** BEWARE OF OVERSHARING
>
> Be mindful how often you're sending design-related articles to the executive team. If you've shared three or four different pieces of content and you haven't seen a response, evaluate if you're creating strong enough ties between design and the company to make the content relevant and worth their time.

Ask Questions to Build Trust and Influence

Many managers and leaders want to appear intelligent, prepared, and like they know everything when working with clients or partner teams. To project this image, they'll often hesitate to ask questions of senior leaders or stakeholders. Others will try to run real-time Root Cause Analyses right in the meeting by asking executives "why?" no fewer than five times per topic.

Margot Bloomstein, a content strategist and founder of her brand and content strategy consultancy Appropriate, Inc., has evolved her approach of influencing executives over her 20-year career.

"Early in my career, I was worried about sounding too naïve, either in asking overly simple questions or in asking too many questions. So I either tried to appear more self-assured than I was, or I avoided speaking up at all. I now know more about what I don't know so I can ask better questions," she said. "Over time, I've gained deeper understanding of industry trends, priorities, and jargon. But I also know that my clients will have the best knowledge of their respective companies, and often, their industries. I know best how to ask questions that will surface that knowledge, help them confront gaps, and apply their knowledge to the medium they've asked me to address."

It's often easy for design leaders to swing the pendulum too far in the other direction, though, and ask questions that don't establish trust or pave the way to influence other leaders. Designers may pose questions that look like their stakeholders or clients don't know anything about their business, customer, or industry. Instead of asking "Do you have business goals?" Bloomstein suggests asking open-ended questions that lead to prioritization, trade-offs, and commitments, such as "What business goals are most important for success?"

Asking these questions doesn't make the leader look unprepared—rather, it looks like the leader is prepared to engage at the same level as the rest of the leadership team.

Use Metrics to State Your Case

Finding causal ties from design output to business success continues to be a struggle for design leaders and parent organizations everywhere, regardless of company size, region, industry, or culture.

Many articles correctly urge caution at relying on *vanity metrics*—numbers that sound important, but don't indicate any significant impact on business objectives. Instead, there are a number of ways to correlate design outcomes to business goals before and during projects, rather than just waiting until after the project is done to determine if you designed the right thing the right way.

Among the most controversial metrics is the Net Promoter Score (NPS). The score, which is derived from organizations asking customers if they would recommend their product or service to a friend, has experienced an exponential rise in corporate America. Now it's expanding beyond the customer service or customer success teams and into design departments. In many cases, NPS is risky because there's little causal tie from what someone says they'd do to what they actually do.

Also, NPS is fraught with a high margin for error and is rife with unintended consequences of people chasing a score instead of providing good service. Anthropologist Marilyn Strathern famously summarized what's known as Goodhart's law as "When a measure becomes a target, it ceases to be a good measure."

Intuit CEO Steve Bennett also echoed Goodhart's law when he said, "A big challenge with the [NPS] methodology is that organizations tend to focus on the metric as the objective instead of gaining the insight to learn and act on to improve the customer experience … When organizations manage to the metric, they find ways to game the system."[4]

If your organization is relying on NPS, try to see if the scoring systems can allow the user to provide their contact information so that you can consider them for more in-depth customer research where you can ask them what led to whatever score they posted. NPS may be as effective as a canary in a coal mine—a catalyst to show that you should be learning more about something, but continue stressing that making short-term business decisions based on NPS alone could lead to even worse outcomes. If prioritization decisions are made primarily from NPS scores, look for other data—qualitative or quantitative—to paint a broader picture with more context to inform what gets decided.

---

4 Khadeeja Safdar and Inti Pacheco, "The Dubious Management Fad Sweeping Corporate America," business, *The Wall Street Journal*, May 15, 2019, www.wsj.com /articles/the-dubious-management-fad-sweeping-corporate-america -11557932084

In many companies, people have a hard time even keeping track of what's trackable by their myriad systems or teams. Others have trouble finding what they're looking for in a format they (or another computer) can easily understand. In some cases, you may luck out and learn you have a lot of metrics easily available; in other situations, you may be at a loss for useful data you can monitor when you want.

Use the following exercise to map what exists and where you can prioritize gaps to learn if it's worth exploring the cost to attain such a metric.

1. Draw a journey map of pre-customer sales, registrations, etc. all the way through post-sale onboarding or support. Each row should represent the readiness of the metrics you want to use in your decision-making, such as easy, difficult, unknown, and doesn't exist.

2. Take one color sticky note—in Figure 15.1, we're using yellow—to describe whatever types of data or metrics you could learn from in each column of the journey, and then put everything in the unknown row.

3. Next, find representatives in your organization who can determine what exists. This may require a lot of detective work, and not every answer you get may be accurate that day, so beware. Take another color sticky note—in this case, pink—to write down the primary point of contact to work with and a brief description of the data.

4. If you learn that the data you want exists, discard the corresponding yellow sticky note from your journey and place the pink note in the row that best describes your ability to access the information.

5. If the data doesn't exist, or isn't exactly what you needed, keep the yellow note in either Unknown (if you can't find the right person) or move it to the Doesn't Exist row so that you can decide if it's worth pursuing later (see Figure 15.2).

You should have a decent picture showing what metrics you have, what will be challenging to access, what doesn't exist, and what you want.

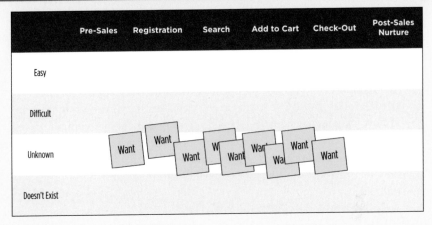

FIGURE 15.1

Create a customer journey where you can write all the data you can use to inform design decisions.

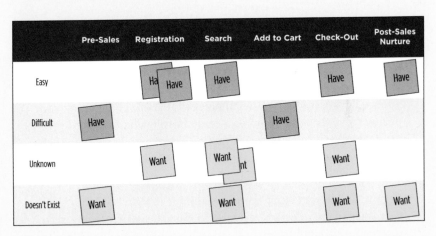

FIGURE 15.2

Interview your colleagues across different teams and departments to find out what data actually exists and place it in the respective columns so that you can spot gaps of data throughout the customer journey.

Know the Data That Influential Teams Measure

Determine what is currently measured at all and then, more importantly, find out how influential teams or stakeholders are measured with that data. For instance, if you're leading a design team in an engineering-dominant culture, find out how those engineers are measured and with what data.

Ideally, your own design team is likely influencing some of those figures today, but those teams aren't considering your own impact as to how those numbers move based on your team's involvement. By tying your own team's work to show how those teams are measured, you'll be demonstrating not only your own team's success, but also how it contributes to the success of those more established or influential teams.

Balance Data with Stories

It's easy, especially in engineering-centric cultures, to let data lead the way. In other situations, an abundance of data can lead to a "dog catches car" scenario, where you as a design leader don't know where to begin with the abundance of data now at your fingertips, for better or worse.

In either case, it's critical to remind your team and your peers that hard performance data is only a piece of what is likely a more nuanced, complex story. The human element of people using your product and services deserves a primary role when analyzing your product or service's success. Human reactions to your organization's work are easily lost when only looking at black-and-white numbers, trend lines, or pie charts.

Be sure to keep transcripts and recordings of your usability tests so that you can share how your participants react when seeing your new features or enhancements, whether good or bad. It's often these emotional reactions that are lost when focusing exactly on what the data indicates, but just as often, such reactions are what can galvanize your team to change something.

Striking that balance can be as easy as presenting data alongside quotes from interviews to paint a picture of activity (the numbers) and impact (the story). Just be sure to be honest in your representation—don't highlight figures that show 80% of your user base *can't* find a key feature and then juxtapose a quote where an outlier usability testing participant exclaims, "This is so easy to find!"

Tying the design team's success to metrics similar to the rest of the product development, engineering, and overall organization shows that you want to play on the same field with the same rules. Instead of positioning design in a value system where their rules don't apply to you and your craft, you create a bond that ties your success to theirs. Keeping qualitative responses to your team's work, both good and bad, also reminds your stakeholders and executives that nurturing a culture of human-centered product development means remembering that those humans should be heard and recognized when measuring success.

Tactics and Exercises

Perhaps the most effective approach to educating the organization—especially senior executives and leaders of your partner teams—starts with making them active participants in the product development process. The following activities, methods, and approaches probably aren't new to many successful designers. But instead of rehashing familiar techniques, the following are pro-tips for tweaking what's familiar to be more inclusive of management and other teams who traditionally aren't in the room when designers are at work.

Include More Leaders

The more people and teams who are included throughout your product development process, the more everyone will have a greater sense of shared ownership in what you're building. You'll also create more familiarity and comfort with what has likely been an obtuse, opaque process called *design*.

We're not advocating for inviting unqualified colleagues to run roughshod over your roadmap with harebrained ideas. As the design leader inviting nondesigners into your world, you should establish limits around the scope of outside participation. You want to be up front about how people can contribute and what your team will do with their contribution. Be careful to emphasize that just because an idea comes from a boss doesn't mean that the idea will automatically make it onto the roadmap and into the product.

Improving Collaboration Between Product Management and Design

by Becki Hyde, product and design leader who builds lean, agile teams

The perspective of disciplines outside of design is immensely valuable to designers. Product managers, in particular, provide perspective on what is most aligned with business goals and what impacts design will have on operations, customer service, and marketing. Some of the most effective products I've built have come from close collaboration between design and product management. Despite their value, the insights of product managers are often left on the table, as designers seek to protect themselves from undue outside influence, from having to explain their process, or from having to justify the value of design. This causes inefficiency and frustration that ripples out to the entire product team, so mitigating this is crucial for design leadership. However, just inviting product managers to the occasional critique often creates more problems than it solves, as occasional attendees, who haven't built up good critique etiquette, do the much-hated "swoop and poop."

As a designer who moved into product management, I learned to work with designers to establish transparency, collaboration, and balance between designers and product managers, so that everyone could benefit from a healthier relationship between these two disciplines. There are a few strategies I've found especially effective for bringing product managers into the design conversation. I'll describe them in rough order of where in the product development lifecycle they occur.

Research and Testing

Working together on user research and usability testing is another way to get product managers involved, gathering their perspectives without letting them become the designers themselves. If a product manager sees what users are struggling with in research and testing, they'll understand design choices more fully, and the team will have a shared context for decision-making throughout product development.

I've found that working together on a research plan is one of the best ways to build shared context between product managers and designers. While designers should take the lead on conducting research, product managers should be involved in the decision of what to test and why, as well as helping to build a script. Product managers also make great note-takers—allowing designers to focus on facilitating research and guiding sessions so that the team gets useful information from participants.

Strategy

Designers and product managers should work together to develop strategy at all levels of product development, from new concept ideation down to the details of individual features. This gets the two disciplines heading in the same direction before anyone has developed an idea in their head of the "right" way to do something. This collaboration involves questions like: "What are we hearing from our users?" and "What problem are we trying to solve?"

Having these discussions at the team level, including not just product management but also engineering, provides several benefits. Most broadly, it creates opportunity for the team to iterate through more ideas more quickly, and better understand what's valuable, feasible, and usable. Collaboration on strategy also improves the team's shared understanding of the context of the product, so that every individual can make more effective choices in their day-to-day work.

For designers specifically, working together, across disciplines, to answer strategic questions is a way for designers to demonstrate the value of design at a level higher than "making things pretty." By facilitating conversations about user pains and needs with product managers, designers can lead without authority and show how their expertise benefits product managers, by helping them prioritize the most valuable features.

Delivery

Most software teams employ user stories to break up development work into small chunks. Unfortunately, the pattern of "product manager writes stories, designers make designs for stories" can prevent designers from leveraging their full skill set, not to mention restricting the possible solutions to what the product manager can imagine. Instead, I like using stories to facilitate conversations between product management and design.

As a product manager (see Figure 15.3), I often write the barest outline of a user story, with no acceptance criteria, and then use these "story sketches" to start a conversation with the design team about what we're trying to accomplish together. By not defining the details up front, I leave the door open for designers to influence the stories—even adding new ones or deleting unnecessary ones—and allowing us to more efficiently craft a product, together.

continues

TITLE: Jane registers for a race

STORY: As JANE
I want to register for a race
So that I can run the race

ACCEPTANCE
CRITERIA

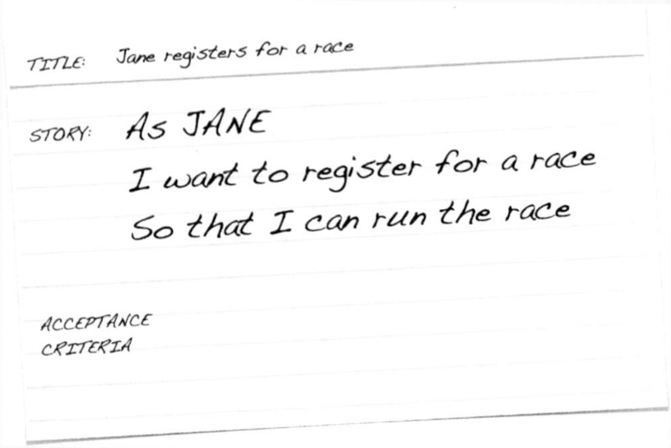

FIGURE 15.3
Becki Hyde clearly distinguishes the story from what will make the story successful to provide designers with clear constraints and expectations, without encroaching on their ability to recommend an approach for solving the problem.

After we have a shared understanding of the user value of the stories, I leave the designers to do the work of design, and let them bring me back into the conversation when they're ready—all with delivery timelines in mind, of course. Once we have designs we all feel good about, I'll write the acceptance criteria based on those designs, so there's no confusion for the team (including developers).

In Closing ...
Healthy collaboration between designers and product managers is built on a foundation of trust and understanding. As a product manager, if I'm having struggles with a designer on my team, I seek to understand where they're coming from and what their concerns are. Often, poor collaboration is the result of poor alignment—perhaps we don't share an understanding of the product goals or timeline. My advice to design managers is that you encourage your designers to do the same—seek to understand and then be understood. Try to get a sense of the constraints that product managers are working within and how they are measuring success. Then work together to come up with a process that ensures that both roles can contribute their best work.

The primary people to include will always be your development and product management colleagues and their leadership. It's arguable that you can never have too collaborative a relationship with these critical pillars for delivering a well-designed, effective, economically viable product to market. In many organizations, the marketing team is also part of this foundational core.

But you can go a step further. Consider leaders from these departments that probably play a role in shaping your product or experience:

- Sales leadership

- Customer success or service teams

- Account management

- Commercial team of business analysts

These people can provide insights and ideas that you may not uncover by only working with product management and engineering alone. If you haven't included these teams before, you'll need to set the stage for what they're doing there and what's expected of them. Reinforce that this is a normal part of the design process, there are no wrong answers, and how you'll use the information they provide.

In many cases, these business leaders will share valuable insights without ever sketching a straight-ish line or touching a Post-it Note.

Beware of Invite Stuffing

Being inclusive and collaborative doesn't mean inviting anyone and everyone all the time. Have a valid purpose for inviting other teams or leaders into your rituals, events, or activities. Be clear why you want them there and how their participation will lead to a wider, shared success than if you acted alone.

We've all likely worked in meeting-centric organizations where the default is to invite everyone. As a result, you spend countless hours in meetings where you don't contribute or know why you're there. That's the antithesis of inclusive, collaborative design. Inviting these people to too many meetings may mean they start prioritizing other meetings when you really need them in yours.

Flip back to Chapter 11, "Presenting Work," to review how we recommend balancing who needs to attend your meetings.

North Star Exercises

Arguably, the most important time to get alignment around the problem to be solved and what value the solution will bring to the business is right at the beginning, with all the stakeholders and leaders approving the direction. North Star exercises are also the easiest way in which to get executive participation—excitement is high, optimism runs rampant, and everyone swears that whatever happened last time, this time will be different.

As the facilitator of whatever North Star exercise you choose to use, whether it's as simple as getting people to commit to what success looks like or writing a press release anticipating a future success (see "Backcasting: Pre-Mortems), you should design your activities to get the alignment you need from the people who matter most.[5] That could mean getting the team to understand their primary user better than last time. Or perhaps everyone needs a clearer understanding of what "done" is supposed to look like, or specifically what measures will be driving future priorities.

In any case, don't just do North Star exercises to get people away from their desks to have a field day in the office. Establish your agenda strategically to get the outcomes you need, record the decisions, and share the results of the time together so that everyone feels accountable to the mission and understands their part in seeing to its success.

Backcasting: Pre-Mortems

Backcasting is a useful, accessible exercise that executives of any background can participate in and bring a new perspective to. Backcasting is a planning method that starts with defining a future and then working backward to identify approaches, tasks, and milestones that create causal ties between the imagined future to the present. The fundamental question of backcasting asks: "If we want to attain a certain goal, what do we all have to do to get there?"

Pre-mortem exercises ask the group to think into the future and imagine why the project was an abject disaster. Since the suggestions

---

5   Jillian D'Onfro, "Why Amazon Forces Its Developers to Write Press Releases," *Business Insider*, March 12, 2015, www.businessinsider.com/heres-the-surprising -way-amazon-decides-what-new-enterprise-products-to-work-on-next-2015-3

haven't happened yet, it's hard to be overly defensive or judgmental, but there can still be useful patterns to uncover.

Take note of who says what as you organize what people think could happen: Do patterns emerge that suggest development is afraid of too many last-minute changes? Or is the commercial team afraid that design may get pulled into a higher priority project midstream, and they'll be left to go right to engineering?

The presence of executives in pre-mortem sessions also helps clear the air and make them aware of where they may need to intervene— especially if possible threats include funding, resources, or changes in priorities.

Critique

If your design organization has established a consistent, repeatable approach to critique, you could likely use design studio as an effective, collaborative event, including diverse teams from across the wider company. Reinforce that nondesign participants are there not just for their sketching ability, but also for the insightful critiques they can offer their designer colleagues.

Ask them to actively listen to the language of design, and they'll likely discover that it's not unlike the language of business. On the other hand, if your critiques generally focus on interface design decisions, colors, typography, and layout, or are more generic show-and-tells, you risk presenting your design team as a production outfit and not a strategic partner in the organization. Consequently, the corresponding feedback might be decidedly less helpful and influential.

Design Research

Design research activities are also a great opportunity for cross-team participation among designers and nondesigners alike. For example, if your sales team or account management organization helps to provide your user research recruiting lists, show them the fruits of their labor by inviting them to the interviews or usability tests.

Ask them to influence the questions or the tasks in the interview script—perhaps they've been hearing a few anecdotes you haven't picked up on, and you all want to see if it's an aberration or a pattern.

When inviting nonresearchers to participate in observing or listening to customers, give them some structure and direction so they feel as if they are part of the team and not in the way. Consider giving them a sheet of paper with prompts such as the following:

- What did you hear or see that surprised you the most?

- What did you hear or see that you've never heard before?

- What did you hear or see that you'd want to know more about?

- Did you assume anything beforehand that turned out to be true? Or different?

At the end of a research campaign, include them in meetings when you present your findings to your team. Go one step further and write a concise one-page report of the campaign that briefly details the customers you talked to, the people who represent each user or account, and what you heard and how that information may be used and send that to the wider sales organization to provide some social proof that others are helping you out. If you have video or audio clips of the sessions, edit a few minutes' worth of reactions or comments that will help galvanize the broader team that you're heading in the right direction, thanks to their help and participation.

Customer Journeys

While the most effective customer journeys are conducted by veteran design researchers, you can ask multiple teams—such as sales, engineering, marketing, etc.—to weigh in on themes that are important to them. We suggest focusing on exposing how they feel about the stages of a journey.

There are a number of different questions about each step or stage of the journey you could ask these diverse teams to answer, ranging from any of the following:

- Where is the most risk?

- What are you most confident in knowing you can do?

- Where are you least confident in this research?

- What step has the most technical challenges?

- Where do we need to know that we're right or wrong?

As an example, with your journey on the wall, provide engineering leadership one color of dot stickers and ask them which phase they think has the most risk assumed in the portrayal. See where the stickers are placed and notice if engineering is aligned with where the most risk exists. Then ask product management to do the same thing to a clean journey and see the degree of overlap or differentiation between the two teams.

Any divergence or similarity will indicate what next steps you now need to prepare to align these teams for your own benefit and for that of the project.

Promote Participation

Remember that unless you work at a design agency, most of the people on the payroll don't know what the design team actually does, or they assume the design team is simply there to add the cosmetic details to an already determined product. You can change this perception by promoting how and when you're collaborating with other teams and the outcomes they helped you achieve.

- Take photos when you have nondesigners in front of the whiteboard with a marker. Use those photos in kickoff decks, final presentations, and in your design room or office.

- Promote a top-five or top-ten list of the people in sales who have signed up the most recruits to participate in your beta.

- Announce when you're talking to customers and what you're hoping to learn from them. Then back that up with what you're doing with the information after those interviews are completed.

- Invite your nondesign colleagues to meetups and design community happy hours—especially if you or someone on your team is speaking or hosting the event.

By making design seem like a more accessible practice and less of a dark art that can only be called upon by trendy artists under 30, your design team will more likely be seen as a partner and strategic contributor across the organization.

In short, including more people, more frequently will increase the total impact on what you deliver and therefore improve your team's standing with those folks you asked to participate.

Designing Culture Change

In Chapter 3, "Designing Your Hiring Process," we mentioned an InVision report that found the number one draw to work for a company was a positive design culture.[6]

The report used innovation and design consultancy IDEO's definition of such a work culture as one consistently demonstrating these rituals and traits:

- **Constant curiosity:** Everyone in the company is expected to be curious and to question what's possible.

- **Frequent experimentation:** Teams have methods in place to systematically test hypotheses before deciding what to do next.

- **Cross-team collaboration:** Diverse teams are expected to work together, share ideas and artifacts, and prevent silos and groupthink.

- **Intentional storytelling:** Stories rely on characters, and storytelling involves characters accomplishing their goals despite the roadblocks in their way. Instead of building things based on a spreadsheet, these teams apply the empathy for their users into narratives and design products that meet their goals.

- **More ideas:** Teams don't settle on one idea or fixate on functionality too early, and frequent feedback loops ensure that more people can contribute their own perspectives more often.

To improve how your organization's culture can evolve to be more pro-design, we recommend turning to the lessons of change management.

Change management encompasses the approaches to inspire a belief that your organization can design better than it does today—and that you can be trusted as a leader to catalyze, nurture, and sustain this new change.

In many cases, these lessons span disciplines and industries. The research behind change management and broad organizational transformation is mature, established, researched, and documented. But applying what may have worked for GM in the 1980s likely won't resonate at a startup that says it wants to be design-led but makes all its decisions in the board room ... with no designers.

---

6   *Design Trends Report: Talent* (InVision, June 2019), www.invisionapp.com/design
   -trends-report-talent

Instead, let's look at some of the fundamentals of change management[7] through a modern design-centric lens. The goal is as simple to set as it is difficult to accomplish: improve the culture in which you design and deliver your products and services.

Assess the Current State

Being able to identify how design is perceived in your own organization is critical to knowing what to change and where to start. But there's also value in knowing how your team compares to those in other organizations, especially teams in similar industries or size.

There have been many useful studies commissioned to understand the maturity of design practices. Many of these studies arrive at similar conclusions: less mature design teams just design screens, and more mature teams infuse design practices throughout the organization. They address product and business problems using design methods, and generally use design tactics to influence business strategy (see Figure 15.4).

These maturity models give a design leader the chance to see where their team and organization measure up, relative to the larger industry, and what behaviors they need to exhibit to move up the model. The benefits of a mature design practice are significant.

	Low Maturity	Medium Maturity	High Maturity
InVision New Design Frontier	Design is making things on a screen	Design is performed at scale via DesignOps & design systems	Design is business strategy
Forrester	Digital only	Multiple digital touchpoints and some research	End to end; establishes a roadmap aligned to business strategy
UK Design Council	Design plays a small or peripheral part in the business	Design is a process and integrated into operations and delivery	Design is a central and determining element in business strategy
McKinsey Business Value of Design	Little or no research or design measurement capability	Break down org silos, increase research, create experiments	Design is measured, embedded throughout the org, with senior leadership

FIGURE 15.4
These different maturity models all arrive at similar conclusions, suggesting the path to design maturity is well established, if not necessarily any easier to accomplish.

---

7 John Kotter, *Leading Change* (Boston, MA: Harvard Business Review Press, 2012).

InVision's New Design Frontier report found that "Companies with high design maturity ... are more likely to see cost savings, revenue gains, productivity gains, speed to market, and brand and market position improvements through their design efforts."[8]

But you can struggle trying to advance if you don't know where you are today.

Figure 15.5 shows a progression of an organization's understanding of design, based on the InVision maturity model. Level 1 represents organizations that perceive design as what gets rendered on a screen, and it progresses to Level 5 where companies employ design methods to address business strategy and enable design as a competitive differentiator. Hand a blank grid to your team, or to your managers if you lead a large team, and ask them to anonymously and individually plot where they think each team or department falls on the maturity scale from 1–5 and return each sheet to you.

Then compile the votes onto one master matrix that can show you where everyone perceives these teams to fall.

"How do each of these teams perceive the design practice here?"

	1	2	3	4	5
	Everyone perceives design as decoration	Little support or attempt to learn about design	Leadership is curious to see design value quantified	Leadership wants design involved in big projects	Design is seen as innovators, differentiators at all levels
Executive Team					
Development/ Engineering					
Product Management					
Marketing					
Line of Business Stakeholder/Client					

FIGURE 15.5

Use a grid to measure to what degree your business partners and stakeholders understand design to identify where you should focus your change management efforts.

---

8 Leah Buley, Chris Avore, Stephen Gates, "The New Design Frontier" (InVision, January 2019), www.invisionapp.com/design-better/design-maturity-model/

Completing this quick exercise should show you where to prioritize your education efforts. In Figure 15.6, for example, it seems that most of the team feels that the engineering team doesn't necessarily understand the design practice. If your development partners generally score about a 2 and are pretty far from a 4, you may be better served by focusing on your Line of Business/Commercial stakeholders who only see design as a 1 and with a little help, could probably get to a 3.

Note any glaring differences between how they view the world and how you perceive the organization. You may have your share of biases that your team is naturally immune to, so it's best to get a broad perception of how the design team thinks their organization understands design.

It's ultimately up to you to prioritize which group you want to focus on, or in what order, or just how tailored of a message you want to craft for each group. Here, we'll focus primarily on the executive team and commercial leaders of the organization since it's those audiences who often control resources, funding, and which projects will ultimately get done.

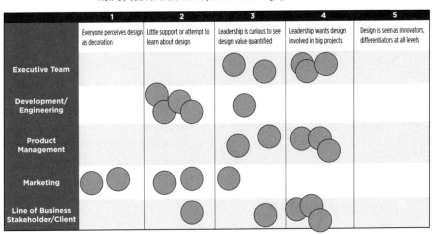

FIGURE 15.6
Individually mapping responses reveals how the team feels without risking groupthink.

Establish a Vision

With a clear understanding of how the company understands design, you can now craft a vision for what your organization, team, and process will look like once you've reached the top of that hill. You'll likely find that with a vision in place, your broader product development organization will be more willing to believe that change is possible and understand how they can contribute to the difference between where you are today and where you want to go.

You can also turn to the characteristics of more mature design organizations to shape your vision via the maturity models we discussed previously in "Assess the Current State" to guide what is a realistic next step for your team.

You should decide how broad you want this vision to be. In larger organizations, keeping your vision focused on how your product development will research, prioritize, and deliver new and existing products in your line of business is likely enough of a challenge. In smaller companies, you may be able to expand the vision to include more themes. Here, we'll focus on how to establish a realistic vision of how products should be designed and delivered.

This vision should be clearly aligned with how you want to prioritize your time coming out of the current state exercise we discussed earlier. Because you will still be doing your day job of leading a design team, you need to concentrate your efforts on creating a vision that is attainable and focused on what is most important, easiest to change, or quickest to change—not all of the above.

The more people outside of your design team you can involve in crafting this vision, the better. After all, a strong organization-wide understanding of design should also be the rising tide that lifts the product management, development, and marketing boats as well. Such participation gives your contributors a greater sense of ownership in making them part of a larger strategic effort, and not just someone who wasn't consulted who now has to deal with the fallout.

Most vision statements can be as simple as a paragraph and a few bullet points on a slide that describe the design team. The most effective vision statements usually include the following characteristics:

- It's clear to others within the organization (not just designers).

- It's easy to repeat, describe, and share with others.

- It's actually attainable.

Likewise, many effective vision statements try to address these questions:

- Why is this important?
- To whom? For whom?
- Why now?
- How will we know when we're there?
- What will we do to get there?

Consider the following example of an effective vision statement when crafting your own.

> The ACME Design Group (yes, we're making that up) researches, prototypes, and consistently tests a more elegant, profitable portfolio of products that serve a customer base of thousands of healthcare administrators. As the health insurance industry undergoes massive disruption from unforeseen threats, regulation, and consumer demand, our distributed team of designers across three lines of business will strive to rely on the latent and primary needs of our customers to identify where and how to prioritize our design work.
>
> Instead of annual planning and roadmaps to drive our product development process, over the next six months, we will shift to building prototypes to test against our hypotheses to determine what we should be building and why. We will share these insights and recommendations early, often, and across diverse teams. As a result, our executives can participate, adapt, and lead the rest of this organization as we undergo our digital transformation to be more customer-centric over the next 18 months.

This vision is brief, understandable, and still suggests concrete change from the current state to an end state, within a window of time. After executives have acknowledged what vision you're setting out to fulfill, you can then use such an agreement to measure if others are keeping up their end of the bargain later down the road. For example, if a stakeholder is averse to signing off on user research prior to a development effort because they see it as taking too much time, reference the vision and reiterate that committing to customer centricity means involving customers before building anything.

It's also tied to larger corporate initiatives, such as the digital transformation and the organization's commitment to customer centricity.

Such a tactic indirectly proves that you're not doing this effort independently of the larger company, and it allows you to tie your efforts to commitments that the organization has already made.

Creating such a vision with your full team ensures that they are buying into their commitments as well, which begets co-ownership and a sustained interest in seeing their mission through. And much like a team charter, it's a good idea to print and post this commitment in a group office space, design room, theater, and digitally for others to see and learn from.

Build a Coalition of Advocates

Most days may seem like you're the only one who can lead the fight for good design in your organization. You probably feel like you're the only one who can pick up your design team and carry them on your back to victory. But the reality is that you need people who support you and believe in what your team can do for the company, if given the chance.

Finding advocates who will support you and your team is where you immerse yourself in the office politics that many others will shy away from—often at the expense of their careers in the company. Making these connections will likely increase your team's responsibilities to the company, ensure they have the resources and time to get their jobs done, get more recognition for their work, and be seen as a critical contributor to the organization's success.

To be most influential, your allies should be a diverse group across the organization—not just your boss or your boss's boss. You want to create a number of ties throughout the company—people who are aware of your work and your vision—but you risk stifling that awareness if you don't cross out of your own business unit or reporting line.

Your allies should know how the big decisions get made. They should know who allocates funds—and how it happens. They have the inside track on the projects that get green-lit, and they are one of the first to know why other projects end up on life support. And to top it off, they're comfortable speaking about these topics in plain, clear language so their help is accessible and, in turn, actionable.

Additionally, the best allies are those who have political capital to spend with you, not just the ability to provide resources. Although often being in a position to assign resources implies some political influence, having politically influential advocates can make problems go away without needing any resources, or can line up resources before you even have to ask.

In Chapter 13, "Developing Designers," we discussed the differences between mentors and sponsors. These allies should not be mistaken for mentors—think of them as sponsors for your entire design practice. Similar to how personal sponsors spur change that actively progresses individual professional opportunities, the best allies are sponsors who can create change—indirectly or directly—that will advance your team and practice in the company.

Finding these advocates can be as easy as learning about what problems they're passionate about solving and showing how your team's design work could or already addresses these challenges.

For example, if a new executive of a line of business other than your own is publicly committed to greater data-informed decision-making, you can have a productive introductory conversation showing how your design team has been successful at applying design research and usage metrics to guide your own design solutions. Revisit how you've been communicating the value of design to your management and see what you can apply to these conversations as well.

Treat these initial conversations much like you would when meeting a neighbor for the first time—you probably wouldn't ask for a favor right away unless you absolutely had to, because there's a great chance you're going to be around each other for the long haul, even if you don't see that person every day.

That said, if you do need something, be specific about how your ally can help—don't just be ambiguous or vague and expect that person to know how to fix something.

Perhaps most important of all is to never stop at one ally or advocate—you want a coalition of diverse supporters who can help you maneuver through the organization. Failing to have a strong network of these allies exposes you to the risk that they won't always be there and able to support you. These advocates may change positions themselves, leave the organization entirely, or perhaps have their own priorities shift that may inadvertently result in them no longer supporting your efforts.

Some people even keep a page in a notebook keeping track of their allies. They'll list their names, when they started supporting them, what business unit, team, or line of business they lead, and even high-level demographic information such as if they're white males or represent an underrepresented group. These lists are simply a quick summary to indicate if you're inadvertently maintaining a coalition of allies that is too similar to one another, and therefore inherently risks limiting the perspective they can offer.

Find and Celebrate Short-Term Wins

Showing evidence of early success is critical to getting senior leadership—and your coalition of allies—to continue their support that design really *does* make a difference to the company. Quick, early wins mean that you build momentum and show the rest of the organization you're capable of leading change for the better. These wins also show that, unlike many corporate initiatives that just fade away or die on the vine, you're backing up your talk with action. John Kotter's model for change management cites the best short-term wins are:

- Easy to understand by others
- Support your vision for the team and organization
- Measurable

These wins can be tactical—even increasing the number of customers you're interviewing or how many different teams have participated in design studio over time are worth celebrating.

In fact, we even encourage you to maintain a log of your victories. Keep a simple shareable, editable spreadsheet for your team with the following info to monitor your victories:

- Short-term win
- Team/individual responsible
- Primary business partner/stakeholder
- So what (outcome)
- Business goal
- Output
- Date
- Evangelized via …
- Celebrated via …
- Notes

It's too easy to get caught up in the day–to-day job of leading your team to realize you've had four successful wins that you haven't shared or celebrated. In other cases, writing down what and how you celebrated will also be a useful exercise to make sure that you're diversifying how you promote your success and who you're championing.

Create a Sense of Urgency

Complacency can creep up and slowly demoralize many organizations over years and decades. For design teams, complacency can destroy a team in months. Designers are hired to challenge the status quo, to do things differently, and to create something today that didn't exist yesterday. As a result, it can be incredibly frustrating to be told either "that's the way it's always been done here," or "that would never work here."

But that's still what many teams hear when they want to improve—or at least try to improve—how they work in their organizations. In many cases, pointing to a maturity model isn't enough to create action where there previously was none. Instead, you'll need to prepare yourself to have some possibly awkward conversations.

Prove Value by Creating Value

by Anne Hjortshoj, Director of UX at CarGurus

Most companies understand that product design requires some level of investment, if only because it's so easy for the layperson (read: *the customer*) to tell when a product isn't usable, seems broken, or feels cheap.

The hard part, for upper management, is understanding the value and capabilities of the designers they've hired. User experience design isn't just surface-level pixels; it's an entire practice that leads to design outcomes. If company leadership doesn't understand this, then the design team is at risk of being seen as an expensive "extra" and as a cost center.

It's incumbent upon design leaders, then, to prove that design is a capability that drives business success, just as engineering, product management, or marketing do. In order for design teams to continue and grow and flourish, design leaders must prove the value of design.

Many years ago, I created a UX team at a startup that had never had a formal UX practice. I was hired by the head of product management, who wanted to see improvement in the front-end design of the company's product. Although there was already an established product management capability, the startup's product managers didn't see designers as partners. Product managers were accustomed to ideating on their own, and believed that the function of design was to polish the ideas that the product managers came up with. As far as product managers were concerned, designers were there to document ideas and to make things pretty.

Unfortunately, designers were consulted too late in the project cycle to add much value, and the solutions that resulted didn't solve actual customer problems very well, or scale over time. Customers were unhappy, and the team was caught in a cycle of releasing features that weren't successful.

It turned out that customer unhappiness was a crucial lever to apply to this situation. If customer pain hadn't been obvious, it would have been much harder to argue that anything needed to change. In this case, it was crystal clear that the designs created by product managers weren't working, and that something needed to shift.

With the support of the head of product management, who was a strong advocate for the UX group, I gently pushed to get designers involved earlier in the process. I pointed out to the product managers that one of design's functions is to reduce risk, and that product management was failing to take advantage of this capability.

Designers helped with this effort by asking probing questions and pushing back on product manager–generated design work. The air cover provided by the head of product management was immensely helpful here; she calmly explained to her product managers that yes, this is how designers should be incorporated into project work, and that getting to the right solution was more important than getting to a solution.

After some minor initial resistance and questioning, product managers were soon asking outright for designer help at the beginning of projects, and the quality of the product UI rapidly improved. This "win" made it easier to advocate for further hiring, and made a case for introducing additional UX-led functions.

A Progression of Wins

On joining an organization that has a very narrow appreciation of the value of design, it may be tempting to jump into the task of defining a broad vision for the new design team, which can be presented to executive stakeholders to get buy-in, extend influence, and gain support.

Unfortunately, top-down declarations of intent are not in themselves very convincing, and if there's no pre-existing understanding of the value of design in an organization, a sweeping vision won't compel or seem realistic.

An alternative approach is to instead survey the organizational and product landscape for immediate wins that demonstrate the value of design team involvement, while quietly keeping the long-term vision in mind as an ultimate target. For example, at a large company, I noticed that UI engineers were isolated on project teams. They complained to me that they felt that it was impossible to coordinate their approach to front-end code, and that code quality was declining as a result.

Additionally, because UI engineers were outnumbered on each team by full-stack engineers, they felt that they didn't have adequate representation to upper management, which resulted in lack of budget for UI-engineer-specific conference attendance and training.

Coincidentally, my UX design team was in charge of leading a product rebrand. We needed the UI engineers to partner with us to coordinate code refactoring and scoping of the rebrand effort. A divided UI engineering function would mean that our project was sunk.

continues

I suggested that the UI engineers create a guild, with the goal of sharing information, coordination of code refactoring efforts, and philosophical alignment. The engineers responded enthusiastically, but wondered: How do we do this without managers trying to be involved?

I answered that I'd commit to actively shielding them from interference until the Guild had established a cadence of meetings and workshops.

It worked beautifully. I provided air cover from management (who did try to get involved; I had total support from people further up the chain, though, which made things easier), and the Guild collectively sorted out an approach to code refactoring.

In the end, the Guild got their conference budget, and even created their own yearly global conference. And they were fantastic partners for my team, going forward.

Adjacent Wins Are Also Wins

It might seem at first that facilitating improvements for design-adjacent areas of the organization isn't helping the design team in a direct way. But these are the first steps to build trust between the design team and the rest of the organization, while in the background the design leader can begin to push more business outcome–driven design work.

In the end, all positive outcomes help to increase the credibility and influence of the design team, no matter if they're "vision-related" or not. To build the influence of the UX team, leverage every opportunity you can—everything counts.

Usually, these meetings are awkward for everyone involved because creating this urgency often means talking about where things have failed, where other competitors have surpassed the company, or where the wrong decision was made. Incredibly, many work cultures don't want to hold people—and teams—accountable because the bar is usually set so low that technically these teams are doing exactly what they're supposed to do.

Fortunately, we can rely on two consistent approaches of the design practice to help set the table for managing conflict and accountability to create a sense of urgency: research and metrics. User reactions tinged with emotional honesty and hard quantitative data representing patterns of missed goals or expectations make the conversation about the work, not the people in the room or the people back at their desks (unless one of the quotes you choose to use is *"Anyone who designed this deserves to be sent to Mars to design their way home"*). Abandonment rates, patterns found in search logs, and customer attrition are all useful indicators that something needs to be improved. Be wary of basing your argument exclusively on NPS scores, due to their high margin of error and questionable value, as discussed earlier in this chapter.

In other cases, design leaders have gone so far as to print disjointed cross-channel experiences—yes, foam-mounted glossy screenshots of mobile apps and desktop interfaces—to show executives how these systems looked and worked like totally different systems, despite everyone regularly committing to a cohesive experience.

Likewise, you can illustrate that a lack of action means that something the company wants will not happen without change. If, for example, the organization says it's customer centric, try to advise that such a culture can't exist if you have to get permission to talk to customers to just test an interface for usability.

As Maria Giudice, a former design executive at Facebook and Autodesk, has said, "aligning your work to customer needs isn't a guarantee to change, but it's certainly harder for skeptics to ignore you or debunk your recommendations when you're saying that something needs to change."[9]

Wrapping Up

Design leaders regularly say they want design to be more influential in the company and have a seat at the executive table. It's not because they're on a power trip. They want influence because they're tired of being brought in too late to make a meaningful impact. They're sick of working on things already decided by others. They're through with designing things that probably don't matter instead of working on more valuable, rewarding, meaningful opportunities.

Such suspicions usually come back to a lack of trust on behalf of the executive team for the larger product development process and the perceived ambiguity of the design process. They just aren't

9   Jamie O'Brien, "6 Rules for Embracing Change at Your Company," *Fortune*, March 19, 2019, https://fortune.com/2019/03/19/design-leadership-change/

convinced, or haven't yet heard a compelling argument tailored for their own organization.

But this tide can be turned.

Those design leaders who have seen themselves and their larger design and product organization become more influential say they knew they were on the right track when their teams were asked for research to explore a new initiative to see if it warranted funding. Or when they presented their team's personas to the heads of the different lines of business to see where there were overlaps and gaps that the design team should explore. Or when they were asked to show how implementing a design system within a greater design operations effort had reduced time to market but increased quality.

There's no better way to convince someone that something can be successful than making them part of the success. Show these executive colleagues how ideas start in research as the voice of the customer and turn into features. Teach them how to critique design work early and often. Continue a drumbeat of asking what the prototype needs to prove with customers before deciding what gets built next. Refer to your team charter—particularly your team motto—early and often, as it crystalizes and catalyzes who you are in the organization.

As you continue your own evangelization and promotion efforts, continue learning more about how your champions, allies, skeptics, and other stakeholders can impact your ability to deliver. Find out what's important to them. Learn if they're even incentivized to work together. Uncover if they've been a change agent somewhere earlier in their career and could help you on this journey.

Be careful you don't find yourself growing frustrated at a lack of perceived buy-in if you're not monitoring positive change step-by-step. Keep tabs on which meetings you're invited to now that you weren't invited to earlier, or if other senior leaders are now actively participating in your meetings, rituals, and events. You can even monitor what you're being asked and by whom. Find out how you got your invite.

Many a management consultant has said that change management is a long game—the proverbial marathon versus a sprint. Usually, the only people who say it can be quick are the authors and speakers who have something to sell. But the framework is sound, and there's no better time to begin fostering the environment for culture change than right now.

Escape Velocity

We chose to title this book *Liftoff!* when we pictured design managers having the tools, training, and vision necessary to elevate themselves and their teams higher than where they were when they started reading this book—and long after they set it down. We hope you'll be higher in the organization, higher in your confidence, and have a loftier perspective to view the systems in which you practice.

If that's indeed the case, then at this point in the book, we're in the final stages of counting down to liftoff. The safety checks have been run, the boosters are lighting up, and the helmets are on. It's *go* time.

The good news—no, the *great* news—is that our design industry is in a great position for liftoff, too. Designers now have the opportunity to lead organizations to deliver better, more useful, sustainable products that can make a meaningful difference in the world.

As more companies invest in design, they will subsequently trust, support, and enact the recommendations of their design, product, and development leadership teams to create a better future. The laggards and skeptics will have little choice but to adapt or cross their fingers and hope this is all a phase, as their revenues dwindle and growing the top line cedes priority to cutting the bottom line.

It's these forward-thinking leaders, some of whom will be leading design teams and others who will lead entire organizations, who will drive this change from how products were designed for decades to this more inclusive, thoughtful, present approach we've been exploring.

The design leaders of these companies or their own firms will manage and lead differently than their colleagues with similar titles and roles just 15 years ago. These leaders won't be limited by hierarchy, specialized roles, or by business requirements documents describing what to build and when it's due.

Their teams will be a diverse organization of designers, content specialists, researchers, and developers who have unique backgrounds, both in their individual lives and their professional discipline. Specialists will help coach and mentor junior generalists. Senior generalists will create their own opportunities and will apply their knowledge of multiple disciplines and experience across many products to be invaluable at helping their partners thrive in this new era of design and product development.

These leaders will enable their teams to focus on complex problems because they'll be working side-by-side with their previously siloed counterparts in their development team and their business stakeholders, sooner and more frequently. They'll use methods like design thinking and design studio throughout the product development process, not just at the start of projects, so that teams are constantly working collaboratively exploring new ideas or new solutions to problems that everyone on the team can understand.

Fluently speaking the language of the business will be natural and comfortable—not just to the design leaders' senior executives, but to their direct managers and the directs of their directs, so that they too understand how their work contributes to the larger success of the company. They'll phrase requirements in relation to the user, and phrase success criteria in relation to the company's overall goals—goals which will be centered around the customer's success.

Instead of inadvertently solving the same problems over and over again, or seemingly creating more and more procedures to make teams more efficient that do anything but, these leaders will enable design operations to allow designers to have the structure, tools, and format they need to focus on solving the most important problems of the business.

Embracing Complexity, Resiliency, and Systems

These new design leaders won't stop at learning more about the primary user. Rather, they'll take a systems-thinking view of the problem space and identify and mitigate downstream consequences of their design recommendations. As automation becomes more widespread, design leaders will have to prioritize learning who else is hurt or empowered by these design choices, such as people who manage inventory in the warehouse, the drivers and delivery staff, and the teams who service these goods when they break down.

The design managers who were leading teams during the 2020 coronavirus pandemic have had a crash course in resiliency that will make them more adaptable to future significant disruptions. It's still far too early to try predicting what a new normal will look like and for whom. The design leaders who were increasing how frequently they checked in with their teams to create more human-centered feedback loops will have the advantage over those managers who tried to enforce a business-as-usual mindset when the world was anything but. These leaders learned how to embrace a remote workforce. Some had to pivot their business model and their customer experience. Others, through no fault of their own, found themselves trying to find their next team to lead while helping their dislocated colleagues also find their next opportunities. Coping with change and instability won't be comfortable, and likely won't be unfamiliar either.

All of which means that the design leaders who will guide teams well into the middle of the 21st century will know how fragile these socioeconomic and technological systems may be. These design leaders will be aware of the inherent biases that may be found in the algorithms of their machine-learning platforms. They'll use their influence to make sure that diverse, inclusive teams are involved early and often to ensure that they don't put their communities—especially those at greatest risk—in harm's way simply because they were only concerned with bringing their AI products to market faster.

And the new design leader of tomorrow will have to confront the challenges of a more connected society that has grown comfortable sharing more data (fake or real), with far more people (both bad actors and beyond friends and family), and at the expense of other activities or norms (as screen time increases exponentially).

Although ethics isn't frequently taught as required material in many higher education curriculums, the design leaders of tomorrow will have to seek out how to educate themselves and their product development colleagues to base their product decisions on a shared foundation of ethical behavior that supports the business, customer, and downstream people who can be affected by the choices they make in the design office. They'll create the time and space necessary for exploring the moral and ethical ramifications of their decisions so their products and services don't stray from their core values and principles.

These responsibilities are more complex and demanding than those of the design manager of a decade ago, and quite possibly more than what's in your remit as you read this today. But these challenges are only going to be compounded as entire populations will have higher expectations of more digital products and services in almost every facet of their lives.

That's not to infer that design leaders can feel like success will just come to them. In fact, a sense of design's entitlement—that the business owes design teams something just because they're designers—could undermine, if not unravel, years of progress.

Adapting to New Challenges and Expectations

There are many roadblocks that can impede organizations from embracing design leadership. Existing attitudes, policies, and cultures may stunt adoption. Champions and sponsors of effective, high-performing design teams can leave the company. CEOs may not really know what their Chief Design Officers are doing, and they may question their value. And just like that, the organization can lurch back to the dark ages of hovering art directors and making the logo bigger.

The most significant threat to creating an environment where designers can do their best work is the company itself. A company that doesn't value design will not be able to support valuable designers.

ADVICE FROM THE FIELD

Know Your Worth

by Adam Fry-Pierce, Director of Design Community at InVision and curator of the Design Leadership Forum

Adam Fry-Pierce has asked designers all over the planet what keeps them awake at night. He says that design leaders struggle to articulate their value clearly and the effectiveness of their contributions, which leads to skeptical stakeholders.

"There's a lot of pressure on design leaders right now, particularly those in enterprise environments," he said. "We have a seat at the strategy table, but most of us don't know how to prove our value in the same way as our peers in engineering or product. The only way we'll keep our seat is by proving and expanding upon the value we offer. This means for leaders at more mature design orgs, the investment in design needs to work out, and they need to tell a clear story on how the business is benefiting from a more mature design organization."

Indeed, design leaders of tomorrow will be measured in how clearly they articulate design's impact to the business. Designers are being asked to solve more complex, compelling problems that can improve the lives of millions of people compared to the earlier projects of the field (cue a side-eye to the still-running legal debates of gig-economy apps and how those businesses define their workforce).

Design leaders will be at the forefront of helping more people across the planet access medical care, connect to the internet, and find employment. It's not unreasonable to think that design managers will be building teams to confront climate change, address homelessness, or improve the political process or judicial system. Yes, those are wicked problems. And no, design won't magically fix everything. It is likely that to reach any milestone of any significance, designers will have some influence in the outcome.

Fortunately, there are more opportunities to learn how to practice effective design leadership than ever (and far more than when we started writing this book). Today, there are books by amazing leaders, such as *Resilient Management* by Lara Hogan, *The Making of a Manager* by Julie Zhuo, and *The Manager's Path* by Camille Fournier. You can also check out conferences that are dedicated exclusively to design leadership and managing design (at least one of which is in Chicago, in the late summer).

You'll even find specialized retreats where design leaders can unplug and share stories, perspectives, and tactics that create a dedicated safe place in a more intimate gathering. Even multiple design leadership-focused Slack communities are available for asking questions, making introductions, and listening and sharing with others who are experiencing similar challenges.

The digital design field is ready to evolve. Some organizations are learning there can be a better way and are more open to changing how they design. Others will need champions and change agents to create a sense of urgency. Design leaders are learning how to elevate and articulate the relationship between their teams' successes and their organizations' outcomes.

Escape velocity, when used in physics, refers to the minimum speed needed for a free object to escape from the gravitational pull of a massive body. In turn, design's escape velocity is the cultural tipping point when an organization understands the possibilities of great design. It's the inflection point when the organization wants to elevate its design maturity *with* you, leaving the gravitational pull of fixed scope, fixed cost, and fixed time that can happen when design is perceived as a service offered. We hope the steps and strategies we've discussed will lead you, your team, and your company to reach that escape velocity and leave the old ways of design far in the past.

The future for design is *now*. Companies of all sizes and industries will be increasingly relying on emerging technologies, and will need better equipped design leaders to fully thrive in these complex, global markets. Let's all design how we'll lead when we lift off to embrace that challenge.

NOTE MORE LEADERSHIP RESOURCES

There are many different opportunities and ways to learning more about design leadership, including the following:

- **leadingdesign.slack.com**
- **designleadership-hq.slack.com**
- **design-dept-leaders.slack.com**
- InVision Design Leadership Forum
- Leadership by Design conference
- Leading Design conferences, meetups, and retreats
- Design Leadership Summit
- DesignOps Summit
- Design Dept. workshops and coaching
- Within.co retreats, community, and magazine

INDEX

Skinner, Kristin, 291

skip-level one-on-ones, 161–163, 254

Slack apps for onboarding, 133

Slack communities for design leaders, 338, 339

Slackground Check, 115

"So You Want to Be a UX Manager?" (Glasson), 9

Society for Human Resource Management, 72

software skills of candidates, 81

solo project team members, 28

Spells, Monet, 10–11

sponsors

  compared with advocates, 325

  in development of designers, 251–255

sprint cadence, DesignOps in practice, 266

status checks, DesignOps in practice, 267

stories, 308–309, 311–312

strategy, collaboration between designers and product managers, 311

Strathern, Marilyn, 305

structured interviews, 40, 45, 99

Swanson, Gail, 14, 200–201

T

tactics and exercises, 309–317. *See also* designing influence

  backcasting, 314

  collaboration between product management and design, 310–312

critique, 315

customer journeys, 316–317

design research, 315–316

include more leaders, 309–313

North Star exercises, 314

pre-mortem exercises, 314–315

promote participation, 317

take-home projects as design exercises, 109–111

team building activities, failure of, 30–32

team charters, 135–148

  advantages of, 138

  areas to grow and improve, 144–145

  defined, 136–137

  defining team purpose, 139–140

  finalizing charter document, 145–146

  how team conducts its business, 143–147

  member-to-member behaviors and expectations, 142–143

  as reflection of team culture, 148, 275

  signing and sharing the charter, 147

  what team does, does not do, 140–142

  workshop to develop, 137–143

technology, for presentations, 187

Textio, 69–70

Thomas, Erin L., 14

threats to scaling design, 261–265

  large number of designers, 263–265

  organizational misunderstanding of design, 263

ACKNOWLEDGMENTS

Our Sincerest Gratitude

We'd both like to thank:

Lou Rosenfeld and Marta Justak have been great shepherds through-out the extended process of writing this book. They were quick with the joke, or to light us up a little bit when we needed some ... motiva-tion. We've been lucky to get to work with them, and the material in this book is much, much better because of them. Danielle Foster was really put through a test to make sure that everything got dropped into place from a graphic design and layout perspective, and Deb Aoki made sure our illustrations conveyed deep messages, often from a single bullet of context. Additionally, Sue Boshers was invalu-able as a proofreader, and Marilyn Augst made sure that everything was indexed in order to make it easily accessible.

When we first started on this journey so many seasons ago, we pulled together a much different outline of ideas and spent time shaping it. Once we'd completed that, we reached out to other leaders to help make sure that we were going in the right direction. We deeply appreciate the time and energy spent reviewing our thoughts, provid-ing key insights, and adding some great feedback quotes for the book. Okay, a lot of time. We truly appreciate our shapers: Cennydd Bowles, Amy Jiménez Márquez, Gabby Hon, Fred Beecher, Will Hacker (who we miss dearly), Nicole Maynard, Eduardo Ortiz, Will Sansbury, Nathan Gao, Dan LeBoeuf, Per Axbom, Christopher McCann, James Royal-Lawson, and Phil Suessenguth. These fine folks all chimed in and provided feedback that we used to help put forth our proposal to write this book. If not for them, we wouldn't have been able to shape a decent idea into what we believe is a solid book.

We wouldn't have been able to make any real progress without being on the shoulders of giants who provided us with the eleva-tion needed. In no particular order, we are infinitely grateful to the stand-out leaders who lent us their wisdom and insight: Monet Spells, Helen Keighron, Alexis Lloyd, Erin Thomas, Ph.D, Lisa Welch-man, Julia Elman, Boon Yew Chew, Amy Johnson, Eli Montgomery, Maria Pereda, Joanne Weaver, Jasmine Friedl, Jen Tress, Randy Ellis, Amanda Schonfeld, Dr. Steve Julius, Richard Dalton, Shay Howe,

Abi Jones, Adam Connor, Elizabeth Goodman, Amy Jiménez Márquez, Brad Nunnally, Gail Swanson, Jason Mesut, Jacqui Frey, Todd Zaki Warfel, Kim Lenox, Becki Hyde, Margot Bloomstein, Anne Hjortshoj, Adam Fry-Pierce, Dani Nordin, Lisa deBettencourt, Nicole Maynard, Alissa Briggs, Ryan Rumsey, Alexa Curtis, Mindaugas Petrutis, and Tutti Taygerly. You'll meet them across the pages of the book—we know you'll learn from them just as we did.

Additionally, we've been really fortunate to have some amazing peer reviewers who have patiently awaited the implementation of their feedback. It takes a really special person to flip through the pages of often-unfinished thoughts (or sentences!), or not-yet-ready-for-prime-time-consumption content. We're not sure if those folks ever thought they'd see a cover design, and yet, here we are, bound and ready to go, thanks to their very significant nudges. Our thanks are extended to: Emily Campbell, Ronnie Battista, David Panarelli, Bibiana Nunes, Emileigh Barnes, Amy Jiménez Márquez, and Eli Montgomery.

We'd be remiss if we also didn't thank the people who have read the much more finalized version, too. It takes a lot of moxy to read some-one's work and then put your personal stamp of approval on it. These folks really stepped up and gave us the last-minute-before-hitting-print boost of confidence: Kristin Skinner, Scott Berkun, Bruno Figueiredo, Eduardo Ortiz, Kara DeFrias, Karen Pascoe, Meriah Garrett, Katja Forbes, Anna Ewing, Johnny Boursiquot, Aaron Snow, and Jesse James Garrett.

Finally, we're over the moon to have Kim Goodwin write our fore-word. We've both been fans of Kim for almost as long as we can remember being in design. When you write a book, you come up with a list of "who would make for a great foreword for this?" and this is one of those cases where the first choice was also the person who agreed. Kim is someone we both look up to and admire and aspire to be more like as we make our way through the world.

Every step of the way, we've found ourselves surrounded by wonder-ful humans who helped us iterate and improve. And then iterate and improve again. Some of the folks we've mentioned have not only read this material once, twice, or three times ... they've seen it at its imperfect worst. It's an amazing community that is home to kind souls like the folks we've been blessed to know and work with, and we don't take that for granted.

Chris would like to thank:

I don't know if I'll write another book again, so I'd better get this right.

First, I have to thank Russ. It was his guidance and leadership early on—including the proposal writing and operations of writing a book—that led to where we are today. His perspective, voice, and approach helped shape my own writing as we adjusted the vision for the text, and the book is better for it.

You can't write a half-decent book on management if you've never managed a team before, so I have to start by thanking the folks who have worked on the teams I've managed. Without our successes and the lessons we learned, this book would have been written by someone else. That means I have to thank Joe McNeil, Megan Grocki, Tami Evnin, Sofia Millares, Casey Hald, Dan Selden, Abby Getman, Aaron Irizarry, Kyle Riedel, Brian Putz, Rich Hemsley, JD Jones, Jon Van Dalen, Lorena Vargas, Drew Griffith, Dmytro Kovalenko, and Sofia Mora for helping shape those experiences. Thank you to Dean Oligino, Jeanne McKenna, Sarah McCasland, and Drew Falkman as peers I could learn from while managing teams.

Likewise, you can't appoint yourself a manager, so I have to thank the executive leaders I've had the privilege of learning from and who have trusted me to lead their organizations over the last ten years, so big thanks to Adam Ross, Nick Pastoressa, Jay Garcia, and Pat Sheridan.

I'm also fortunate to have a great support system of folks with whom I can discuss either the design industry or the benefits of two yurts versus one while walking the fairway (but more likely the rough): Pete Kim, Matt Ventre, Ashley Mayo, Justin Davis, Hally Leadbetter, Michelle Wie, and Jeremy Breslau. Kevin Baxter and Jeremy Entwistle have also provided much needed advice, wisdom, and encouragement my whole career, which has been captured throughout this book, so thank you both.

Throughout the speaking and travel circuit, I've been able to have amazing conversations with design leaders who have also helped me reflect on how to frame the recommendations in this book. Many of the folks change over the years (especially when it takes you over four years to write a book, so recency bias is in play here), but thank you to Steve Baty, Bennett King, Elina Ollila, Corey Vilhauer, Jason Mesut, Charlene McBride, Margot Bloomstein, Boon Sheridan, Peter Boersma, Andy Budd, Cennydd Bowles, and many others. And even though New York City doesn't exactly count as travel and I don't get to see you all enough, it's great knowing that Whitney Hess, Donna Lichaw, and Andi Mignolo are a few miles away and have amazing insights to offer as friends and colleagues.

Matt Grocki has also been an amazing friend, confidant, and world explorer with me. Whether discussing the influence chapter in Kansas or the hiring chapters in Nova Scotia, he's always had a caring, empathetic, and kind view of what lessons could help people and how to communicate those in a way that inspires learning and self-improvement. Thank you.

Lastly, I have to thank my family for their love, understanding, and support throughout this process. Most of this book was written not on nights and weekends, but on tarmacs, in airline lounges, and in the air when I've been away and missing good-night kisses and morning drop-offs at school. Thank you Karen, Riley, Courtney, and Graeme.

Russ would like to thank:

Chris is the obvious first person to thank: he's been a great partner—great friction and grease when either were needed—and always without a worry of staying our course as authors and friends.

There are always more people to thank than there is room for—and I'd like to start by thanking everyone who has ever been a part of my ever-learning work experiences. Every context has been something to learn from, and I've been grateful for that.

There are always folks who are quick to prop me up, lend me an ear, or show me a better path. I'm ever grateful and thankful for some of the best partners and pals a person could get to share time and space with, including Lena Trudeau, Khalid Hassouneh, John Galeziowski, Ahmad Ishaq, Mike Pansky, Brad Nunnally, Brad Simpson, probably another Brad I'm forgetting, Matthew Milan, Jennifer Tress, Kara DeFrias, Bill Rooney, Eduardo Ortiz, Dr. Steve Julius, Aaron Snow, Gabby Hon, Yoni, Shay Howe, Emileigh Barnes, Steve Baty who happily reviewed all kinds of poorly written stuff in my first books and showed me that there's no harm in early reviews, and Christina Wodtke, who gently nudged me in the direction of Michael Nolan, who in turn got all this writing business started in the first place.

I've been thoroughly moved by the strength, courage, and wisdom of the following amazing people: Anne Hjortshoj, Helen Keighron, Maria Pereda, Liz Goodman, Lisa deBettencourt, Alyssa Boehm, Dani Nordin, Jasmine Friedl, Jane Austin, Kara DeFrias, Andrea Mignolo, and the others who are part of this ever-evolving crew. Pay attention conference organizers—that's an entire event of keynote speakers who were just listed!

If you ever get the chance to do public service work, please do so. Public service was so very rewarding, and I was lucky to be able to spend time doing that awesome work. I'm overcome with the gratitude that I have for all public servants—the ones I got to work with who were near, the ones somewhere adjacent, and the ones that I got to learn from yet never got to meet. There are so many great public servants working across the globe to make living our lives ... just better. They're everywhere, and they're talented and gifted, and they do the work for the rest of us. Thank you, each and every one of you.

And to the people who always make me want to squeeze extra hours out of the days, carry the load and keep me grounded when I'm in other places, and who make me laugh a lot more than a person really has any business doing, a big, hearty thank you. Nicolle, Sydney, and Avery, you make me do those things, whether you know it or not. And I guess you do now.

 **Rosenfeld**

Dear Reader,

Thanks very much for purchasing this book. There's a story behind it and every product we create at Rosenfeld Media.

Since the early 1990s, I've been a User Experience consultant, conference presenter, workshop instructor, and author. (I'm probably best-known for having cowritten *Information Architecture for the Web and Beyond*.) In each of these roles, I've been frustrated by the missed opportunities to apply UX principles and practices.

I started Rosenfeld Media in 2005 with the goal of publishing books whose design and development showed that a publisher could practice what it preached. Since then, we've expanded into producing industry-leading conferences and workshops. In all cases, UX has helped us create better, more successful products—just as you would expect. From employing user research to drive the design of our books and conference programs, to working closely with our conference speakers on their talks, to caring deeply about customer service, we practice what we preach every day.

Please visit **rosenfeldmedia.com** to learn more about our **conferences**, **workshops**, **free communities**, and **other great resources** that we've made for you. And send your ideas, suggestions, and concerns my way: louis@rosenfeldmedia.com

I'd love to hear from you, and I hope you enjoy the book!

Lou Rosenfeld,
Publisher

RECENT TITLES FROM ROSENFELD MEDIA

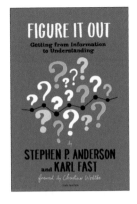

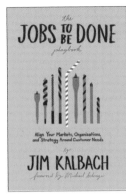

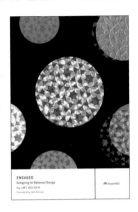

Get a great discount on a Rosenfeld Media book:
visit rfld.me/deal to learn more.

SELECTED TITLES FROM ROSENFELD MEDIA

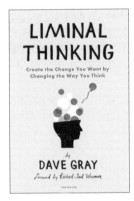

View our full catalog at rosenfeldmedia.com/books

ABOUT THE AUTHORS

Chris Avore is an experienced design manager who leads teams, coaches design leaders, and helps executives understand the value of design. He's championed design, research, and content strategy to improve the services people use every day in organizations of all sizes and industries around the globe. You can follow him on Twitter @erova.

Russ Unger is an experience design leader who has built teams across enterprise, government, and private organizations. He is also coauthor of the books: *A Project Guide to UX Design*, *Designing the Conversation*, and *Speaker Camp* for New Riders (Voices That Matter).